PREFACE

The first edition of subclass KE, *Law of Canada*, developed by Ann Rae and Guy Tanguay as the result of a cooperative effort between the Library of Congress and Library and Archives Canada (then called the National Library of Canada) was published in 1976. A 1999 edition cumulated all changes that had been made to the schedule since the 1976 edition was published. This 2008 edition cumulates changes made since the 1999 edition was published. It includes significant changes and simplifications that were made to form division tables KE4 and KE5 in 2008.

Classification numbers or spans of numbers that appear in parentheses are formerly valid numbers that are now obsolete. Numbers or spans that appear in angle brackets are optional numbers that have never been used at the Library of Congress but are provided for other libraries that wish to use them. In most cases, a parenthesized or angle-bracketed number is accompanied by a "see" reference directing the user to the actual number that the Library of Congress currently uses, or a note explaining Library of Congress practice.

Access to the online version of the full Library of Congress Classification is available on the World Wide Web by subscription to *Classification Web*. Details about ordering and pricing may be obtained from the Cataloging Distribution Service at:

<http://www.loc.gov/cds/>

New or revised numbers and captions are added to the L.C. Classification schedules as a result of development proposals made by the cataloging staff of the Library of Congress and cooperating institutions. Upon approval of these proposals by the weekly editorial meeting of the Cataloging Policy and Support Office, new classification records are created or existing records are revised in the master classification database. Weekly lists of newly approved or revised classification numbers and captions are posted on the World Wide Web at:

<http://www.loc.gov/aba/cataloging/classification/weeklylists/>

Paul Weiss, senior subject cataloging policy specialist in the Cataloging Policy and Support Office, is responsible for coordinating the overall intellectual and editorial content of subclass KE. Kent Griffiths, assistant editor of classification schedules, is responsible for creating new classification records, maintaining the master database, and creating index terms for the captions.

Barbara B. Tillett, Chief
Cataloging Policy and Support Office

March 2008

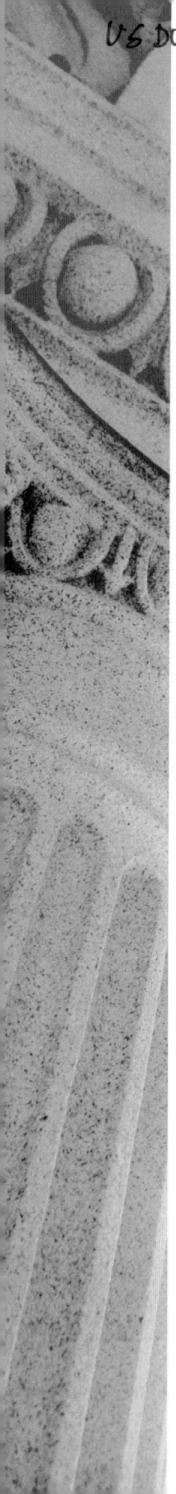

KE

Law of Canada

Library of Congress Classification 2008

Prepared by the Cataloging Policy and Support Office
Library Services

LIBRARY OF CONGRESS
Cataloging Distribution Service
Washington, D.C.

This edition cumulates all additions and changes to class KE through Weekly List 2008/11, dated March 12, 2008. Additions and changes made subsequent to that date are published in weekly lists posted on the World Wide Web at

<http://www.loc.gov/aba/cataloging/classification/weeklylists/>

and are also available in *Classification Web*, the online Web-based edition of the Library of Congress Classification.

Library of Congress Cataloging-in-Publication Data

Library of Congress.

Library of Congress classification. KE. Law of Canada / prepared by the Cataloging Policy and Support Office Library Services. — 2008 ed.

p. cm.

"This edition cumulates all additions and changes to class KE through Weekly List 2008/11, dated March 12, 2008. Additions and changes made subsequent to that date are published in weekly lists posted on the World Wide Web ... and are also available in *Classification Web*, the online Web-based edition of the Library of Congress classification."

Includes index.

ISBN-13: 978-0-8444-1205-4

ISBN-10: 0-8444-1205-8

1. Classification, Library of Congress. 2. Classification—Books—Law. 3. Classification—Boooks—Canada. 4. Law—Canada—Classification. I. Library of Congress. Cataloging Policy and Support Office. II. Title. III. Title: Law of Canada.

Z696.U5K4 2008 025.4'634971—dc22 2008013715

Copyright ©2008 by the Library of Congress except within the U.S.A.

For sale by the Library of Congress Cataloging Distribution Service, 101 Independence Avenue, S.E., Washington, DC 20541-4912. Product catalog available on the Web at **www.loc.gov/cds**.

OUTLINE

Call Number	Subject
KE1-9450	Law of Canada
KE1-8	Bibliography
KE78-107	Statutes
KE111-125	Subordinate [Delegated] legislation
KE132-176	Law reports and related materials
KE198-206	Judicial statistics
KE211-216	Directories
KE225-237	Trials
KE225-229	Criminal trials
KE234-237	Civil trials
KE250-259	Legal research. Legal bibliography
KE269	Law reporting
KE273-322	Legal education
KE325	Law institutes, societies, etc.
KE330-372	The legal profession
KE335-355	Practice of law
KE359-372	The organized bar. Law societies. Bar associations
KE376-378	Community legal services. Legal aid
KE380	Lawyer referral services
KE427	Jurisprudence and philosophy of Canadian law
KE429-430	Criticism. Law reform
KE454	Common law
KE457	Equity
KE470-474	Conflict of laws
KE476	Retroactive law
KE495	Private (Civil) law
KE498-606	Persons
KE499-521	Natural persons
KE531-606	Domestic relations. Family law
KE618-781	Property
KE625-754	Real property. Land law
KE765-781	Personal property
KE787-799	Trusts and trustees
KE806-833	Succession upon death
KE850-1225	Contracts
KE899-906	Government contracts
KE924	Contract of service. Master and servant
KE928-936	Contract for work and labor
KE943-966	Sale of goods
KE970-972	Contracts involving bailments
KE980-986	Negotiable instruments
KE991-1026	Banking

OUTLINE

Law of Canada

Contracts - Continued

Call Number	Subject
KE1030-1034	Loan of money
KE1042-1056	Secured transactions
KE1060-1089	Investments
KE1093-1094	Commodity exchanges
KE1099-1135	Carriers. Carriage of goods and passengers
KE1141-1220	Insurance
KE1225	Aleatory contracts
KE1229	Restitution. Quasi contracts. Unjust enrichment
KE1232-1312.5	Torts (Extracontractual liability)
KE1312-1312.5	Compensation to victims of crime. Reparation
KE1328-1332	Agency
KE1335-1465	Associations
KE1351-1361	Unincorporated associations
KE1369-1465	Corporations. Juristic persons
KE1485-1520	Insolvency and bankruptcy. Creditors' rights
KE1570-1575	Economic policy. Economic planning. Economic development
KE1591-2742	Regulation of industry, trade, and commerce. Occupational law
KE1591-1660	Trade regulation. Control of trade practices. Consumer protection
KE1610-1614	Advertising
KE1616-1618	Labeling
KE1620-1622	Weights and measures. Containers
KE1631-1655	Competition. Restraint of trade. Combines, monopolies, mergers
KE1671-1830	Primary production. Extractive industries
KE1671-1745	Agriculture. Forestry
KE1760-1765	Fishery
KE1790-1830	Mining. Quarrying. Petroleum. Oil and gas
KE1840-1858	Manufacturing industries
KE1867-1906	Food processing industries
KE1915	Construction and building industry. Contractors
KE1935-1999	Trade and commerce
KE2020-2061	Public utilities
KE2071-2649	Transportation and communication
KE2700-2742	The professions
KE2771-2999	Intellectual property
KE3098-3542	Social law and legislation
KE3575-3635	Public health. Sanitation. Environmental pollution

OUTLINE

Law of Canada - Continued

Call Number	Subject
KE3646-3663	Medical legislation
KE3696-3725	Food. Drugs. Cosmetics
KE3756-3778	Public safety
KE3788-3798	Control of social activities
KE3805-3920	Education
KE3950-4010	Science and the arts. Research
KE4120	Public law in general
KE4125-4775	Constitutional law
KE4228	Amending process
KE4270-4285	Structure of government
KE4310	Foreign relations
KE4335	Public policy. Police power
KE4345-4486	Individual and state. Civil and political rights
KE4502-4514	Church and state
KE4526-4775	Organs of the government
KE4529-4665	The legislature
KE4705-4765	The Crown and the Executive branch
KE4775	The Judiciary
KE4900-4934	Local government
KE4940-4995	Public service. Government officials and employees
KE5006-5010	Police and power of the police
KE5015-5036	Administrative organization and procedure
KE5105-5420	Public property. Public restraints on private property
KE5145-5165	Water resources
KE5184-5217	Public land law
KE5258-5284	Regional and city planning
KE5460-5484	Government measures in time of war, national emergency, or economic crisis
KE5600-6328	Public finance
KE6800-7240	National defense. Military law
KE7701-7749	Native peoples. Indians. Inuit
KE8200-8605	Courts. Procedure
KE8200	Administration of justice
KE8212-8332	Court organization and procedure
KE8341-8605	Civil procedure
KE8615	Negotiated settlement. Compromise
KE8618	Arbitration and award
KE8801-9443	Criminal law. Criminal procedure
KE9445-9450	Juvenile criminal law and procedure

OUTLINE

Code	Description
KEA-KEN	Law of Alberta, British Columbia, Manitoba, New Brunswick, Newfoundland and Labrador, Northwest Territories, Nova Scotia
KEO1-(1199.5)	Law of Ontario
KEO1	Bibliography
KEO49-95	Legislation
KEO104-144	Law reports and related materials
KEO152-154	Judicial statistics
KEO156	Legal research. Legal bibliography
KEO162-168	The legal profession
KEO202-230	Persons
KEO234-280.5	Property
KEO282-284.5	Trusts and trustees
KEO286-295	Succession upon death
KEO299-353	Contracts
KEO358-377	Torts (Extracontractual liability)
KEO385-412.5	Associations
KEO430-618	Regulation of industry, trade, and commerce. Occupational law
KEO628-710	Social law and legislation
KEO713-721	Public health
KEO724-730	Medical legislation
KEO759-764	Public safety
KEO770-795	Education
KEO798-802	Science and the arts. Research
KEO804-858	Constitutional law
KEO860-879	Local government
KEO881-885	Public service
KEO895-937	Public property
KEO950-1029	Public finance
KEO1054-1157	Courts. Procedure
KEO1165-1193	Criminal law
KEO1195-1196.7	Juvenile criminal law and procedure
KEP	Law of Prince Edward Island
KEQ1-(1199.5)	Law of Québec
KEQ1	Bibliography
KEQ48-89	Legislation
KEQ100-126	Law reports and related materials
KEQ136-138	Judicial statistics
KEQ140-142	Legal research. Legal bibliography

OUTLINE

Law of Québec - Continued

Classification	Subject
KEQ149	Law institutes, societies, etc.
KEQ151-176	The legal profession
KEQ151-166	Lawyers
KEQ153-157.5	Practice of law
KEQ159-166	The organized bar. Bar associations
KEQ169-176	Notaries
KEQ180-181	Community legal services. Legal aid
KEQ196	Law reform. Criticism
KEQ205.3	Common law (in Québec)
KEQ205.6	Equity
KEQ205.9	Retroactive law
KEQ208-209	Conflict of laws. Private international law
KEQ211-470	Civil law
KEQ228-260.5	Persons
KEQ229-236	Natural persons
KEQ237-258	Domestic relations. Family law
KEQ260-260.5	Tutorship and curatorship
KEQ264-340	Property
KEQ345-357	Succession and gifts
KEQ365-470	Obligations
KEQ390-446	Contracts
KEQ415-420	Sale. Exchange
KEQ424-431	Lease and hire
KEQ433	Agency
KEQ435-436	Loan
KEQ439	Deposit. Sequestration
KEQ441	Life-rents
KEQ443	Transaction. Negotiated settlement. Compromise
KEQ444	Gaming contracts and bets
KEQ448	Quasi contracts. Unjust enrichment
KEQ451-470	Delicts and quasi delicts. Torts
KEQ473	Compensation to victims of crime. Reparation
KEQ477-477.5	Commercial law. Mercantile transactions
KEQ479-480.8	Negotiable instruments
KEQ481-482.5	Banking
KEQ484-485.8	Investments
KEQ487-490.9	Insurance
KEQ492-500.7	Associations
KEQ503-503.7	Insolvency and bankruptcy
KEQ506-506.5	Economic policy. Economic planning. Economic development

OUTLINE

Law of Québec - Continued

KEQ510-635	Regulation of industry, trade, and commerce
KEQ510-519	Trade regulation. Control of trade practices. Consumer protection
KEQ522-540	Primary production. Extractive industries
KEQ544-545	Manufacturing industries
KEQ548-549	Food processing industries
KEQ553	Construction and building industry. Contractors
KEQ558-568	Trade and commerce
KEQ575-580	Public utilities
KEQ585-635	Transportation and communication. Carriers
KEQ637	Intellectual and industrial property
KEQ640-728	Social law and legislation
KEQ735	Public law in general
KEQ738-787	Constitutional law
KEQ798-988	Administrative law
KEQ800-811	Administrative functions
KEQ814-834	Administrative organization
KEQ837-840.5	Public service. Government officials and employees
KEQ842	Police and power of the police
KEQ844-878	Public property. Public restraints on private property
KEQ882-890	Public health. Sanitation. Environmental pollution
KEQ893-898	Medical legislation
KEQ906-906.5	Alcohol. Liquor laws
KEQ909-910	Public safety
KEQ914	Control of individuals
KEQ918-919	Control of social activities. Recreation
KEQ922-962	Education
KEQ968-975	Science and the arts. Research
KEQ980-988	The professions
KEQ995-1048	Public finance
KEQ1052-1056	Military law
KEQ1060-1062	Native peoples. Indians. Inuit
KEQ1068-1162	Courts. Procedure
KEQ1068	Administration of justice. Organization of the judiciary
KEQ1070-1098	Court organization and procedure
KEQ1101-1162	Civil procedure
KEQ1124-1141	Trial
KEQ1143-1144.5	Judgment
KEQ1146-1157	Remedies and special proceedings
KEQ1162	Arbitration and award. Commercial arbitration
KEQ1168-1197	Criminal law. Criminal procedure

OUTLINE

KES, KEY Law of Saskatchewan, Yukon

KEZ Law of cities, towns, etc.

LAW OF CANADA

Law of Canada

Canadian statutory law, and civil and common law and equity as developed by the courts of Canada and its provinces in general and collectively

Class here also materials relating to the period of the Province of Canada, 1841-1867

For the law of particular provinces and territories, see the relevant jurisdictions

Bibliography

For bibliography of special topics, see the topic, e.g. KE273, Legal education

For manuals on legal bibliography, legal research, and the use of law books see KE250+

Number	Description
1	General bibliography
2	Checklists of statutes, regulations
3	Checklists of law reports
4	Library catalogs. Union lists
6	Sales catalogs. Want lists. Lists of duplicates
8	Indexes to periodical literature, society publications, collections

For indexes to particular publications, see the publication

<12> Periodicals

For periodicals consisting primarily of informative material (Newsletters, bulletins, etc.) relating to a particular subject, see the subject and form division for periodicals

For law reports, official bulletins or circulars, and official gazettes intended chiefly for the publication of laws and regulations, see appropriate entries in the text or form division tables

For periodicals consisting predominantly of legal articles, regardless of subject matter and jurisdiction see K1+

16 Monographic series

Canada Gazette (1841-1869) see KE111

Canada Gazette (1867-1946) see KE112

Canada Gazette, Part I (1947-) see KE117

Canada Gazette, Part II (1947-) see KE118

Canada Gazette, Part III (1974-) see KE91

<25-68> Parliamentary publications (Province of Canada)

see J102 (Province of Canada); J103 (Dominion of Canada)

By period

If necessary to class more than one serial publication in a particular number, use successive cutter numbers (.A1-.A9) to arrange the sets chronologically

Province of Canada (1841-1867)

Number	Description
<25>	Both houses (Table KE14)
<26>	Legislative Council (Table KE14)
<27>	Legislative Assembly (Table KE14)

Dominion of Canada (1867-)

KE LAW OF CANADA KE

Parliamentary publications
By period
Dominion of Canada (1867-) -- Continued

<31-38>	Both houses (Table KE13)
<41-48>	Senate (Table KE13)
<51-58>	House of Commons (Table KE13)
	Bills
<65>	Senate
<68>	House of Commons
72	Other materials relating to legislative history
	e.g. Current Legislative Digest
	Legislation
	For statutes, regulations, etc. on a particular subject, see the subject
	Treaties
	General
	see KZ
	Treaties on international uniform law
	see K
	Indian treaties see KE7702.7
	Statutes
	By period
	Province of Canada (1841-1867)
78	Sessional volumes
80	Consolidations
	By date of consolidation
85	Indexes and tables to statutes
	Dominion of Canada (1867-)
	Public general acts
	Official editions
	Sessional volumes and revised statutes
87.A2-.A29	Serial sessional volumes
	Arrange chronologically
88	Monographic sessional volumes to 1885
89	Revised statutes and sessional volumes, 1886-
	Arrange chronologically by date of revision, treating sessional volumes as supplements to the latest revision
91	Canada Gazette, Part 3
94	Other
97	Unofficial compilations and collections
101	Statute revision commission acts and reports
	By date of publication
103	Local and private acts
	By date of publication
105	Abridgments and digests of statutes
106	Citators to statutes

Legislation
Statutes
By period
Dominion of Canada (1867-) -- Continued
Indexes and tables to statutes
106.5.A-Z
Serials, A-Z
107
Monographs. By date
Subordinate [Delegated] legislation
Statutory orders and regulations. Statutory instruments
Official editions
Before 1947
Serials
Canada Gazette
111
1841-1869
112
1867-1946
114
Consolidations
By date of consolidation
116
Monographic collections
By initial date of period covered
1947-
117
Canada Gazette, Part I
118
Canada Gazette, Part II
119
Consolidations
Arrange chronologically by date of consolidation
122
Unofficial editions
123
Abridgments and digests of regulations and proposed regulations
124
Citators to statutory instruments and regulations
125
Indexes and tables to regulations
For the Consolidated Index to Statutory Orders and Regulations see KE119
Law reports and related materials
For reports and materials on particular subjects, see the subject
Law reports
National reports
132
Several courts (Table KE8)
Particular courts
136
Judicial Committee of the Privy Council (Table KE8)
138
Federal courts (Table KE8)
Class here the National Reporter
140
Supreme Court of Canada (Table KE8)
142
Federal Court of Canada (Table KE8)
Formerly the Exchequer Court
143
Appeal Division (Table KE8)
144
Trial Division (Table KE8)
Regional reports
By region

Law reports and related materials
Law reports
Regional reports
By region -- Continued

150	Eastern provinces (Table KE8)
156	Western provinces (Table KE8)

Provincial and territorial reports
see the relevant jurisdiction

<170.A-Z>	Particular subjects, A-Z

This is an optional number provided for law libraries using this classification. Such libraries may wish to class the decisions of administrative boards on particular subjects here as well

173	Comprehensive digests and abridgments
176	Citators. Indexes. Tables

For citators, indexes, etc. related to particular reports or digests and abridgments, see those works

Administrative decisions on a particular subject
see the subject

180	Encyclopedias

Law dictionaries. Words and phrases
For law dictionaries on a particular subject, see the subject

183	Unilingual
184	Bilingual

Class here English-French or French-English only
For other bilingual dictionaries see K52.A+

Multilingual see K54

186	Legal maxims. Quotations
<189.A-Z>	Looseleaf services. By subject, A-Z
192	Form books

General only
For form books on a particular subject, see the subject

195	Yearbooks

Class here only publications issued annually, containing information, statistics, etc., about the year just passed
For other publications appearing yearly see K1+

Judicial statistics

198	General
203	Criminal statistics
204	Juvenile crime
206.A-Z	Other. By subject, A-Z
206.F6	Food and drug convictions

Directories

211	National or regional
213.A-Z	Provincial. By province, A-Z
214.A-Z	Local. By county or city, A-Z
216.A-Z	By specialization, A-Z

Directories
By specialization, A-Z -- Continued
Law schools see KE322.A+
Law teachers see KE280
Legal aid agencies see KE376.A65
Trials
For "reference cases" (i.e. advisory opinions on constitutional questions) see KE4216.3+
Criminal trials
For courts-martial see KE7165+
Collections

225 General
Class here collections of both criminal and civil trials
Particular offenses, A-Z

226.A2 Abortion

226.M8 Murder. Assassination

226.P6 Political offenses
Including treason, sedition, etc.
Particular trials
Including records, briefs, commentaries and stories on a particular trial

228.A-Z Early through 19th century
By defendant or by best known name, A-Z

229.A-Z 20th century
By defendant or by best known name, A-Z
Civil trials

234 Collections
Particular trials
Including records, briefs, commentaries and stories on a particular trial
Class individual trials with "Particular cases" or "Particular companies" only if specifically provided for in the schedule, e.g. KE3234, Railway labor disputes; KE4655, Contested elections; KE2649.C3, Litigation involving the Canadian Broadcasting Corporation

236.A-Z Early through 19th century
By plaintiff, A-Z

237.A-Z 20th century
By plaintiff, A-Z
Legal research. Legal bibliography
Methods of bibliographic research and how to find the law

250 General (Table KE5, modified)

250.A65 Indexes of legal research projects
Electronic data processing. Information retrieval

252 General (Table KE5)

254.A-Z By subject, A-Z

254.C6 Court administration

KE LAW OF CANADA KE

Legal research. Legal bibliography
Electronic data processing. Information retrieval
By subject, A-Z -- Continued
254.L36 Land titles
259 Systems of citation. Legal abbreviations
265 Legal composition and draftsmanship
For legislative drafting see KE4560
269 Law reporting (Table KE5)
For parliamentary reporting see KE4540
For court reporters see KE8315
Legal education
273 Bibliography
274 Periodicals
For periodicals consisting predominantly of legal articles,
regardless of subject matter, see K1+
For periodicals consisting primarily of informative material
(Newsletters, bulletins, etc.) relating to a particular subject,
see subject and form division for periodicals
For law reports, official bulletins or circulars, and official
gazettes intended chiefly for the publication of laws and
regulations, see appropriate entries in text or form division
tables
279 Yearbooks. Annual and periodical surveys
280 Directories
281 Society publications
282 Congresses. Conferences
286.A-Z Law school catalogs and bulletins
By name of school, A-Z
289 General works. Treatises
290 Addresses, essays, lectures
Continuing (post-admission) legal education
294 General works
296 Judicial education
Study and teaching
General works see KE289
298.A-Z Particular subjects, A-Z
298.C4 Children, Law pertaining to
298.C6 Commercial law
298.L4 Legal writing
Teaching methods
300 General works
301 Case method
Moot courts
302 General works
302.3.A-302.3Z Particular. By name of school, A-Z
303 Clinical methods

KE LAW OF CANADA KE

Legal education

Study and teaching -- Continued

307 Students' guides and textbooks

For introductions to legal literature (Legal bibliography) see KE250+

For introductory surveys of the law see KE444

Prelaw-school education. Admission to law school

For study and teaching of law in elementary and secondary schools see KE3883.L3

309 General works

309.3 Examination aids

Law students

Including sociology and psychology of law students

313 General works

315 Student associations, fraternities, etc.

318.A-Z Particular groups of students, A-Z

318.N3 Native peoples. Indians. Inuit

318.W6 Women

322.A-Z Particular law schools. By name, A-Z

Table KE10 is provided as an optional subarrangement for libraries using this classification. The Library of Congress does not apply Table KE10

325.A-Z Law institutes, societies, etc. By name, A-Z

Including the journals, proceedings, annual reports, etc. of such societies

For law societies incorporated to regulate the profession see KE359+

The legal profession

Including works on law as a career

330 General (Table KE5)

331 Special aspects

e.g. The lawyer and society

332.A-Z Particular classes of lawyers and types of careers, A-Z

332.G6 Government service

332.M45 Mennonite lawyers

332.M56 Minority lawyers

Patent attorneys see KE2975

332.P82 Public interest lawyers

332.W6 Women lawyers

Practice of law

335 General (Table KE5)

336 Surveys of the legal profession

Biography of lawyers see KE395+

337 Admission to the bar. Bar examinations

For examination questions and answers see KE446

The legal profession

Practice of law -- Continued

Legal ethics and etiquette

Cf. KE8218 Courtroom decorum

Cf. KE8293.J8 Judicial ethics

339 General (Table KE5)

Discipline. Unauthorized practice. Disbarment

342 General works

343.A-Z Particular cases. By attorney, A-Z

344.A-Z Special topics, A-Z

344.A38 Advertising

344.C58 Conflict of interests

344.C6 Contingent fees

Attorney and client

346 General works

347.A-Z Special topics, A-Z

Liability see KE347.M3

347.M3 Malpractice. Liability

Cf. KE1264+ Negligence

Economics of law practice

349 General (Table KE5)

Surveys see KE336

Fees

Cf. KE8517+ Costs (Civil procedure)

Cf. KE9358 Costs (Criminal procedure)

350 General (Table KE5)

Contingent fees see KE344.C6

350.5 Marketing of legal services (Table KE5)

Law office management

352 General (Table KE5)

353 Attorneys' and legal secretaries' handbooks, manuals, deskbooks, etc.

Form books see KE192

355.A-Z Special topics, A-Z

355.A3 Accounting

For general works on accounting for the use of lawyers, see HF

355.A96 Automation

355.L4 Legal assistants. Paralegal personnel

The organized bar. Law societies. Bar associations

For monographs and other publications of law societies or bar associations on a particular subject, see the subject

359 General works

Law societies

360 General works

KE LAW OF CANADA KE

The legal profession
The organized bar. Law societies. Bar associations
Law societies -- Continued

361.A-Z	Particular law societies. By province, A-Z (except Quebec)
	For collective biography see KE395+
	For individual biography (To 1867) see KE406.A+
	For individual biography (1867-1931) see KE411.A+
	For individual biography (1931-) see KE416.A+
	Bar associations
363	General works
	Particular associations
	National
	Canadian Bar Association
365.A2	Journals
365.A3	Proceedings. Yearbooks
365.A4	Papers
365.A5	Incorporating statutes. Bylaws. Regulations. By date
365.A7	Other documents
366	General works. History
	For collective biography see KE395+
	For individual biography (To 1867) see KE406.A+
	For individual biography (1867-1931) see KE411.A+
	For individual biography (1931-) see KE416.A+
	Subordinate organizations
366.4.A-Z	Subject sections. By subject, A-Z
366.7.A-Z	Provincial branches
	By province, A-Z
	Provincial (except Quebec)
	General works see KE363
370.A-Z	Particular associations, A-Z
372.A-Z	Local associations, lawyers clubs, etc. By place, A-Z (except Quebec)
	Law and lawyers in literature see PN6110.L2
	Legal anecdotes, wit and humor see K183+
	For purely fictitious works see PN6231.L4
	Community legal services. Legal aid. Legal assistance to the poor
	For collections of, and works on, substantive law see KE452.P6
376	General (Table KE5, modified)
376.A65	Directories of legal aid agencies
378.A-Z	Legal aid services to particular groups, A-Z

KE LAW OF CANADA KE

Community legal services. Legal aid. Legal assistance to the poor

Legal aid services to particular groups, A-Z -- Continued

378.J8	Juveniles
378.N3	Native peoples. Indians. Inuit
378.W65	Women
380	Lawyer referral services
	Public defenders see KE9289
	History
	For works on the history of a particular subject, see the subject
392	Sources
394	General (Table KE5)
	Biography
	Collective
395	General
396.A-Z	By province, A-Z
397.A-Z	By county, city, etc., A-Z
	Individual (To 1867) see KE406.A+
	Individual (1867-1931) see KE411.A+
	Individual (1931-) see KE416.A+
399	Special aspects. Influence of foreign (e.g. Roman) law
	By period
	To 1867
	Sources see KE392
404	General works
	Biography
	For biographies of Supreme Court of Canada justices see KE8246+
405	Collective
	For provincial biography see KE396.A+
	For local biography see KE397.A+
406.A-Z	Individual, A-Z
	Subarrange each by Table KE11
407.A-Z	Special topics, A-Z
	1867-1931
	Sources see KE392
409	General works
	Biography
	For biographies of Supreme Court of Canada justices see KE8246+
410	Collective
	For provincial biography see KE396.A+
	For local biography see KE397.A+
411.A-Z	Individual, A-Z
	Subarrange each by Table KE11
412.A-Z	Special topics, A-Z
	1931-

KE — LAW OF CANADA — KE

History
By period
1931- -- Continued
Sources see KE392

414 — General works
Biography
For biographies of Supreme Court of Canada justices see KE8246+

415 — Collective
For provincial biography see KE396.A+
For local biography see KE397.A+

416.A-Z — Individual, A-Z
Subarrange each by Table KE11

417.A-Z — Special topics, A-Z

427 — Jurisprudence and philosophy of Canadian law (Table KE5)
Class here doctrines peculiar to Canadian legal institutions
For works on the philosophy of particular branches of the law (e.g. Constitutional or criminal law), see those subjects
For works by Canadian authors on legal philosophy in general see K201+

Relationship of law to other disciplines, subjects, or phenomena see K486+

Criticism. Law reform. General administration of justice
Cf. KE8199.2+ Judiciary
Cf. KE8813+ Criminal justice

429 — General (Table KE5)

430 — Law Reform Commission of Canada (Table KE5)

432 — Uniformity of legislation (Table KE5, modified)
Class here general works only
For uniform provincial laws on a particular subject, see the subject

432.A65 — Proceedings of the Uniform Law Conference of Canada
Formerly Commissioners on Uniformity of Legislation in Canada

436 — Congresses. Conferences
Collected works (nonserial)
For monographic series see KE16

439 — Several authors

440 — Individual authors
Under each:
.x — *By date*
.xA-.xZ — *By editor*
Including collected opinions

442 — Casebooks. Readings
Class here general works only
For casebooks on particular subjects, see the subject

444 — General works. Treatises

445 — Compends. Outlines, syllabi, etc.

KE LAW OF CANADA KE

446	Examination aids
447	Popular works
448	Addresses, essays, lectures
	Including single essays, collected essays of several authors, festschriften, etc.
450.A-Z	Works for particular groups of users, A-Z
450.A3	Accountants
450.B87	Businesspeople
	Including foreign investors
450.C7	Credit managers
	Draft evaders see KE450.I4A+
450.E3	Educators
	Foreign investors see KE450.B87
450.I4A-.I4Z	Immigrants. By nationality, A-Z
	Including draft evaders
450.M87	Musicians
450.O43	Older people. Retired persons
450.P5	Physicians
	Retired persons see KE450.O43
450.W6	Women
452.A-Z	Works on diverse legal aspects of a particular subject and falling within several branches of the law. By subject, A-Z
452.A5	Animals
452.C6	Computers
452.M44	Meetings
452.P6	Poverty. Legal protection of the poor. Handbooks for legal services
452.U7	Urban studies
452.W35	Waiver
454	Common law
457	Equity (Table KE5)
	Usage and custom see KE482.U8
	Conflict of laws
	For conflict of laws between the United States and Canada see KF416.A+
470	General (Table KE5)
471.A-Z	Special aspects, A-Z
	Foreign judgments see KE8222
474.A-Z	Particular branches and subjects of the law, A-Z
474.C64	Contracts. Obligation. Debtor and creditor (Table KE6)
	Criminal jurisdiction see KE8828
	Debtor and creditor see KE474.C64
	Obligations see KE474.C64
476	Retroactive law
	General principles and concepts
	Comprehensive works see KE444
482.A-Z	Particular principles and concepts, A-Z

KE LAW OF CANADA KE

General principles and conflicts

Particular principles and concepts, A-Z

Classification of library collections of legal literature see Z697.L4

482.S83	Stare decisis
482.S84	Statutory construction and interpretation
482.U8	Usage and custom
484.A-Z	Concepts applying to several branches of law, A-Z
484.D3	Damages
484.L5	Liability
484.L54	Limitation of actions
	Cf. KE8386+ Civil procedure
484.N8	Nullity
495	Private (Civil) law
	Persons
498	General works
	Natural persons
	Civil status
499	Domicile
501	Name
503	Absence. Missing persons. Presumption of death
	Capacity and disability
507	General (Table KE5)
509	Women (Table KE5)
	For married women see KE552
512	Minors. Children (Table KE5)
	Including liability
	Mentally ill. People with mental or physical disabilities
	For care of the mentally ill see KE3658
514	General (Table KE5)
515	Mental incompetency proceedings (Table KE5)
516.A-Z	Particular diseases or impairments, A-Z
516.B5	Blindness
517	Unborn children. Nasciturus (Table KE5)
518.A-Z	Other groups of persons, A-Z
518.A4	Aliens
	Cf. KE621+ Alien property
	Cf. KE4452+ Control of individuals
521	Recording and registration (Table KE5)
	Including registers of births, marriages, deaths; birth and death certificates; census; vital statistics
	Juristic persons, corporate persons, associations, etc. see KE1369+
	Domestic relations. Family law
531-540	General (Table KE4)
542	Family courts and procedure (Table KE5)
	For juvenile court proceedings see KE9446

Persons

Domestic relations. Family law -- Continued

Marriage. Husband and wife

544	General (Table KE5)
545	Special aspects
546	Certificates. Premarital examinations
548	Performance of marriage. Civil and religious celebrations
550	Void and voidable marriages. Nullity
	Rights and duties of husband and wife
552	Civil status of married women
	Property relationships
554	General (Table KE5)
	Particular modes of property relationships
556	Community property
557	Separate property
559	Marriage settlements. Antenuptial contracts
	Divorce. Annulment. Separation
561-570	General (Table KE4)
572	Relationship between civil and religious divorces (Table KE5)
574	Special aspects
	Parliamentary divorce
576	Rules and procedure. By date of publication
578	General works. Treatises
	Grounds for divorce
581	General works
582.A-Z	Particular grounds, A-Z
582.M4	Mental cruelty
585	Separation. Judicial separation
589	Maintenance. Alimony (Table KE5)
590	Unmarried couples (Table KE5)
591	Same-sex marriage. Civil unions (Table KE5)
	Including quasi-marital relationships
	Parent and child
593	General (Table KE5)
595	Legitimacy. Legitimation. Paternity
596	Illegitimate children. Affiliation
598	Adoption
	Parental rights and duties. Property of minors. Custody. Access to children
	Including parental kidnapping
600	General (Table KE5)
602	Child support. Desertion and nonsupport (Table KE5)
606	Guardian and ward
	Agency see KE1328+
	Property
618	General. Ownership. Possession (Table KE5)

Property -- Continued

Special aspects and relationships

619

Particular kinds of property

621 Alien property. Enemy property

Government property see KE5323+

Matrimonial property see KE554+

Real property. Land law

625 General (Table KE5)

626 Special aspects and relationships. Alien landownership

Land tenure

628 General works

Seigneurial tenure see KEQ271+

Estates and interests

630 General works

Particular estates and interests (legal or equitable)

Freehold estates

Fee simple

632 General works

Extent of ownership above and below surface

634 Airspace

636 Minerals. Metals

Cf. KE1790+ Mining. Quarrying

Particular kinds

641 Housing condominium. Horizontal property (Table KE5)

Life interests. Possessory estates

648 General works

Fixtures. Improvements see KE702

Rights of user. Waste. Dilapidations. Repairs see KE703

Dower. Curtesy. Homestead rights see KE684

Estates less than freehold

Leasehold interests. Landlord and tenant see KE690+

Future estates and interests

Including works on future interests in both real and personal property

660 General. Limitations. Rule in Shelley's case

662 Power of appointment

663 Reversions. Reversionary interests

664 Remainders. Contingent remainders. Executory interests

668 Rule against perpetuities

Concurrent ownership. Co-ownership

Including works on concurrent ownership in both real and personal property

673 General (Table KE5)

Property
Real property. Land law
Land tenure
Estates and interests
Particular estates and interests (legal or equitable)
Concurrent ownership. Co-ownership -- Continued
Joint tenancy. Tenancy in common

675	General works
678	Partition
680	Housing cooperatives
	Estates and interests arising from marriage
684	Dower. Curtesy. Homestead rights
	Tenancy. Leaseholds. Landlord and tenant
690	General (Table KE5)
692	Rent. Rent control (Table KE5)
695.A-Z	Particular kinds of leaseholds, A-Z
695.C6	Commercial leases
695.G7	Ground leases. Building leases
	Oil and gas leases see KE1822
	Rights and interests incident to ownership and possession. Interests less than estates
700	General works
702	Fixtures. Improvements
703	Rights of user. Waste. Dilapidations. Repairs
705	Boundaries. Fences
707	Riparian rights. Water rights of individuals
709	Action to recover possession of land. Ejectment
	For trespass to land see KE1257
	Right to dispose of land
711	Restraints on alienation
	Rights as to the use and profits of another's land. Incorporeal hereditaments
714	General works
	Easements
715	General works
716.A-Z	Particular kinds, A-Z
716.P3	Party walls
	Covenants running with the land
719	General works
720	Restrictive covenants
725.A-Z	Special topics, A-Z
725.P7	Prescription
	Transfer of rights in land
	Transfer inter vivos
729	General. Vendor and purchaser. Real estate transactions (Table KE2)
	Real estate agents see KE1987.R4

Property

Real property. Land law

Transfer of rights in land

Transfer inter vivos

Conveyances. Title investigation. Abstracts

731 General. Deeds (Table KE5)

Title investigation. Abstracts

738 General (Table KE5)

739 Registration. Land titles system (Table KE5)

742 Description of land. Surveying (Table KE5)

Transfer by will see KE808+

Intestate succession see KE827+

746.A-Z Other modes of transfer, A-Z

Prescription see KE725.P7

Mortgages

752 General (Table KE5)

754.A-Z Special topics, A-Z

754.D5 Distress, Mortgagees' right to. Attornment clause

754.F6 Foreclosure

754.I5 Interest

Personal property

765 General. Personal actions (Table KE5)

Choses in action

766 General works

Negotiable instruments see KE980+

Stocks and shares (Stock exchange transactions) see KE1065+

Stocks and shares (Issuing and sale of securities) see KE1411+

Intellectual and industrial property see KE2771+

Ownership and possession

Fixtures see KE702

Acquisition of property

770 General works

772 Original acquisition

Transfer

Choses in possession

775 General works

Sale see KE943+

779 Bailment

For contracts involving bailments see KE970+

Transfers as security see KE1042+

781 Actions to recover personal property. Replevin

For trover and conversion see KE1261

Trusts and trustees

787 General (Table KE5)

Particular kinds of trusts

KE LAW OF CANADA KE

Trusts and trustees
Particular kinds of trusts -- Continued

793	Charitable trusts
795	Land trusts
	Trustees
797	Trust companies (Table KE5)
798.A-Z	Special topics, A-Z
798.A3	Accounting
	Legal investments. Trust investments see KE1085.L4
798.L5	Liability. Breach of trust
799.A5-Z	Particular trust companies. By name, A-Z
	Estate planning see KE5974
	Succession upon death
806	General (Table KE5)
	Testate succession. Wills
808	General (Table KE5)
	Texts of wills see CS1+
812.A-Z	Contested wills. By testator, A-Z
814.A-Z	Special topics, A-Z
814.D42	Decedents' family maintenance
	Error see KE814.M57
814.M57	Mistake. Error
	Probate law and practice
820	General. Surrogate courts (Table KE5)
824.A-Z	Special topics, A-Z
	Intestate succession
827	General (Table KE5)
829.A-Z	Special topics, A-Z
	Subarrange each by Table KE5
	Dower, curtesy, homestead rights see KE684
	Administration of decedents' estates. Execution of wills.
	Personal representatives
831	General (Table KE5)
833.A-Z	Special topics, A-Z
833.A3	Accounting
	Estate taxes, death duties see KE5976+
	Contracts
850	General (Table KE5)
	Formation of contract
857	General (Table KE5)
860	Conditions (Table KE5)
	Parties to contract
863	General works
865	Assignment of contracts. Subrogation
	Void and voidable contracts
869	General works
871.A-Z	Unlawful contracts, A-Z

Contracts
Void and voidable contracts
Unlawful contracts, A-Z -- Continued
Restraint of trade see KE1631+
Sunday legislation see KE1971
871.U8 Usury
Cf. KE1030+ Loan of money
Wager see KE1225
872 Immoral contracts. Unconscionable transactions
Lack of genuine consent
874 Duress. Undue influence
875 Mistake. Misrepresentation. Fraud
Discharge of contract
880 General works
882 Performance
884 Accord and satisfaction
886 Supervening impossibility
Limitation of actions (General) see KE484.L54
Limitation of actions (Civil procedure) see KE8386+
Bankruptcy see KE1491+
Breach of contract. Remedies
890 General works
Particular remedies
892 Damages. Quantum meruit
894 Specific performance
896 Rescission and restitution
Government contracts. Public contracts. Purchasing and procurement
899 General works
900 Municipal contracts
902 War contracts. Defense contracts. Military procurement (Table KE5)
905 Construction and building contracts (Table KE5)
906 Research and development contracts
Cf. KE3960.D4 Science and the arts
Particular contracts
911-920 General. Commercial law. Mercantile law (Table KE4)
Agency see KE1328+
Banking see KE991+
Business associations see KE1356+
Carriers. Carriage of goods and passengers see KE1099+
Companies. Business corporations see KE1381+
Contracts involving bailments see KE970+
Cooperatives see KE1454
Corporations see KE1369+
Insurance see KE1141+
Investments see KE1060+

Contracts

Particular contracts -- Continued

Loan of money see KE1030+

Negotiable instruments see KE980+

Partnership see KE1356+

Sale of goods see KE943+

Secured transactions see KE1042+

Stock exchange transactions see KE1065+

Suretyship. Guaranty see KE1039

Contract of service. Master and servant

924	General (Table KE5)
	Merchant mariners see KE1121+
	Public service see KE4940+

Contract for work and labor (Contract for services). Independent contractors

928	General works
930	Mechanics' liens (Table KE5)
931	Repairmen's liens (Table KE5)

Particular types of contracts

933	Building and construction. Engineering
936.A-Z	Other, A-Z

Sale of goods

943	General (Table KE5)
945.A-Z	Particular goods and chattels, A-Z
945.H6	Horses

Formation of contract

948	General works
949.A-Z	Special topics, A-Z
	C.I.F. and F.O.B. clauses see KE964
949.C6	Conditions and warranties. Implied warranties
	Products liability see KE1282+
951	Transfer of property and title. Auction sales

Documents of title

955	General works
956	Bills of lading
	For ocean bills of lading see KE1110
957.A-Z	Other, A-Z

Conditional transfer, conditional sale, installment sale see KE1047

Performance

963	General works
964	Overseas sales. C.I.F. clause. F.O.B. clause
966	Other clauses

Rights of unpaid seller

Liens see KE1050+

Contracts involving bailments

Cf. KE779 Bailment

Contracts

Particular contracts

Contracts involving bailments -- Continued

970 General works

972.A-Z Particular contracts, A-Z

Carriers see KE1099+

Partnership see KE1361

Negotiable instruments

980 General (Table KE5)

981 Bills of exchange (Table KE5)

Checks

983 General (Table KE5)

984 Travelers' checks (Table KE5)

986 Promissory notes (Table KE5)

Securities (Stock exchange transactions) see KE1065+

Securities (Issuing and sale) see KE1411+

Banking

991-1000 General (Table KE4)

Particular kinds of banks and other deposit taking and financing companies and institutions

1008 Credit unions. Cooperative credit associations (Table KE5)

1012.A-Z Other, A-Z

1012.B8 Building societies

Trust companies see KE797

Particular banking transactions

1016 Deposits (Table KE5)

1018 Collection of accounts. Collection law (Table KE5)

For collection agencies see KE1987.C6

1022 Letters of credit (Table KE5)

1024.A-Z Other, A-Z

Bank secrets see KE1024.R42

Money laundering see KE1024.R42

1024.R42 Record keeping (Table KE6)

Including bank secrets, money laundering

1026.A-Z Particular banks. By name, A-Z

1026.I5 Industrial Development Bank (Table KE6)

Foreign exchange regulation see KE5612

Loan of money. Interest. Usury

Including debtor and creditor in general

Cf. KE872 Unconscionable transactions

1030 General (Table KE5)

1034 Consumer credit. Small loans. Finance charges (Table KE5)

1039 Suretyship. Guaranty (Table KE5)

For suretyship insurance, bonding see KE1211+

Secured transactions

Contracts

Particular contracts

Secured transactions -- Continued

1042	General (Table KE5)
1045	Chattel mortgages (Table KE5)
1047	Conditional sale. Installment sale. Lease purchase (Table KE5)

Liens

1050	General works
1052.A-Z	Particular kinds, A-Z

Maritime liens see KE1114.B6

Mechanics' liens see KE930

Repairmen's liens see KE931

1056.A-Z	Other, A-Z

Suretyship. Guaranty see KE1039

Investments

For foreign investments see KE1575

1060	General (Table KE5)
1062	Stockbrokers (Table KE5)

Securities. Stock exchange transactions

For issuing and sale of securities see KE1411+

1065	General (Table KE5)
1067.A-Z	Particular transactions, A-Z
1067.I5	Insider trading

Particular securities

Mortgages see KE752+

1085.A-Z	Special topics, A-Z
1085.L4	Legal investments. Trust investments
1089	Investment trusts. Investment companies. Mutual funds

Commodity exchanges. Produce exchanges

1093	General. Futures trading (Table KE5)
1094.A-Z	Particular commodities, A-Z

Carriers. Carriage of goods and passengers

1099	General. Liability (Table KE5)
1100	Carriage by land (Table KE5)

For motor carriers see KE2130+

For railways see KE2141+

1102	Carriage by air (Table KE5)

Cf. KE2273+ Regulation of commercial aviation

Carriage by sea. Maritime (Commercial) law. Admiralty

1105	General (Table KE5)

Liability

1107	General. Maritime torts. Collisions at sea (Table KE5)
1110	Ocean bills of lading
1112	Admiralty proceedings (Table KE5)
1114.A-Z	Special topics, A-Z

Contracts
Particular contracts
Carriers. Carriage of goods and passengers
Carriage by sea. Maritime (Commercial) law. Admiralty
Special topics, A-Z -- Continued

1114.B6	Bottomry and respondentia. Ship mortgages.
	Maritime liens
	Maritime labor law. Merchant mariners
1121	General (Table KE5)
1124	Citizenship requirements (Table KE5)
1126	Certification. Suspension. Revocation (Table KE5)
	Coastwise navigation see KE2372
	Inland water transportation see KE2440
1135	Marine insurance
	Insurance
	Including regulation of insurance business
1141-1150	General (Table KE4)
1154	Insurance business. Agents. Brokers (Table KE5)
1157	Foreign insurance companies (Table KE5)
1163.A-Z	Special topics, A-Z
1163.B33	Bad faith. Good faith
	Good faith see KE1163.B33
1163.W3	Waiver
	Personal insurance
	Life
1165	General (Table KE5)
1171.A-Z	Special topics, A-Z
1174	Health. Medical care
	For state medicine see KE3405
1179.A-Z	Other, A-Z
	Property insurance
1181	General (Table KE5)
1184.A-Z	Particular types, A-Z
1184.A9	Aviation (Table KE6)
1184.B87	Business interruption (Table KE6)
1184.F5	Fire (Table KE6)
	Marine see KE1135
1187.A-Z	Particular kinds of property, A-Z
1187.C6	Condominiums (Table KE6)
	Casualty insurance
1198	General liability
	Particular risks
	Motor vehicle (Automobile) insurance
1202	General (Table KE5)
1204	Unsatisfied judgment funds
	For financial responsibility laws, compulsory insurance see KE2105

KE LAW OF CANADA KE

Contracts
Particular contracts
Insurance
Casualty insurance
Particular risks
Motor vehicle (Automobile) insurance -- Continued

1205	No-fault
1207.A-Z	Other, A-Z
1207.P64	Pollution (Table KE6)

Suretyship. Guaranty. Title insurance
For contract of suretyship see KE1039

1211	General works
1213	Bonding
1217	Guaranty
1220	Title insurance

Social insurance see KE3400+
Aleatory contracts

1225	Gambling. Wagering. Speculation
	Lotteries (Regulation) see KE3795
	Lotteries (Criminal law) see KE9066
	Insurance see KE1141+
1229	Restitution. Quasi contracts. Unjust enrichment (Table KE5)

Torts (Extracontractual liability)

1232	General. Liability. Damages (Table KE5)
1233	Special aspects

Particular torts
Torts in respect to the person

1237	Personal injuries. Death by wrongful act (Table KE5)
	Cf. KE8432.P4 Trial practice

Violation of privacy
Cf. KE8940 Criminal law

1240	General (Table KE5)
1242.A-Z	Special aspects, A-Z
1242.C6	Computers and privacy
1242.U5	Unauthorized publication of picture
1243.A-Z	Special topics, A-Z

Torts in respect to reputation
Cf. KE8948+ Criminal law

1246	General. Libel and slander (Table KE5)
1248.A-Z	Particular instances of tort liability, A-Z
1248.C7	Credit information
1250.A-Z	Defenses, A-Z
1252	Torts in respect to domestic relations

Abuse of legal process

1253	Malicious prosecution
1255	Deceit. Fraud

Unfair competition see KE2988+

Torts (Extracontractual liability

Particular torts

1257 Trespass to land

For ejectment see KE709

1259 Nuisance

1261 Torts affecting chattels. Trespass to goods. Conversion. Trover

Replevin see KE781

Negligence

Cf. KE8432.N4 Trial practice

1264 General (Table KE5)

1266 Contributory negligence (Table KE5)

1269 Liability for condition and use of land. Occupiers' liability (Table KE5)

1271 Malpractice (Table KE5)

1274.A-Z Particular types of accidents, A-Z

1274.A8 Automobile accidents (Table KE6)

For financial responsibility laws see KE2105

Cf. KE1204 Unsatisfied judgment funds

1274.A9 Aviation accidents

For liability of common air carriers see KE2280

1274.F57 Fire accidents (Table KE6)

Marine accidents see KE1107+

Railway accidents (General. Damage to property) see KE2197+

Railway accidents (Personal injuries) see KE2203

1274.S65 Sports accidents (Table KE6)

Strict liability. Liability without fault

Cf. KE8834 Criminal liability

1277 General (Table KE5)

1279 Damages caused by animals (Table KE5)

Products liability

Cf. KE3763+ Product safety

1282 General (Table KE5)

1283.A-Z By product, A-Z

1283.C48 Chemical products

1285 Environmental damages (Table KE5)

1288.A-Z Parties to actions in torts, A-Z

1288.L3 Labor unions (Table KE6)

Minors. Children see KE512

1288.M8 Municipalities (Table KE6)

1288.P8 Public officers and government employees (Table KE6)

1288.S3 School boards. Teachers (Table KE6)

Liability for torts of others. Vicarious liability

1295 General works

1301 Employers' liability

Cf. KE3414+ Workers' compensation

Torts (Extracontractual liability

Liability for torts of others. Vicarious liability -- Continued

1305	Government torts. Crown liability (Table KE5)
1309	Remedies. Defenses
	Compensation to victims of crimes. Reparation
	Including injuries to both person and property and compensation by government
1312	General (Table KE5)
1312.5.A-Z	Particular crimes, A-Z
1312.5.C56	Child sexual abuse
1314	Assistance in emergencies. Good Samaritan laws (Table KE5)
	For medical emergency assistance see KE2706+
	Agency
1328	General (Table KE5)
	Special topics
1330	Power of attorney
1332.A-Z	Particular types of agency, A-Z
1332.B7	Brokers. Commission merchants. Factors
	For insurance brokers see KE1154
	For real estate agents see KE1987.R4
	Associations
	Including business enterprises in general, regardless of form of organization
1345	General (Table KE5)
1347	Accounting law. Auditing. Financial statements (Table KE5)
	For corporation accounting see KE1430
	For practice of accountancy see KE2722
	Unincorporated associations
1351	General (Table KE5)
1353.A-Z	Particular types of associations, A-Z
	Building societies see KE1012.B8
	Labor unions see KE3170
	Business associations. Partnership
1356	General (Table KE5)
1361	Partnership (Table KE5)
	For joint-stock companies see KE1381+
1362	Joint ventures (Table KE5)
	Corporations. Juristic persons
1369	General (Table KE5)
1369.5	Indexes to incorporated bodies
1371.A-Z	Special topics, A-Z
1371.U4	Ultra vires doctrine
	Nonprofit corporations
1373	General (Table KE5)
1375.A-Z	Particular types, A-Z
1375.E5	Endowments. Foundations
	Religious corporations and societies see KE4502

Associations

Corporations. Juristic persons -- Continued

Business corporations. Companies

1381-1390	General. Joint-stock companies (Table KE4)
1394	Special aspects
	Government regulation and control. Licensing
1396	General (Table KE5)
1398	Foreign corporations. Multinational enterprises. Extra-provincial corporations (Table KE5)
1400	Incorporation. Corporate charters and bylaws. Promoters. Prospectus (Table KE5)
1402	Management. Board of directors. Officers (Table KE5)
1403	Corporate legal departments (Table KE5)
	Corporate finance. Capital. Dividends
1408	General (Table KE5)
1411-1420	Issuing of securities and their sale in general (Table KE4)
	For stock exchange transactions see KE1065+
1424.A-Z	Particular types of stocks, A-Z
1424.W5	Without par value (Table KE6)
1430	Accounting. Auditing. Financial statements (Table KE5)
	Shares and shareholders' rights. Stock transfers
1432	General (Table KE5)
1434	Shareholders' meetings (Table KE5)
	Class here works on procedure at public meetings in general
	Particular types of corporations
1448	Subsidiary and parent companies. Holding companies
	Combines, monopolies see KE1631+
1450	Private companies. Family companies. Close companies (Table KE5)
1454	Cooperatives (Table KE5)
	Credit unions, cooperative credit associations see KE1008
	Building societies see KE1012.B8
	Professional corporations see KE2700+
1459	Dissolution. Liquidation (Table KE5)
1462	Consolidation and merger (Table KE5)
	Corporate reorganization see KE1518.C6
1465	Crown corporations. Government-owned corporations and business organizations (Table KE5)
	Class here general works only
	For particular industries see KE2020+
	For public utilities (Railways, etc.) see KE2141+
	Municipal corporations see KE4904+
	Insolvency and bankruptcy. Creditors' rights

Insolvency and bankruptcy. Creditors' rights -- Continued

1485	General (Table KE5)
	Bankruptcy
1491-1500	General (Table KE4)
1503	Procedure (Table KE5)
1506.A-Z	Special topics, A-Z
1506.F7	Fraudulent conveyances
1506.P74	Priority of claims
1506.R43	Receivers in bankruptcy
	Spouses see KE1506.T56
1506.T56	Third parties
	Including spouses
	Debtors' relief
1515	General (Table KE5)
1518.A-Z	Particular forms of debt relief, A-Z
1518.A8	Assignments for benefit of creditors (Table KE6)
1518.C6	Corporate reorganization (Table KE6)
1520.A-Z	Particular classes or groups of debtors, A-Z
1520.F3	Farmers (Table KE6)
	Economic policy. Economic planning. Economic development
	Class here works on programs to overcome regional economic disparities
	For economic emergency legislation see KE5460+
1570	General (Table KE5)
1575	Foreign investment (Table KE5)
	Cf. KE626 Alien landownership
	Cf. KE1398 Foreign corporations
	Regulation of industry, trade, and commerce. Occupational law
	Trade regulation. Control of trade practices. Consumer protection
	For consumer credit see KE1034
	For foreign trade regulation see KE1940+
	For economic emergency legislation see KE5460+
	Cf. KE2908+ Patent law, trademarks, etc.
1591-1600	General (Table KE4)
	Advertising
1610	General (Table KE5)
1612.A-Z	By industry or product, A-Z
1612.A4	Alcoholic beverages. Liquor
1614.A-Z	By medium, A-Z
	Signboards see KE5134
	Labeling
	Including misbranding
1616	General (Table KE5)
1618.A-Z	By product, A-Z
	Subarrange each by Table KE5

KE LAW OF CANADA KE

Regulation of industry, trade, and commerce. Occupational law

Trade regulation. Control of trade practices. Consumer protection

Labeling

By product, A-Z -- Continued

Drugs, pharmaceutical products, narcotics see KE3714+

Hazardous substances see KE3763+

Weights and measures. Containers

1620	General. Standards (Table KE5)
1622.A-Z	By products, A-Z
1622.P7	Precious metals

Competition. Restraint of trade. Combines, monopolies, mergers

For works on the competition, etc. aspects of a particular industry or profession, see the industry or profession

1631-1640	General (Table KE4)
	Investigation of particular combines, etc. Official reports
1643	To 1958
	By date of publication
1644	1959-
	By report number
1646	Special aspects
	Restrictive and unfair trade practices
	Cf. KE2988+ Trademarks and unfair competition
1649	General (Table KE5)
1651	Price discrimination. Price fixing (Table KE5)
1653	Resale price maintenance (Table KE5)
	Dumping see KE6129
1655.A-Z	Other, A-Z
1658	Small business (Table KE5)
1660	Trade associations
	Professional associations see KE2703

Primary production. Extractive industries

Agriculture. Forestry

1671-1680	General (Table KE4)
1686	Conservation of agricultural and forest lands. Soil conservation. Erosion control (Table KE5)
	For development and rehabilitation programs see KE1691
	Cf. KE5194+ Land reclamation
	Control of agricultural pests, plant diseases, predatory animals. Weed control. Plant quarantine
	Cf. KE3668+ Veterinary law
1687	General (Table KE5)
	Pesticides, insecticides see KE3766.P5

Regulation of industry, trade, and commerce. Occupational law

Primary production. Extractive industries

Agriculture. Forestry -- Continued

Economic assistance

1691	General. Rural development and rehabilitation (Table KE5)
	Price supports. Price stabilization. Guaranteed prices
1693	General (Table KE5)
1694.A-Z	By commodity, A-Z
1694.G7	Grain (Table KE6)
	Including wheat, barley, oats, etc.
1700	Farm loans. Farm mortgage credit (Table KE5)
	Marketing
	For produce exchanges see KE1093+
1712	General (Table KE5)
1714.A-Z	Particular commodities, A-Z
1714.G7	Grain
	Including wheat, barley, oats, etc.
	Standards and grading. Inspection
	For containers, measurements see KE1620+
1717	General (Table KE5)
1719.A-Z	Particular commodities, A-Z
1719.G7	Grain (Table KE6)
	Including wheat, barley, oats, etc.
	Livestock industry and trade. Cattle raising
	For standards and grading see KE1717+
	For the meat packing industry see KE1878+
	Cf. KE3668+ Veterinary laws. Veterinary hygiene
1723	General. Cattle industry (Table KE5)
1726	Sheep raising (Table KE5)
1729	Poultry industry (Table KE5)
	Dairy industry see KE1887
1740	Forestry. Timber laws (Table KE5)
	For national forests see KE5203
1745	Beekeeping. Apiculture (Table KE5)
	Game laws see KE5210
	Fishing industry
1760	General (Table KE5)
1761	Special aspects
1765.A-Z	Particular fish or marine fauna, A-Z
	Including conservation, control, and regulation of the industry
1765.C6	Cod (Table KE6)
	Mining. Quarrying
1790	General (Table KE5)
1795	Coal (Table KE5)

KE LAW OF CANADA KE

Regulation of industry, trade, and commerce. Occupational law

Primary production. Extractive industries

Mining. Quarrying -- Continued

Nonferrous metals

1800	General works
1802.A-Z	Particular metals, A-Z
1802.C6	Copper (Table KE6)
1802.G6	Gold (Table KE6)
	Petroleum. Oil and gas
1808	General (Table KE5)
1809	Special aspects
1811	Conservation (Table KE5)
1815	Submerged land legislation. Tidal oil. Offshore drilling (Table KE5)
1822	Oil and gas leases (Table KE5)
1827	Natural gas (Table KE5)
	Pipelines see KE2230+
1830	Other nonmetallic minerals and gases (Table KE5)
	Manufacturing industries
	Chemical industries
1840	General works
1842.A-Z	Particular products, A-Z
1842.F4	Fertilizers and feed stuffs
1855.A-Z	Major and heavy industries, A-Z
1855.E4	Electric industries (Table KE6)
1855.S5	Shipbuilding (Table KE6)
1858.A-Z	Consumer products. Light industries, A-Z
1858.B56	Biotechnology industries (Table KE6)
1858.T6	Toys (Table KE6)
	Food processing industries
	Cf. KE3705 Food adulteration
1867	General works
	Agricultural products
1870	General (Table KE5)
1874	Fruits and vegetables (Table KE5)
1876.A-Z	Other, A-Z
	Meat industry
1878	General. Meat inspection (Table KE5)
1882	Poultry products. Eggs and egg products (Table KE5)
1887	Dairy industry. Dairy products industry. Milk production and distribution (Table KE5)
	Fishery products. Seafood industry
1896	General (Table KE5)
1898.A-Z	Particular products, A-Z
1906.A-Z	Beverages, A-Z
	Liquor, alcoholic beverage production see KE3736

Regulation of industry, trade, and commerce. Occupational law -- Continued

1915 Construction and building industry. Contractors (Table KE5)
For building contracts see KE933
For building laws see KE5268+

Trade and commerce
For commercial law (General) see KE911+
For trade regulations see KE1591+

1935 General (Table KE5)
International trade
For foreign investment control and regulation see KE1575

1940 General. Export and import controls and regulations (Table KE5)
For trade agreements see K4600+

Export trade. Export controls and regulations

1950 General (Table KE5)

1952.A-Z Particular commodities, A-Z

1952.E43 Electricity (Table KE6)

1952.P4 Petroleum. Oil and gas (Table KE6)

1952.W43 Weapons (Table KE6)
Including arms transfers

1955-1957 Import trade. Import controls and regulations
For tariff see KE6081+
For dumping see KE6129

1955 General works

1957.A-Z Particular commodities, A-Z

1957.T4 Textiles. Clothing (Table KE6)

1961 Wholesale trade (Table KE5)
Retail trade

1967 General (Table KE5)
Conditions of trading

1971 Sunday legislation (Table KE5)
Resale price maintenance see KE1653

1973 Franchises (Table KE5)

1976.A-Z Particular modes of trading, A-Z

1980.A-Z Particular products, A-Z

1980.A3 Automobiles

1980.G3 Gasoline

Service trades

1985 General. Licensing (Table KE5)

1987.A-Z Particular trades, A-Z

1987.C6 Collection agencies (Table KE6)
For collection laws see KE1018

1987.C7 Credit bureaus (Table KE6)

1987.D3 Day care centers. Nursery schools (Table KE6)

1987.E5 Employment agencies (Table KE6)

Regulation of industry, trade, and commerce. Occupational law

Trade and commerce

Service trade

Particular trades, A-Z -- Continued

Funeral services see KE1987.U5

1987.H6 Homemakers. Visiting nurses (Table KE6)

1987.H65 Hotels. Restaurants (Table KE6)

Insurance brokers see KE1154

Nursery schools see KE1987.D3

1987.R4 Real estate agents (Table KE6)

Restaurants see KE1987.H65

Stockbrokers see KE1062

1987.T73 Travel agents (Table KE6)

1987.U5 Undertakers. Funeral services (Table KE6)

Cf. KE3581 Disposal of the dead

Visiting nurses see KE1987.H6

Warehouses

1995 General (Table KE5)

Special-purpose warehouses

1999 Bonded warehouses (Table KE5)

Public utilities

Including both privately and publicly owned utilities

2020 Regulated industries in general (Table KE5)

Particular industries

Power supply

Including energy resources and development

2035 General (Table KE5)

2036 National Energy Board (Table KE5)

2041 Electricity (Table KE5)

2046 Gas (Table KE5)

2051 Water (Table KE5)

Including water supply

For water power development see KE5145

2056 Atomic power (Table KE5)

2061.A-Z Other sources of power, A-Z

Transportation and communication see KE2071+

Transportation and communications

Including government-owned and municipal services

2071-2080 General (Table KE4 modified)

Decisions of regulatory agencies. Orders. Rulings

2076.54 Decisions and orders (CTC Review Committee). By date

2082 Procedure. Canadian Transport Commission (Table KE5)

Road traffic. Automotive transportation

Motor vehicles

2095 General (Table KE5)

KE **LAW OF CANADA** KE

Regulation of industry, trade, and commerce. Occupational law

Transportation and communications

Road traffic. Automotive transportation

Motor vehicles -- Continued

2097	Safety equipment
2100	Registration. Title transfer
2103	Drivers' licenses
2105	Safety responsibility laws. Financial responsibility laws. Compulsory insurance (Table KE5) Cf. KE1204 Unsatisfied judgment funds
2107.A-Z	Other vehicles, A-Z
2107.B5	Bicycles (Table KE6)
2107.S6	Snowmobiles. All-terrain vehicles (Table KE6)
2107.T7	Trailers (Table KE6)
	Traffic regulation and enforcement
2112	General (Table KE5)
2114	Criminal offenses. Traffic violations. Drunk driving (Table KE5)
2122	School buses
	Carriage of passengers and goods
2130	General motor carrier regulation (Table KE5)
2135.A-Z	Particular types of motor carriers, A-Z
2138.A-Z	Special topics, A-Z
	Railways
2141-2150	General. Corporate structure. Regulation of industry (Table KE4)
2152	Canadian Transport Commission Railway Transport Committee (Table KE5) Established in 1904, the Board of Railway Commissioners was renamed the Board of Transport Commissioners in 1938. With proclamation of Part I of the National Transportation Act on September 19, 1967, the Board became part of the Canadian Transport Commission and was designated the Railway Transport Committee Class here works about the Committee and its predecessors
	Operation of railways
	Railway safety. Railway sanitation
2170	General (Table KE5)
2172.A-Z	Particular types of freight, A-Z
2172.D3	Dangerous goods
	Rates and ratemaking
2177	General works
2179	Freight. Freight classification
2189	Passenger fares
	Liability

KE LAW OF CANADA KE

Regulation of industry, trade, and commerce. Occupational law

Transportation and communications

Railways

Operation of railways

Liability -- Continued

2197	General. Damage to property
2203	Personal injury
2210.A-Z	Particular railways and railway companies, A-Z
	Including litigation, decisions, rulings, etc.
2220	Local transit. Electric railways. Streetcar lines. Subways (Table KE5)
	Pipelines
2230	General (Table KE5)
2231	Oil and gas (Table KE5)
2233	Other commodities (Table KE5)
	Aviation
2241-2250	General (Table KE4, modified)
	Statutes. Regulations. Orders. Rules of practice, etc.
	Regulations. Orders. Rules of practice, etc.
2244.73	Air navigation orders
2265	Airports (Table KE5)
	Particular types of aircraft
2268	Helicopters
	Commercial aviation. Airlines
2273	General (Table KE5)
2275	Finance
2280	Liability (Table KE5)
	For general tort liability for aviation accidents see KE1274.A9
2287.A-Z	Particular airlines. By name, A-Z
2287.A4	Air Canada
	Water transportation. Navigation and shipping
2345	General (Table KE5)
	Merchant mariners see KE1121+
	Ships
2350	General (Table KE5)
2352	Registration (Table KE5)
	Safety regulations
2355	General. Inspection (Table KE5)
2357	Lifesaving apparatus (Table KE5)
2359	Load line (Table KE5)
2365.A-Z	Particular types of vessels, A-Z
2365.G7	Ground-effect machines (Table KE6)
2365.M6	Motor boats (Table KE6)
2365.P5	Pleasure craft. Yachts (Table KE6)
2365.S7	Steamboats (Table KE6)

KE LAW OF CANADA KE

Regulation of industry, trade, and commerce. Occupational law

Transportation and communications

Water transportation. Navigation and shipping

Ships

Safety regulations -- Continued

2367.A-Z	Particular types of cargo, A-Z
2367.D3	Dangerous goods (Table KE6)
2367.G7	Grain (Table KE6)

Navigation and pilotage

For international rules of the road at sea see K4184

2372	General. Coastwise navigation (Table KE5)

Particular waterways

Cf. KE5155.A+ Waterway development

2377	Great Lakes (Table KE5)
2379	Saint Lawrence Seaway (Table KE5)
2381	Canals (Table KE5)
2383	Rivers (Table KE5)
2387	Harbors and ports (Table KE5)

Bridges see KE5142

2392	Lighthouses (Table KE5)

Shipping laws. The merchant marine

2402	General (Table KE5)
2440	Domestic shipping. Inland water carriers. Coastwise shipping (Table KE5)

Communication. Mass media

2460	General (Table KE5)

Postal service

2464	General (Table KE5)
2468	Organization and administration (Table KE5)

Classification of mails. Rates

2488	General (Table KE5)
2490.A-Z	Special classes, A-Z
2490.P3	Parcel post
2550	Press law (Table KE5)

For freedom of the press see KE4422

Telecommunication

2560	General (Table KE5)
2565	Artificial satellites in telecommunication

Particular companies engaged in telecommunication or any of its branches see KE2649.A+

2575	Telegraph. Teletype (Table KE5)

Including radiotelegraph

2580	Telephone (Table KE5)
2601-2644	Radio communication

Including radio and television combined

2601	General (Table KE5)

Regulation of industry, trade, and commerce. Occupational law

Transportation and communication

Communication. Mass media

Telecommunication

Radio communication

Canadian Radio-Television Commission see KE2614

2605	Radio stations. Frequency allocations. Licensing. Networks (Table KE5)
2607	Amateur stations

Radio broadcasting

Including radio and television broadcasting combined

2612	General (Table KE5)
2614	Canadian Radio-Television Commission

Television broadcasting

2640	General (Table KE5)
2644	Community antenna television (Table KE5)
2649.A-Z	Particular companies, A-Z
	Including litigation, decisions, rulings, etc.
2649.C3	Canadian Broadcasting Corporation (Table KE6)
2649.T4	Telesat Canada (Table KE6)

The professions

Including occupations

2700	General. Professional corporations
2703	Professional associations
	General only
	For particular associations, see the profession

Particular professions

The health professions

For malpractice see KE1271

For medical legislation see KE3646+

2706	General (Table KE5)

Physicians

Including legal status, etc.

2708	General (Table KE5)
2710.A-Z	Special topics, A-Z
2710.M34	Malpractice (Table KE6)
2714.A-Z	Other health professions, A-Z
2714.A5	Anesthesiologists (Table KE6)
	Chiropodists see KE2714.P6
2714.D4	Dentists and dental specialists (Table KE6)
2714.N8	Nurses (Table KE6)
2714.P4	Pharmacists (Table KE6)
2714.P6	Podiatrists. Chiropodists (Table KE6)
2714.S9	Surgeons (Table KE6)

Other health practitioners, A-Z

2717.C5	Chiropractors

Regulation of industry, trade, and commerce. Occupational law

The professions

Particular professions -- Continued

Economic and financial advisors

2722 Accountants. Auditors

For accounting law see KE1347
For corporation accounting see KE1430

Lawyers see KE330+

Engineering and construction

2727 Architects (Table KE5)

2730 Engineers (Table KE5)

Building contractors see KE1915

2742.A-Z Other professions, A-Z

2742.G4 Geologists

Journalists see KE2550

Social workers see KE3502

Teachers see KE3850+

Intellectual property

For relationship with competition laws see KE2923

2771-2780 General (Table KE4)

2781 Special aspects

Including relationship with law of master and servant
For employees' inventions see KE2945

Copyright

2791-2800 General (Table KE4)

Formalities. Administration

2808 General (Table KE5)

2810 Registration (Table KE5)

2815 Scope of protection. Duration and renewal (Table KE5)

Particular branches

Literary copyright

2825 General works. Authorship

Protected works

2826 General (Table KE5)

2829.A-Z Particular types of works, A-Z

2829.M32 Machine-readable bibliographic data (Table KE6)

Scope of protection

General see KE2825

2835 Mechanical reproduction. Reprinting. Dissemination (Table KE5)

2839 Public lending rights

2850 Musical copyright

Works of art and photography

2868 General works

2885 Designs and models

2900 Author and publisher. The publishing contract (Table KE5)

Intellectual property -- Continued

2905 Design protection (Table KE5)
Cf. KE2885 Design copyright
Cf. KE2952 Design patent

Industrial property

Including patents, industrial designs, trademarks, and unfair competition

2908 General (Table KE5)

Patent law

2911-2920 General (Table KE4)
2923 Special aspects

Including relationship with competition laws

Procedure. Patent and Copyright Office

2929 General (Table KE5, modified)

Statutes. Regulations. Orders. Rules of practice, etc.

Regulations. Orders. Rules of practice, etc.

2929.A34 Rules of practice. By date of publication
2935.A-Z Special topics, A-Z
2935.F4 Fees

Scope of protection see KE2911+

Invention

2941 General (Table KE5)
2943.A-Z Particular products and processes, A-Z
2945 Employees' inventions
2952 Designs and models
2955 Licenses. Compulsory licenses (Table KE5)
2975 Patent attorneys. Patent practice (Table KE5, modified)
2975.A65 Canadian Institute of Patent Solicitors. Bylaws. Reports

By date of publication

Trademarks and unfair competition

Cf. KE1649+ Unfair trade practices

2988 General (Table KE5)
2990 Procedure. Registration (Table KE5)
2998 Expungement of trademarks
2999 Trade secrets. Industrial espionage. Commercial espionage

Social law and legislation

3098 General (Table KE5)

Labor law

Including wartime legislation

3101-3110 General (Table KE4)
3113 Special aspects
3117 Administration. Department of Labour

Management-labor relations

3141-3150 General (Table KE4)

Social law and legislation
Labor law
Management-labor relations -- Continued

3151	Special aspects
	Labor relations boards
3153	General (Table KE5)
3156	Judicial review of board decisions
	Cf. KE3208 Judicial review of labor arbitration
3160	Fair and unfair labor practices
	For specific practices, see the subject
	Labor unions
3170	General (Table KE5)
3172	Union security. Union shop
3182	Union organization
	Tort liability see KE1288.L3
	Collective bargaining. Collective labor agreements
3193	General (Table KE5)
	Particular clauses and benefits
	see the subject
3196.A-Z	Particular industries, occupations, or groups of employees, A-Z
3196.A25	Actuaries (Table KE6)
3196.A34	Aeronautics (Table KE6)
3196.A37	Agriculture (Table KE6)
3196.A4	Air traffic controllers (Table KE6)
3196.A7	Architecture and town planning (Table KE6)
3196.A9	Auditors (Table KE6)
3196.B36	Banking (Table KE6)
3196.C67	Corrections. Correctional institutions (Table KE6)
3196.D4	Dentistry (Table KE6)
3196.E37	Education (Table KE6)
	Cf. KE3196.T4 Teachers
3196.E43	Electronic data processing personnel (Table KE6)
3196.E44	Electronic industries (Table KE6)
3196.E5	Engineers (Table KE6)
3196.F4	Federal public service employees (Table KE6)
	For particular occupations or groups of employees within the service, see the occupation or group
3196.F6	Foreign service officers (Table KE6)
3196.F67	Forestry (Table KE6)
	Government employees see KE3196.P9
3196.H43	Heating plants. Steam power-plants (Table KE6)
3196.H57	Historians (Table KE6)
3196.H6	Home economics (Table KE6)
3196.H65	Hospitals (Table KE6)
3196.L38	Lawyers (Table KE6)
3196.L5	Library science (Table KE6)

Social law and legislation
Labor law
Management-labor relations
Labor unions
Collective bargaining. Collective labor agreements
Particular industries, occupations, or groups of
employees, A-Z -- Continued

3196.L53	Lightkeepers (Table KE6)
3196.M27	Mathematicians (Table KE6)
3196.M35	Medical personnel (Table KE6)
3196.M4	Meteorology (Table KE6)
	Occupational therapists see KE3196.P58
3196.P5	Pharmacy (Table KE6)
3196.P58	Physical therapists. Occupational therapists (Table KE6)
3196.P65	Postal service (Table KE6)
3196.P7	Printing industry (Table KE6)
3196.P8	Provincial and municipal public service employees (Table KE6)
3196.P87	Psychologists (Table KE6)
3196.P9	Public employees (Table KE6)
	Cf. KE3196.F4 Federal public service employees
	Cf. KE3196.P8 Provincial and municipal service employees
3196.S34	Scientists (Table KE6)
3196.S54	Shipbuilding workers
3196.S62	Social scientists (Table KE6)
3196.S63	Social workers
	Steam power-plants see KE3196.H43
3196.T4	Teachers
3196.T44	Telephone workers
	Town planning see KE3196.A7
3196.T73	Translators

Collective labor disputes

3204	General (Table KE5)
3206	Arbitration. Conciliation (Table KE5)
3208	Judicial review of arbitration (Table KE5)
	Particular industries, occupations, or groups of employees see KE3232+
	Strikes and lockouts. Boycotts. Picketing
	For particular industries, occupations, or groups of employees see KE3232+
3213	General (Table KE5)
3217	Labor injunctions (Table KE5)
3226	Wartime disputes
	By industry, occupation, or group of employees

Social law and legislation
Labor law
Management-labor relations
Labor unions
Collective labor disputes
By industry, occupation, or group of employees -- Continued
Railways

3232	General (Table KE5)
3234.A-Z	Particular cases. By company, A-Z
3236.A-Z	Other, A-Z

Under each:
.x General
.x2 Particular cases. By employer, A-Z

3236.P6-.P62	Postal workers
3236.P8-.P82	Public employees
	Including public service employees
3236.S8-.S82	Steel industry
3240.A-Z	Particular industries, occupations, or groups of employees, A-Z
3240.C6	Construction industry (Table KE6)
3240.F4	Federal public service employees (Table KE6)
3240.P8	Provincial and municipal public service employees (Table KE6)
3240.P9	Public employees (Table KE6)

Labor standards

3244	General. Labor conditions (Table KE5)
3245	Special aspects

Employment and dismissal
For individual labor contracts see KE928+
Preferential employment

3247	General (Table KE5)
	Veterans see KE7240.E4

Discrimination in employment and its prevention
Including equal pay for equal work

3254	General. Racial discrimination (Table KE5)
3256.A-Z	Particular groups, A-Z
3256.A4	Aged. Older people
3256.R44	Religious discrimination
	Including Jews
3256.W6	Women

Dismissal. Resignation. Job security

3262	General (Table KE5)
3266.A-Z	Special topics, A-Z
3266.S9	Subcontracting (Table KE6)

Wages. Minimum wage
Including wage and hour laws

Social law and legislation
Labor law
Labor standards
Wages. Minimum wage -- Continued

3275 General (Table KE5)
Wartime and emergency legislation
For particular industries, occupations, or groups of
employees see KE3292.A+

3277 1939-1945 (Table KE5)
Wage discrimination. Equal pay for equal work see
KE3254+

3292.A-Z Particular industries, occupations, or groups of
employees, A-Z

3292.F5 Fishing industry (Table KE6)
Nonwage payments. Fringe benefits

3298 General (Table KE5)

3300 Pension and retirement plans (Table KE5)

3303 Other (Table KE5)
Hours of labor. Night work
Including weekly day of rest legislation
For Sunday observances see KE1971+

3312 General (Table KE5)
Women see KE3352
Children see KE3348

3318 Vacations. Holidays. Leaves of absence (Table KE5)

3320 Sick leave (Table KE5)
Labor discipline. Work rules

3328 General (Table KE5)

3329 Suspension (Table KE5)
Grievances. Grievance procedure

3332 General (Table KE5)

3336.A-Z Particular industries, occupations, or groups of
employees, A-Z

3336.F4 Federal public service employees (Table KE6)

3336.P9 Public employees (Table KE6)

3340 Labor supply. Manpower controls
Protection of labor. Labor hygiene and safety

3346 General (Table KE5)

3348 Child labor (Table KE5)
Including hours of labor

3352 Woman labor (Table KE5)
Including hours of labor
Labor hygiene and safety. Hazardous occupations.
Safety regulations

3365 General (Table KE5)

3367 Factory inspection (Table KE5)

3370.A-Z By industry or type of labor, A-Z

Social law and legislation
Labor law
Protection of labor. Labor hygiene and safety
Labor hygiene and safety. Hazardous occupations.
Safety regulations
By industry or type of labor, A-Z -- Continued

Call Number	Topic
3370.C6	Construction industry
3370.L8	Lumbering
3372.A-Z	By machinery, equipment, etc., A-Z
	For machinery, equipment, etc. used in a particular industry see KE3370.A+
3380.A-Z	Labor law of particular industries, occupations, or types of employment, A-Z
	Social insurance
3400	General (Table KE5)
	Health insurance. Medical care
	Cf. KE1174 Private insurance
3404	General (Table KE5)
3405	Medicare (Table KE5)
3408.A-Z	Special topics, A-Z
3408.S9	Subrogation. Third party liability
	Worker' compensation
3414	General (Table KE5)
3420.A-Z	Particular industries, occupations, or groups of employees, A-Z
3420.F5	Fishing industry
	Retirement and disability pensions. Survivors' benefits
	For old age security pensions see KE3524
3432	General. Canada Pension Plan (Table KE5)
3440.A-Z	Special topics, A-Z
	Mothers' allowances see KE3517
	Unemployment insurance
3451-3460	General (Table KE4)
3461	Special aspects
	Public welfare. Public assistance. Private charities
3500	General (Table KE5)
3502	Social work. Social workers
3505.A-Z	Special topics, A-Z
3505.D6	Domicile requirements
	Particular groups
3510	Maternal and infant welfare (Table KE5)
	Children. Child welfare. Youth services
3515	General (Table KE5)
3517	Family allowances. Mothers' allowances (Table KE5)
	Older people
3522	General (Table KE5)
3524	Old age pensions (Table KE5)

Social law and legislation
Public welfare. Public assistance. Private charities
Particular groups
Older people -- Continued

3526	Living accommodations. Housing. Old age homes (Table KE5)
	People with disabilities. Vocational rehabilitation
3532	General (Table KE5)
3534	Blind (Table KE5)
	Veterans see KE7230+
3542	Private charities (Table KE5)
	Public health. Sanitation. Environmental pollution
3575	General (Table KE5)
	Particular public health hazards and measures
3581	Disposal of the dead. Burial and cemetery laws (Table KE5)
	For undertakers see KE1987.U5
	Contagious and infectious diseases
3589	General. Reporting
3593.A-Z	Particular diseases, A-Z
3593.A54	AIDS
3593.V4	Venereal diseases
	Particular measures
	Meat inspection see KE1878+
3599	Immigration inspection. Quarantine (Table KE5)
3606.A-Z	Other, A-Z
3606.R4	Refuse disposal (Table KE6)
	Environmental pollution
	Including abatement of public nuisance
3611-3620	General (Table KE4)
3622	Special aspects
3625	Water pollution. Drainage (Table KE5)
	Air pollution. Control of smoke, noxious gases, etc.
3630	General (Table KE5)
3632	Tobacco smoking (Table KE5)
3635	Noise control (Table KE5)
	Medical legislation
	For physicians and related professions see KE2706+
3646	General (Table KE5)
3648	Patients' rights (Table KE5)
	Hospitals and other medical institutions
3650	Hospitals (Table KE5)
	For psychiatric hospitals and mental health facilities see KE3658
	For Armed Forces hospitals see KE6919
3652.A-Z	Other health services, A-Z
3652.C47	Child health services

Medical legislation -- Continued

Pharmacies see KE2714.P4

3654.A-Z Special topics, A-Z

Hospital records see KE3654.R42

3654.R42 Medical records. Hospital records. Records management (Table KE6)

Records management see KE3654.R42

3658 The mentally ill (Table KE5)

Including psychiatric hospitals and mental health facilities
For civil status of insane persons see KE514+
For mental incompetency proceedings see KE515
For criminal liability see KE8841

3659 Mental health courts (Table KE5)

3660.A-Z Disorders of character, behavior, and intelligence, A-Z

3660.A4 Alcoholism

Including works on the treatment and rehabilitation of alcoholics within the criminal justice system

3660.N3 Narcotic addiction. Drug addiction

3660.5 Human reproductive technology (Table KE5)

3661 Eugenics. Sterilization (Table KE5)

3663.A-Z Special topics, A-Z

3663.B44 Behavior modification (Table KE6)

3663.D43 Death, Definition of (Table KE6)

3663.D65 Donation of organs, tissues, etc. (Table KE6)

3663.E94 Euthanasia. Right to die. Living wills (Table KE6)

3663.G45 Genetics, Medical (Table KE6)

3663.I54 Informed consent (Table KE6)

Living wills see KE3663.E94

3663.M43 Medical experiments with humans (Table KE6)

Right to die see KE3663.E94

Veterinary medicine and hygiene. Veterinary public health

3668 General. Reporting (Table KE5)

3670.A-Z Particular measures, A-Z

3676 Animal protection. Animal welfare. Animal rights (Table KE5)

Including prevention of cruelty to animals
For animal rights as a social issue see HV4701+

Food. Drugs. Cosmetics

For regulation of the food processing industries see KE1867+

3696 General (Table KE5)

Food law

3702 General (Table KE5)

3705 Adulteration. Inspection (Table KE5)

3707.A-Z Particular food and food related products, A-Z

Drug laws

3714 General. Labeling (Table KE5)

Food. Drugs. Cosmetics
Drug laws -- Continued
Narcotics
Cf. KE9050+ Illicit possession, use of, or traffic in narcotics

3720	General (Table KE5)
3722.A-Z	Particular narcotics, A-Z
3722.M3	Marijuana
3725.A-Z	Other, A-Z
3725.P3	Patent medicines. Proprietary drugs (Table KE6)

Pharmacies see KE2714.P4

Alcohol. Alcoholic beverages. Prohibition. Liquor laws
Cf. KE9090 Illicit liquor traffic

3734	General (Table KE5)
3736	Alcohol production. Distilleries (Table KE5)
3740.A-Z	Special topics, A-Z

Advertising see KE1612.A4

Public safety

3756	General (Table KE5)
3758	Weapons. Firearms. Munitions (Table KE5)

Hazardous articles and processes. Product safety
For transportation of goods by rail see KE2172.D3
For transportation of goods by sea see KE2367.D3
Cf. KE1282+ Products liability

3763	General (Table KE5)
3766.A-Z	Particular products and processes, A-Z
3766.E9	Explosives (Table KE6)
	Herbicides see KE3766.P5
3766.P5	Pesticides. Herbicides (Table KE6)
3766.P64	Polychlorinated biphenyls (Table KE6)

Toys see KE1858.T6

Accident control

3773	Steam boilers
3778	Fire prevention and control (Table KE5)

Control of social activities. Recreation

3788	General (Table KE5)
3792	Sports. Prizefighting. Horse racing (Table KE5)
3795	Lotteries. Games of chance. Gambling (Table KE5)
	Cf. KE9066 Criminal law
3798.A-Z	Other, A-Z

Education
Including public education

3805	General (Table KE5)
3809	Church and education. Denominational schools (Table KE5)
3810	Other special aspects

School government and finance

3812	General (Table KE5)

KE LAW OF CANADA KE

Education

School government and finance -- Continued

3814 School districts. School boards. Boards of education (Table KE5)

> For individual school districts, see the jurisdiction from which they derive their authority, e.g. KEO774, Ontario For tort liability for school accidents see KE1288.S3

3820 School lands

Including community use of school facilities

3822 Finance. Federal aid to education

Students. Compulsory education

3835 General (Table KE5)

3839.A-Z Special topics, A-Z

3839.R4 Religious and patriotic observances. Bible reading. Religious instruction (Table KE6)

Teachers

For tort liability for school accidents see KE1288.S3

3850 General. Legal status, etc. (Table KE5)

3854.A-Z Special topics, A-Z

3854.S3 Salaries, pensions, etc. (Table KE6)

Elementary and secondary education

3865 General (Table KE5)

3871 Secondary education (Table KE5)

Curricula. Courses of instruction

3873 General works

3878 Language training

Including bilingual instruction

3883.A-Z Particular courses, A-Z

3883.L3 Law (Table KE6)

> Educational services for particular classes or types of students

3887 General works

3890.A-Z Particular classes or types, A-Z

3890.M46 Mental disabilities, Students with (Table KE6)

3895 Private education. Private schools

For denominational schools see KE3809

Higher education. Colleges and universities

3904 General (Table KE5)

3917 Faculties. Legal status of teachers. Academic freedom

3920 Students (Table KE5)

Including legal status, discipline, student government, etc.

Science and the arts. Research

3950 General (Table KE5)

3960.A-Z Particular branches and subjects, A-Z

3960.D4 Defense research and development (Table KE6)

Cf. KE906 Research and development contracts

The arts

Science and the arts. Research

The arts -- Continued

3968 Fine arts

Performing arts

3972 General works

Motion pictures

3980 General works

3982 Censorship (Table KE5)

3986.A-Z Other, A-Z

3990 Museums and galleries

3995 Historic buildings and monuments. Architectural landmarks (Table KE5)

Including preservation of cultural property

4000 Libraries

4010 Archives (Table KE5)

Cf. KE5325 Access to public records

4120 Public law in general

Constitutional law

Sources

4125 Bibliography

4128 Collections

Individual pre-Confederation sources

4136 Quebec Act, 1774

4138 Constitutional Act, 1791

4142 Quebec Conference, 1864

4143 Confederation Debates, 1865

4143.5 Indexes

4155 Other documents

4157 Contemporary writings

Texts of the British North America Act of 1867 and subsequent (i.e. amending) acts

Including the 1982 Constitutional Act

4165 Unannotated

By date of publication

4168 Annotated

4170 Commentaries

Other post-Confederation sources

4179 Constitutional (and Federal-provincial) conferences

By conference date

Under each:

.A2 *Proceedings*

.A3-.A49 *Other documents (reports, submissions, etc.)*

4184 Other

Constitutional history

4191-4200 General (Table KE4)

Constitutional law
Constitutional history -- Continued

4205.A-Z Special topics, A-Z
For the history of a particular subject of constitutional law, see the subject

4211-4220 Constitutional law in general (Table KE4, modified)
Court decisions
Reports

4216.2 Decisions of the Judicial Committee of the Privy Council
"Reference cases." Advisory opinions
Collections

4216.3 General

4216.32.A-Z Special topics, A-Z

4216.35.A-Z Particular references
By best known name of case or topic, A-Z

4226 Canadian and foreign constitutions compared

4228 Amending process (Table KE5)
Constitutional principles

4238 Rule of law

4239 Legality. Legal certainty

4241 Sovereignty of Parliament. Responsible government. Representative government
Crown privilege see KE4715

4244 Conflict of interests (General). Incompatibility of offices. Ethics in government (Table KE5)

4248 Judicial review of legislation (Table KE5)
Cf. KE5036 Judicial review of administrative acts
Sources and relationships of law

4252 International and municipal law. Treaties and agreements

4254 Statutory law and delegated legislation. Ordinances. Rules
Cf. KE5024+ Administrative law
Structure of government. Federal-provincial relations. Interprovincial relations. Jurisdiction

4270 General (Table KE5)

4275 Distribution of legislative power. Exclusive and concurrent legislative powers (Table KE5)
Class works dealing with legislative competence in relation to particular subjects of law, e.g. taxation, trade and commerce, labor law, etc., with those subjects, using "Special aspects" where provided
For "reference cases" see KE4216.3+

4278 Declaratory power of Parliament

4280 Disallowance and reservation of provincial legislation (Table KE5)

Constitutional law
Structure of government. Federal-provincial relations.
Interprovincial relations. Jurisdiction -- Continued
Federal-provincial disputes. Interprovincial disputes

4285	Boundary disputes
	Including litigation, decisions, rulings, etc.
4310	Foreign relations (Table KE5)
	Cf. KE4719 Prerogative in foreign affairs. Treatymaking power
4335	Public policy. Police power
	Individual and state
	Nationality and citizenship
4345	General (Table KE5)
	Acquisition and loss
4349	General (Table KE5)
4351	Naturalization (Table KE5)
4360.A-Z	Particular groups, A-Z
	Civil and political rights and liberties
4381	General. Canadian Bill of Rights (Table KE5)
4381.5	Canadian Charter of Rights and Freedoms (Table KE5)
4382	Special aspects
	Particular groups
4390	Gays
	Cf. KE591 Same-sex marriage
4395	Racial and ethnic minorities. Discrimination in general (Table KE5)
	For Indians see KE7722.C5
4399	Sex discrimination (Table KE5)
	Particular rights and freedoms
4408	Due process of law (Table KE5)
4410	Equality before the law (Table KE5)
4413	Linguistic and cultural rights. Bilingualism (Table KE5)
	Freedom of expression
4418	General works
4420	Freedom of speech
4422	Freedom of the press and of information. Press censorship (Table KE5)
	For press law see KE2550
	For crime and publicity see KE8817
4425	Freedom of assembly and association
4430	Freedom of religion and of conscience
	Cf. KE3809 Church and education
	Cf. KE4502+ Church and state
	Habeas corpus see KE8569
	Right of privacy (Criminal law) see KE8940
	Right of privacy (Torts) see KE1240+
4438	Political parties (Table KE5)

Constitutional law
Individual and state -- Continued
Control of individuals

4445	Passports (Table KE5)
	Aliens
	Cf. KE518.A4 Capacity and disability
4452	General (Table KE5)
	Immigration
4454	General (Table KE5)
4456	Immigration Appeal Board (Table KE5)
4458.A-Z	Temporary admission of particular groups, A-Z
4458.B87	Businesspeople (Table KE6)
4458.S76	Students (Table KE6)
	Particular controls and procedures
	Public health inspection, quarantine see KE3599
	Particular classes of immigrants
	Racial and ethnic groups see KE4479+
4472	Refugees (Table KE5)
4475	Deportation and expulsion (Table KE5)
	Particular racial and ethnic groups
4479	Chinese (Table KE5)
4482.A-Z	Other, A-Z
4486	Internal security. Control of subversive activities (Table KE5)
	Cf. KE9005 Criminal law
	Church and state
4502	General. Religious corporations (Table KE5)
	Church property
4505	General works
4507	Church lands. Clergy reserves (Table KE5)
4508	Jesuit estates (Table KE5)
4512.A-Z	Other topics, A-Z
	Church and education. Denominational schools see KE3809
4512.P3	Parishes
4514.A-Z	Particular denominations, A-Z
4514.C3	Catholic Church
4514.P7	Presbyterians
	Organs of the government
4526	General works
	The people
4527	Initiative and referendum (Table KE5)
	The legislature
4529	General. Legislative power
	Parliament
4533	General. Organization (Table KE5)
4535	Rules and procedure

KE LAW OF CANADA KE

Constitutional law
Organs of the government
The legislature
Parliament -- Continued

4540	Parliamentary reporting
	The legislative process
4550	General works
	Committees
4555	General works
	Joint committees
	Class here only works about joint committees
	General see KE4555+
4557.A-Z	Particular committees, A-Z
4559	Lobbying (Table KE6)
	Legislative investigations
	see the subject
4560	Bill drafting (Table KE5)
	For legal composition, language of the law (General) see K94
	For legal composition, language of the law (Canadian law) see KE265
4564	Private bill procedure (Table KE5)
4572	Discipline of legislators
	Including individual cases
	Legal status of legislators
4578	Parliamentary immunity and privileges
4579	Salaries, pensions, etc.
4582	Conflict of interests (Table KE5)
	Cf. KE9022 Criminal law
	The Senate
4593	General works
4595	Rules and procedures
	By date of publication
	Including rules, etc., of the Legislative Council (Province of Canada, 1847-1867)
	For divorce rules and orders see KE576+
	Committees
	Class here only works about committees
4599	General works
4601.A-Z	Particular committees, A-Z
	The House of Commons
4620	General works
	Election law
	Including the conduct of elections and general election instructions
	For municipal elections see KE4917
4622	General (Table KE5)

Constitutional law
Organs of the government
The legislature
Parliament
The House of Commons
Election law -- Continued
Suffrage. Electoral franchise
Including voting age

4627	General (Table KE5)
	Particular groups of voters
4629	Armed Forces electors. Soldiers (Table KE5)
4631.A-Z	Other, A-Z
4633	Registration. Qualification. Enumeration (Table KE5)
4636	Absentee voting (Table KE5)
	For Armed Forces electors, soldiers see KE4629
4640	Election districts. Apportionment (Table KE5)
4646	Campaign expenditures (Table KE5)
4648	Corrupt practices. Illicit political activities (Table KE5)
	Cf. KE9020 Criminal law
	Contested elections
4652	General works
	Cases
4654	Collections
	By date
4655.A-Z	Particular cases
	By incumbent or best known name, A-Z
	Organization. Legislative process
4658	Rules and procedure (Table KE5, modified)
	Including rules, etc., of the Legislative Assembly (Province of Canada, 1841-1867)
	Statutes. Regulations. Orders. Rules of practice, etc.
	Standing orders. Rules
	Official editions
4658.A351A-.A351Z	Serials
4658.A352	Monographs
	By date of publication
4658.A354	Compilations
	By editor, compiler, etc.
4658.A356	Parliamentary precedents (Speakers' decisions)
	Committees
	Class here only works about committees
4664	General works
4665.A-Z	Particular committees, A-Z

KE LAW OF CANADA KE

Constitutional law
Organs of the government
The legislature
Parliament
The House of Commons
Organization. Legislative process -- Continued
Private bill procedure see KE4564
Contested elections see KE4652+
The Crown and the Executive branch of government
4705 General. Executive power
The Crown
Prerogative powers
4709 General works
Prerogative in domestic affairs
4713 War and emergency powers (Table KE5)
4715 Crown privilege (Table KE5)
4719 Prerogative in foreign affairs. Treatymaking power (Table KE5)
Including questions of provincial competence to conduct foreign relations
4723 Governor-General (Table KE5)
4726 Lieutenant-Governors (Table KE5)
4730 The Prime Minister and the Cabinet (Table KE5)
Government departments and non-departmental organizations of government
For Crown corporations see KE1465
For public service of Canada see KE4940+
For regulatory bodies in general see KE5019+
For administrative tribunals in general see KE5029
4750 General (Table KE5)
Particular departments, boards, commissions, etc.
Including proposed ones
For such bodies dealing with a particular subject, see the subject
4752 Department of Justice (Table KE5)
Commissions of inquiry, royal commissions, task forces, etc.
4765 General (Table KE5)
Particular
see the subject
4775 The Judiciary. Judicial power
Class here constitutional status only
For judicial review of legislation see KE4248
For judicial review of administrative acts see KE5036
Cf. KE8200 Courts, administration of justice, and organization of the judiciary

KE LAW OF CANADA KE

4795	National emblem. Flag. Seal. Seat of government. National anthem
	Local government
4900	General (Table KE5)
	Units of local authority
	Municipal government. Municipal services
	Including regional governments and rural municipalities and districts
4904	General. Municipal corporations (Table KE5)
4913	Charters and ordinances. Local law (Collections)
4915.A-Z	Special topics, A-Z
	Tort liability see KE1288.M8
4917	Municipal elections
	Municipal officials. Organs of government
4919	General works
4921.A-Z	Particular officers or organs, A-Z
4923.A-Z	Special topics, A-Z
4923.A2	Abuse of power
4923.C6	Conflict of interests
	Municipal public service see KE4995
	Municipal finance see KE6265+
4934	Special districts. Special authorities and boards
	General only
	For particular kinds of districts, etc., see the subject, e.g. KE3814, School districts
	For individual special districts, see the jurisdiction from which they derive their authority
	Public service. Government officials and employees
	Federal public service
4940	General. Qualification for employment (Table KE5)
4941	Public Service Commission (Table KE5)
	Conditions and restrictions of employment. Employment discipline
4944	General works
4948	Political activities
	Special classes of employees
4955	Women (Table KE5)
	Employment relations
	General see KE3240.F4
	Collective bargaining see KE3196.F4
	Collective labor disputes see KE3236.P8+
	Grievance procedures see KE3336.F4
	Tenure and remuneration
4962	General (Table KE5)
4964	Classification (Table KE5)
4967	Salaries (Table KE5)
4969	Promotions

Public service. Government officials and employees
Federal public service
Tenure and remuneration -- Continued

4972	Retirement. Pensions (Table KE5)
4976	Leave regulations
4978	Other benefits
	e.g. Life insurance, health insurance
4979	Health and safety regulations (Table KE5)
4980	Travel regulations
	Particular departments, etc.
	see the department
4985	Provincial public service
	General and comparative only
	Employment relations
	General see KE3240.P8
	Collective bargaining see KE3196.P8
	Collective labor disputes see KE3236.P8+
4995	Municipal public service
	General and comparative only
	Employment relations
	General see KE3240.P8
	Collective bargaining see KE3196.P8
	Collective labor disputes see KE3236.P8+
	Police and power of the police
	Including works about police constables
	For police handbooks, manuals, etc., of criminal law and procedure see KE8809.8.P6
5006	General (Table KE5)
5008	Royal Canadian Mounted Police (Table KE5)
5010.A-Z	Special topics, A-Z
5010.P74	Private police (Table KE6)
	Administrative organization and procedure
5015	General. Administrative law (Table KE5)
	The administrative process. Regulatory agencies
	For particular agencies, see the relevant subject
5019	General (Table KE5)
	Legislative functions. Rulemaking power. Delegated legislation
5024	General (Table KE5)
5026	Citizen participation (Table KE5)
5029	Judicial functions. Procedure. Administrative tribunals (Table KE5)
	For particular tribunals, see the relevant subject
	Commissions of inquiry see KE4765+
5034	Abuse of administrative power. Ombudsman (Table KE5)

Administrative organization and procedure
The administrative process. Regulatory agencies --
Continued

5036 Judicial review of administrative acts (Table KE5)
For judicial review of labor board decisions see KE3156
For judicial review of labor arbitration see KE3208
Cf. KE4248 Judicial review of legislation
Tort liability of the government and of public officers see
KE1305
Public property. Public restraints on private property

5105 General (Table KE5)
Conservation and management of natural resources.
Environmental planning
Cf. KE3611+ Environmental pollution

5110 General (Table KE5)
5111 Special aspects
Roads

5126 General. Highway law (Table KE5)
5134 Roadside protection. Rights of way (Table KE5)
Including restrictions on signboards, advertising, etc.
Cf. KE5284 Structures other than buildings

5142 Bridges (Table KE5)
Water resources. Watersheds. Rivers. Lakes. Water
courses

5145 General. Conservation and management. Water
resources development (Table KE5)
Including water power development

5146 Special aspects
Riparian rights see KE707
Water pollution see KE3625

5155.A-Z Particular inland waterways and channels, A-Z
5157 Saint Lawrence Seaway
5159 Canals
For navigation see KE2381

5165.A-Z Particular bodies of water, water districts, etc., A-Z
5175 Expropriation (Table KE5)
Public land law

5184 General. Crown lands (Table KE5)
5185 Special aspects
Reclamation. Irrigation. Drainage

5194 General (Table KE5)
5196.A-Z Particular types of land, A-Z
Marshes see KE5196.S9

5196.S9 Swamps. Marshes. Wetlands
Wetlands see KE5196.S9

5198 Shore protection. Coastal zone management
National preserves

KE LAW OF CANADA KE

Public property. Public restraints on private property
Public land law
National preserves -- Continued

5201	Grazing lands (Table KE5)
5203	Forest preserves (Table KE5)
	National parks and monuments . Wilderness preservation
5207	General (Table KE5)
	Wildlife protection
	Including game, bird, and fish protection
	Cf. KE1760+ Fishing industry
5210	General. Game laws. Protection of migratory birds (Table KE5)
5215.A-Z	Particular animals and birds, A-Z
5215.S4	Seals
5217.A-Z	Particular parks, monuments, etc., A-Z
5217.L3	Lake Louise
	Architectural and historic monuments see KE3995
	Indian reserves and settlements see KE7715
	Clergy reserves see KE4507
5232	Homesteads (Table KE5)
	Land grants
5237	General works
	Particular groups receiving grants
5240	Veterans (Table KE5)
	Regional and city planning. Zoning. Building
5258	General (Table KE5)
5263	Land use. Zoning. Land subdivision (Table KE5)
	Building laws
5268	General (Table KE5)
5270.A-Z	Particular types of buildings, A-Z
5270.F37	Farm buildings (Table KE6)
5270.T4	Theaters (Table KE6)
5275	Electrical installations
5281	Plumbing
5284	Structures other than buildings
	Including billboards and outdoor advertising in cities
	Cf. KE5134 Roadside protection
	Housing. Slum clearance. City redevelopment
5295	General (Table KE5)
5296	Special aspects
	Housing finance
5300	General works (Table KE5)
5302	Central Mortgage and Housing Corporation (Table KE5)
5307	Discrimination in housing (Table KE5)
5312.A-Z	Particular types of accommodation, A-Z
	Low-rental housing. Public housing see KE5295+
5312.M6	Mobile homes (Table KE6)

KE LAW OF CANADA KE

Public property. Public restraints on private property --
Continued
Government property

5323	General (Table KE5)
5325	Access to public records. Freedom of information (Table KE5)
5420	Public works (Table KE5)

Government measures in time of war, national emergency, or economic crisis. Emergency economic legislation

5460	General (Table KE5)

By period

In case of doubt, see the general subject

5461-5464	To 1914 (Table KE12)
5466-5469	1914-1918 (Table KE12)
5471-5474	1918-1939 (Table KE12)
5476-5479	1939-1945 (Table KE12)
5481-5484	1945- (Table KE12)

Public finance

5600	General (Table KE5)
5602	Money. Currency. Coinage
5612	Foreign exchange regulation (Table KE5)
5617	Budget. Government expenditures. Government spending power (Table KE5)
5622	Expenditure control. Public auditing and accounting
5627	Public debts. Loans. Bond issues

National revenue

History

Wartime finance

General only

For works on the history of particular taxes, see the relevant tax

5632	General works

By period

5636	World War I (Table KE5)
5637	World War II (Table KE5)
5645	General works

Taxation

For works on intergovernmental tax relations see KE6166

5661-5670	General. Allocation of taxing power (Table KE4, modified)
5669.8.A-Z	Works for particular groups of users, A-Z
5669.8.B8	Building contractors
5669.8.E94	Executives

KE LAW OF CANADA KE

Public finance
National revenue
Taxation -- Continued
Tax saving. Tax planning
Including income tax
For tax planning relating to other particular taxes, see the taxes

5682	General (Table KE5)
5683	Tax shelters (Table KE5)

Tax administration and procedure
Including administration and procedure relating to federal taxes in general and to federal income tax
For works on topics relating to other taxes, see the taxes
Cf. KE6190+ Provincial taxation
Cf. KE6275+ Local taxation

5688	General (Table KE5)
5690	Department of National Revenue
5695	Double taxation (Table KE5)
	Tax collection
5700	General (Table KE5)
5705	Tax accounting (Table KE5)
	Procedure. Practice
5710	General (Table KE5)
	Remedies. Tax appeals
5715	General (Table KE5)
5717	Tax Court of Canada. Tax Review Board (Table KE5)
	Including predecessor boards
5723	Exemption
	General only
	For exemptions under particular taxes, see the relevant tax
	Tax treatment of special activities
5726	Divorce (Table KE5)
5728	Tax evasion. Criminal offenses (Table KE5)
	Particular taxes
5734	Several. Collective (Table KE5)
	e.g. Income, estate and gift taxes
	Income tax
5751-5760	General. Personal income tax (Table KE4, modified)
5759.8.A-Z	Works for particular groups of users, A-Z
5759.8.A3	Accountants
5759.8.F37	Farmers

Administration see KE5688+
Procedure, practice see KE5710+
Tax planning see KE5682+
Estate planning see KE5974
Income

KE **LAW OF CANADA** KE

Public finance
National revenue
Taxation
Particular taxes
Income tax
Income -- Continued

5764	General. Exclusion form income. Exempt income (Table KE5)
5775	Income from office or employment. Salaries and wages
	Including fringe benefits
	Income from business of property
5779	General works
5781.A-Z	Special topics, A-Z
5781.G6	Goodwill, Sale of
	Income from investments. Capital investment. Capital gains
5785	General. Securities. Dividends. Interest
5787	Foreign investments (Table KE5)
	For foreign investors in Canada see KE5864.N6
	Capital gains
5791	General (Table KE5)
5793	Valuation of assets
5799.A-Z	Other sources of income, A-Z
5799.A44	Alimony and support (Table KE6)
5799.C6	Compensatory payments. Unusual receipts (Table KE6)
5799.L5	Life insurance proceeds (Table KE6)
5799.P4	Pensions and annuities (Table KE6)
	Support and alimony see KE5799.A44
	Allowances and deductions. Personal exemptions
5808	General (Table KE5)
5810	Depreciation allowances. Capital cost allowances (Table KE5)
5814	Charitable contributions (Table KE5)
	Expenses
5820	General (Table KE5)
5822.A-Z	Particular kinds, A-Z
5822.A9	Automobile expenses
5825	Losses
	Computation of tax
5835	General works
5840	Income averaging (Table KE5)
5842	Tax credits
	Cf. KE5787 Foreign investments
	Particular methods of assessment and collection

Public finance
National revenue
Taxation
Particular taxes
Income taxes
Particular methods of assessment and collection -- Continued
Payment at source
Payroll deduction. Withholding tax
5855 General (Table KE5)
5855.5 Tables
5864.A-Z Particular classes of taxpayers, A-Z
Aliens see KE5864.N6
5864.F3 Farmers. Fishermen (Table KE6)
Indians see KE7722.T39
Inuit see KE7722.T39
Native peoples see KE7722.T39
5864.N6 Nonresidents. Aliens (Table KE6)
Including foreign corporations
5864.T7 Trusts (Table KE6)
5870 Income of nonprofit organizations, corporations,
foundations, endowments, pension trust funds
(Table KE5)
Income of business organizations
5875 General (Table KE5)
5878 Partnerships and joint ventures (Table KE5)
Juristic persons. Corporations
For foreign corporations see KE5864.N6
For nonprofit corporations see KE5870
5884 General. Corporation income tax (Table KE5)
5890 Surtaxes. Excess profits tax (Table KE5)
5900 Cooperatives (Table KE5)
Private corporations. Small business
corporations
5906 General (Table KE5)
5908 Associated corporations
5914.A-Z Particular lines of corporate business, A-Z
5914.C6 Construction industry (Table KE6)
5914.M5 Mining. Petroleum (Table KE6)
Petroleum see KE5914.M5
5914.P7 Professional corporations (Table KE6)
5914.R4 Real estate business (Table KE6)
5920.A-Z Special topics, A-Z
5920.C6 Corporate reorganizations
5920.D3 Damages
Other taxes on capital and income
Capital gains see KE5791+

Public finance
National revenue
Taxation
Particular taxes
Other taxes on capital and income -- Continued
Estate, inheritance, and gift taxes
Class here works on federal estate and gift taxes and provincial succession duties combined

5970	General (Table KE5)
5974	Estate planning. Estate tax planning (Table KE5)

Estate tax
Class here works on the Dominion succession duty

5976	General (Table KE5)
5979	Life insurance proceeds (Table KE5)
5985	Gift tax (Table KE5)

Excise taxes. Taxes on transactions

5996	General (Table KE5)
6002	Sales tax (Table KE5)
	Including value-added tax
6005	Excise duties (Table KE5)
6009.A-Z	Particular commodities, services, transactions, A-Z
6009.A43	Alcoholic beverages. Liquor taxes (Table KE6)
6009.B85	Building materials (Table KE6)
	Liquor taxes see KE6009.A43

Taxation of natural resources

6030	General works
6035.A-Z	Particular resources and resource industries, A-Z
6035.M5	Mining. Petroleum (Table KE6)

Particular methods of assessment and collection
For assessment and collection of particular taxes, see the taxes, e.g., Income tax, excise taxes

6060	Stamp duties (Table KE5)

Tariff. Custom duties
For trade agreements see K4600+
For foreign trade regulation see KE1940+
For tariff agreements between the United States and Canada see KF6668.C3+

6081-6090	General (Table KE4)
6096	Tariff Board (Table KE5)

Particular tariffs

6104	General works
6109.A-Z	Particular commodities, A-Z

Customs administration

6118	General. Procedure. Remedies (Table KE5)
6123	Enforcement. Criminal offenses. Smuggling
6129	Dumping. Antidumping duties (Table KE5)
6132.A-Z	Other topics, A-Z

Public finance -- Continued
Provincial and local finance

6155	General works
6164	Provincial and local taxation
6166	Federal grants, loans, etc. Revenue sharing. Intergovernmental tax relations (Table KE5)
	Provincial finance
6172	General. Administration (Table KE5)
6174	Jurisdiction. Limitations on provincial powers of taxation Cf. KE6166 Intergovernmental tax relations
6178	Budget. Expenditure control. Auditing and accounting
6182	Public debts. Securities. Bonds
	Taxation
6190	General (Table KE5)
6194	Income tax (Table KE5)
	Property taxes. Taxation of capital
6204	Real property taxes
6214	Business taxes
6222	Succession duties. Gift tax
	Excise taxes. Taxes on transactions
6230	General works
6232	Retail sales tax (Table KE5)
	Taxation of natural resources
6242	General works
6244.A-Z	Particular resources and resource industries, A-Z
6244.F6	Forestry. Logging
6256.A-Z	Other sources of revenue, A-Z
6256.F4	Federal grants, loans, etc.
	Local finance
6265	General (Table KE5)
6267	Budget. Expenditure control. Auditing and accounting
6270	Local government debts. Municipal bonds and debentures
	Taxation
6275	General. Tax powers of municipalities (Table KE5)
	Property taxes
6280	General. Assessment (Table KE5)
	Real property taxes
6283	General (Table KE5)
6285	Real property assessment. Land valuation (Table KE5)
	Including works on assessment for tax and other purposes
6289	Exemptions
	General only
	For particular exemptions see KE6291.A+

KE --- LAW OF CANADA --- KE

Public finance
- Provincial and local finance
  - Local finance
    - Taxation
      - Property taxes
        - Real property taxes -- Continued

Call Number	Description
6291.A-Z	Particular kinds of land, tax-exempt lands, special modes of taxation, A-Z
6291.F3	Farm land (Table KE6)
6291.G6	Golf courses (Table KE6)
6295.A-Z	Special topics, A-Z
6295.I4	Improvements (Table KE6)
6300	Personal property taxes
6310	Business taxes. Licenses (Table KE5)
6320.A-Z	Other taxes, A-Z
6328.A-Z	Other sources of revenue, A-Z
6328.F4	Federal grants, loans, etc (Table KE6)
6328.P7	Provincial grants, loans, etc. (Table KE6)

National defense. Military law

Call Number	Description
6800	General (Table KE5)

Wartime and emergency legislation

For wartime labor disputes see KE3226
For economic controls see KE5460+

Call Number	Description
6810	General (Table KE5)

By period

Call Number	Description
6813	1914-1918
6816	1939-1945 (Table KE5)
6818	1945- (Table KE5)

The military establishment. Armed Forces

Call Number	Description
6845	General works
6848	Organization and administration. Department of National Defense (Table KE5)

Armed Forces

General works see KE6848

Conscription. Draft

Call Number	Description
6860	General (Table KE5)

Deferment. Exemptions. Disqualification

Call Number	Description
6863	General works
6865.A-Z	Particular groups, A-Z
6868.A-Z	Special topics, A-Z

Personnel. Services

Call Number	Description
6870	General (Table KE5)
6872	Enlistment. Recruiting. Discharge (Table KE5)

Education. Training

Call Number	Description
6874	General (Table KE5)

Military colleges. Schools. Courses of instruction

Call Number	Description
6875	General works

National defense. Military law
The military establishment. Armed Forces
Armed Forces
Personnel. Services
Education. Training
Military colleges. Schools. Courses of instruction --
Continued
Particular colleges

6877	Royal Military College (Table KE5)
	Pay, allowances, benefits
6880	General (Table KE5)
6882	Retirement pensions (Table KE5)
	Disability pensions and benefits
	Including survivors' pensions and benefits
	For war veterans' pensions see KE7230+
6884	General (Table KE5)
6886	Canadian Pension Commission (Table KE5)
6892	Medical care
6894.A-Z	Other, A-Z
6902	Officers (Table KE5)
	Including appointments, promotions, retirement
6904	Enlisted personnel
6906	Reserves. Cadets (Table KE5)
	For The Militia see KE6966
6913.A-Z	Special services, A-Z
6916	Equipment. Weapons. Plants. Supplies and stores (Table KE5)
6919	Hospitals (Table KE5)
	Particular branches of service
	The Canadian Forces Reorganization Act, which came into force on February 1, 1968, "unified" the Royal Canadian Navy, the Canadian Army and the Royal Canadian Air Force into a single service called the Canadian Armed Forces
	Army (Land forces after February 1, 1968)
6928	Organization. Administration (Table KE5)
	Personnel. Services
6930	General (Table KE5)
6932	Enlistment. Recruiting. Discharge (Table KE5)
	Education. Training
6934	General (Table KE5)
6935	Military colleges. Schools. Courses of instruction (Table KE5)
	Pay, allowances, benefits
6940	General (Table KE5)
6942	Retirement pensions (Table KE5)

National defense. Military law
The military establishment. Armed Forces
Armed Forces
Particular branches of service
Army (Land forces after February 1, 1968)
Personnel. Services
Pay, allowances, benefits -- Continued

6944	Disability pensions and benefits (Table KE5)
	Including survivors' pensions and benefits
	For war veterans' pensions see KE7230+
6952	Medical care
6954.A-Z	Other, A-Z
6962	Officers (Table KE5)
	Including appointments, promotions, retirement
6964	Enlisted personnel
6966	Reserves. The Militia. Cadets (Table KE5)
6973.A-Z	Special services, A-Z
6976	Equipment. Weapons. Plants. Supplies and stores (Table KE5)
6979	Hospitals (Table KE5)

Navy (Maritime forces after February 1, 1968)

6997	Organization. Administration (Table KE5)
	Personnel. Services
7000	General (Table KE5)
7002	Enlistment. Recruiting. Discharge (Table KE5)
	Education. Training
7004	General (Table KE5)
7005	Military colleges. Schools. Courses of instruction (Table KE5)
	Pay, allowances, benefits
7010	General (Table KE5)
7012	Retirement pensions (Table KE5)
7014	Disability pensions and benefits (Table KE5)
	Including survivors' pensions and benefits
7022	Medical care
7024.A-Z	Other, A-Z
7032	Officers (Table KE5)
	Including appointments, promotions, retirement
7034	Enlisted personnel
7036	Reserves. Cadets (Table KE5)
7043.A-Z	Special services, A-Z
7046	Equipment. Weapons. Plants. Supplies and stores (Table KE5)
7049	Hospitals (Table KE5)

Air Force (Air forces after February 1, 1968)

7057	Organization. Administration
	Personnel. Services

National defense. Military law
The military establishment. Armed Forces
Armed Forces
Particular branches of service
Air Force (Air forces after February 1, 1968)
Personnel. Services -- Continued

Number	Topic
7060	General (Table KE5)
7062	Enlistment. Recruiting. Discharge (Table KE5)
	Education. Training
7064	General (Table KE5)
7065	Military colleges. Schools. Courses of instruction (Table KE5)
	Pay, allowances, benefits
7070	General (Table KE5)
7072	Retirement pensions (Table KE5)
7074	Disability pensions and benefits (Table KE5)
	Including survivors' pensions and benefits
7082	Medical care
7084.A-Z	Other, A-Z
7092	Officers (Table KE5)
	Including appointments, promotions, retirement
7094	Enlisted personnel
7096	Reserves. Cadets (Table KE5)
7103.A-Z	Special services, A-Z
7106	Equipment. Weapons. Plants. Supplies and stores (Table KE5)
7109	Hospitals (Table KE5)
7135	Military discipline
	Military criminal law and procedure
7146	General (Table KE5)
	Criminal law
7152	General works
7155.A-Z	Particular offenses, A-Z
	Criminal procedure. Military justice
7160	General works
	Courts-martial
7165	General (Table KE5)
7168	Evidence
	Trials
7175	Collections
7177.A-Z	Particular trials. By defendant, A-Z
	Appellate procedure
7185	General (Table KE5)
7187	Court Martial Appeal Court (Table KE5)
7197	Execution of sentence. Penalties. Punishment

KE LAW OF CANADA KE

National defense. Military law

The military establishment. Armed Forces -- Continued

7205 Civil status of members of the Armed Forces. Civil law relating to soldiers, sailors, airmen, etc. (Table KE5) For suffrage see KE4629+ For veterans' re-employment rights see KE7240.E4

7210.A-Z Other defense and intelligence services, A-Z

7210.C35 Canadian Security Intelligence Service (Table KE6) Defense Research Board see KE3960.D4

7213 Civil defense (Table KE5)

7223.A-Z Other topics, A-Z Defense research and development see KE3960.D4 War veterans For Canadian Pension Commission see KE6886

7230 General. Pensions and allowances (Table KE5)

7240.A-Z Special types of benefits and assistance, A-Z

7240.E3 Education. Training (Table KE6)

7240.E4 Employment and assistance preference (Table KE6) Land grants see KE5240+

7240.M4 Medical care and treatment (Table KE6) Veterans' land act benefits see KE5240+

Native peoples. Indians. Inuit

For materials relating to a particular group or tribe, see the group or tribe below

Federal law

Including provincial law collectively

7701-7710 General (Table KE4, modified)

7702.7 Treaties By date of publication

7715 Land laws. Reserves and settlements (Table KE5)

7718 Claims (Table KE5)

7722.A-Z Other topics, A-Z

7722.C5 Civil rights (Table KE6)

7722.C67 Courts (Table KE6)

7722.C75 Criminal law (Table KE6) Cultural rights see KE7722.I58

7722.D6 Domestic relations (Table KE6)

7722.E3 Education (Table KE6)

7722.H8 Hunting and fishing rights (Table KE6)

7722.I58 Intellectual property (Table KE6) Including cultural rights Legal aid see KE378.N3 Legal education see KE318.N3

7722.P8 Public welfare (Table KE6)

7722.T39 Taxation (Table KE6)

7722.W6 Women (Table KE6)

Indigenous legal systems

KE LAW OF CANADA KE

Native peoples. Indians. Inuit
Indigenous legal systems -- Continued

7735	General works
7739.A-Z	Special topics, A-Z
7739.L3	Land tenure. Aboriginal title
7742	Administration (Table KE5)
7749.A-Z	Particular groups or tribes, A-Z

Courts. Procedure
Administration of justice. Organization of the judiciary
Judicial statistics see KE198+
History see KE392+

8200	General (Table KE5)
	Department of Justice, Attorney General see KE4752

Court organization and procedure
For procedure in general, or before several courts see KE8341+

8212	General (Table KE5)
	Special aspects
8218	Conduct of court proceedings. Decorum (Table KE5)
8220	Congestion and delay (Table KE5)
8222	Foreign judgments (Table KE5)

Administration and management
For information storage and retrieval systems see KE254.C6

8226	General (Table KE5)
8226.5	Finance (Table KE5)
8227	Bilingualism (Table KE5)

Particular courts and procedure (General) before such courts
For particular subjects, e.g. actions, special pleading, trial evidence, see the relevant subject

Federal courts

8240	General (Table KE5)

Supreme Court of Canada

8244	General. History (Table KE5)
	Biography of justices
8246	Collective
8248.A-Z	Individual justices, A-Z
	Including appointments
8251-8260	Procedure (Table KE4)

Federal Court of Canada

8265	General (Table KE5)
8268	Procedure (Table KE5)
	For Admiralty rules and practice see KE1112

Provincial and territorial courts
Class here general and comparative works only

8273	General works

KE --- LAW OF CANADA --- KE

Courts. Procedure
Court organization and procedure
Particular courts and procedure (General) before such courts
Provincial and territorial courts -- Continued

8276 --- Small claims courts (Table KE5)
Magistrates' courts see KE9365+
Courts of special jurisdiction
see the subject, e.g. KE2082 Canadian Transport Commission; KE7187 Court Martial Appeal Court; KE5717 Tax Review Board; KE542 Family courts; KE9446 Juvenile courts; KE820 Probate courts; KE3659 Mental health courts
Judicial officers. Court employees

8285 --- General works
Judges
Including provincial superior and intermediate court judges
For biography of judges see KE395+
For Supreme Court of Canada justices see KE8246+

8290 --- General (Table KE5)

8293.A-Z --- Special topics, A-Z

8293.A6 --- Appointment. Tenure. Retirement (Table KE6)
Continuing education for judges see KE296

8293.J8 --- Judicial ethics. Corruption (Table KE6)

8293.R4 --- Removal. Impeachment (Table KE6)
Including invididual cases

8293.S3 --- Salaries. Pensions (Table KE6)

8298 --- Administrative officers. Clerks of the court

8308 --- Constables (Table KE5)
Cf. KE5006+ Police
Cf. KE8809.8.P6 Criminal law

8312 --- Coroners. Medical examiners (Table KE5)
For medical evidence see KE8475
Cf. RA1001+ Medical jurisprudence

8315 --- Court reporters (Table KE5)
For technique of law reporting see KE269

8325 --- Justices of the peace. Magistrates
Including civil jurisdiction

8328 --- Notaries (Table KE5)

8332 --- Sheriffs (Table KE5)
Civil procedure
Including common law and equity
For works on procedure and practice in general before a particular court, see the court

8341-8350 --- General (Table KE4)

8360 --- Equity practices and procedure

8364 --- Jurisdiction. Venue

KE LAW OF CANADA KE

Courts. Procedure
Civil procedure -- Continued
Actions

8370	General works
8372	Process and service
	Pleading and motions
8375	General (Table KE5)
	Defenses and objections (Exceptions)
8386	Limitation of actions
8388	Lis pendens
8392	Counterclaims and cross claims
	Parties
8394	General (Table KE5)
8396	Standing. Locus standi (Table KE5)
8399	Interpleader (Table KE5)
8402	Class action (Table KE5)
8404	Citizen suits (Table KE5)
	Pretrial procedure
8408	General. Deposition and discovery. Interrogatories (Table KE5)
8410.A-Z	Special topics, A-Z
	Settlement see KE8615
	Trial
8420	General works
	Trial practice. Trial tactics
8422	General (Table KE5)
8427	Cross examination (Table KE5)
8429	Forensic psychology
8432.A-Z	Particular types of cases or claims, A-Z
8432.M34	Malpractice (Table KE6)
8432.N4	Negligence (Table KE6)
8432.P4	Personal injuries (Table KE6)
8432.P76	Products liability (Table KE6)
	Trial by jury see KE8495+
	Evidence
	Including works on both civil and criminal evidence For works on evidence pertaining to particular proceedings see KE8452.A+
8440	General (Table KE5)
	Burden of proof
8445	General (Table KE5)
8447.A-Z	Special topics, A-Z
8447.P7	Presumptions
8452.A-Z	Particular proceedings, A-Z
	For works on evidence before courts classed with particular subjects, see the relevant subject, e.g. KE820, Evidence before probate courts

KE LAW OF CANADA KE

Courts. Procedure
Civil procedure
Trial
Evidence -- Continued
Particular kinds of evidence

8455	Circumstantial
	For techniques of identification (Criminology) see HV8073+
	For techniques of identification (Forensic medicine) see RA1001+
8457	Documentary
	Witnesses
8460	General works
8464	Oath and affirmation
	Contempt of court see KE9028+
	Perjury see KE9033
	Privileged (confidential) communications
8468	General works
8470.A-Z	Particular relationships, A-Z
	Expert evidence. Expert witnesses
8472	General (Table KE5)
	Particular kinds
8475	Medical evidence. Medical witnesses (Table KE5)
8478.A-Z	Other, A-Z
8478.A28	Actuarial evidence
	Presumptions see KE8447.P7
	Admissibility and exclusion of evidence
8485	Hearsay
	Jury and jurors
8495	General (Table KE5)
8505	Instructions to juries
	For individual instructions see KE448
	Judgment
8512	General (Table KE5)
8514	Res judicata. Estoppel by judgment
	Costs. Fees
	For legal aid see KE376+
8517	General (Table KE5)
	By particular court
8519	Supreme Court of Canada
8522.A-Z	Particular types of judgments, A-Z
8522.D42	Declaratory judgments
8522.S8	Summary judgment
	Remedies and special proceedings
8532	General (Table KE5)

Courts. Procedure
Civil procedure
Remedies and special proceedings -- Continued
8536 Injunctions. Provisional remedies (Table KE5)
For labor injunctions see KE3217
Interpleader see KE8399
Possessory actions, ejectment see KE709
Replevin see KE781
8540 Receivers
Execution of judgment
8550 General works
Attachment. Garnishment
8552 General (Table KE5)
8554 Attachment proceedings against property of absconding debtor
8560.A-Z Exemptions, A-Z
8560.C4 Chattels
Extraordinary remedies
Including older remedies
8566 General works
Particular remedies
8568 Certiorari
8569 Habeas corpus (Table KE5)
8570 Mandamus
8571 Prohibition
8572 Quo warranto
8575 Other
Appellate procedure
8585 General (Table KE5)
Supreme Court of Canada see KE8251+
Proceedings by or against the Crown
For tort liability of the government see KE1305
8595 General works
Federal Court see KE8268
Proceedings relating to particular branches of the law or special subjects, or governed by special rules.
Noncontentious (ex-parte) jurisdiction
8605 General works
Admiralty see KE1112
Bankruptcy see KE1491+
Divorce see KE561+
Parliamentary divorce see KE576+
Mental incompetency proceedings see KE515
Mortgage actions, foreclosures see KE754.F6
Probate see KE820+
Tort claims procedure see KE1232+
8615 Negotiated settlement. Compromise

KE LAW OF CANADA KE

8618	Arbitration and award. Commercial arbitration (Table KE5)
	Criminal law
	Cf. KE7146+ Military criminal law and procedure
	Cf. KE9445+ Juvenile criminal law and procedure
8801-8810	General (Table KE4, modified)
8809.8.A-Z	Works for particular groups of users, A-Z
	Constables see KE8809.8.P6
	Justices of the peace, magistrates see KE9365+
8809.8.P6	Police. Constables
	Administration of criminal justice. Reform of criminal law, enforcement and procedure
8813	General (Table KE5)
8815	Speedy trial
8817	Crime and publicity (Table KE5)
	Cf. KE9028+ Contempt of court
	Punishment and penalties
	For theory and philosophy of criminal punishment see K5103
	Cf. HV6001+ Criminology
8820	General works
8822	Habitual criminals. Recidivists. Preventive detention (Table KE5)
8824.A-Z	Particular penalties, A-Z
8824.C3	Capital punishment
	Penal institutions see KE9415+
	Criminology see HV6001+
8828	Criminal jurisdiction (Conflict of criminal law)
	Burden of proof see KE9312+
	Criminal liability
8833	General (Table KE5)
8834	Culpability. Mens rea. Criminal intent. Strict liability. Criminal negligence (Table KE5)
	Exemption from liability. Defenses. Diminished responsibility
8839	General works
	Particular defenses
8841	Insanity (Table KE5)
8843	Drunkeness
8845	Other
	Particular offenses
8900	General (Table KE5)
8903	Preliminary crimes. Inchoate offenses (Table KE5)
	Offenses against the person
8905	General (Table KE5)
	Homicide
8908	General (Table KE5)
8910	Murder (Table KE5)

Criminal law
Particular offenses
Offenses against the person
Homicide -- Continued

8912	Manslaughter (Table KE5)
8920	Abortion. Procuring miscarriage
8925	Assault and battery
8925.5	Conjugal violence. Wife abuse. Husband abuse (Table KE5)
8926	Child abuse (Table KE5)
	Including child sexual abuse
	Sexual offenses
	Including works on legal implications of sexual behavior in general
8928	General (Table KE5)
8930.A-Z	Particular offenses, A-Z
	Abduction see KE8935+
	Child sexual abuse. Child molesting see KE8926
8930.R3	Rape (Table KE6)
8930.S43	Seduction (Table KE6)
	Offenses against personal liberty
8935	Kidnapping. Abduction (Table KE5)
8940	Invasion of privacy. Wiretapping (Table KE5)
	Cf. KE1240+ Tort liability for invasion of privacy
	Offenses against reputation
8948	Libel. Slander. Defamation (Table KE5)
	Cf. KE1246+ Tort liability for libel and slander
8952	Hate propaganda (Table KE5)
	Offenses against property
	Including works on white collar crime and on offenses against the economic order in general
8958	General works (Table KE5)
8960	Thievery. Larceny (Table KE5)
8968	Embezzlement (Table KE5)
8973	Fraud. False pretenses
	Threats. Extortion. Blackmail
8980	General works
8984	Racketeering. Organized crime
8986	Arson
8988	Other
	Offenses against the state and public order
	Political offenses
8998	General (Table KE5)
9000	Treason
9002	Espionage. Illegal disclosure of official secrets (Table KE5)
9005	Sedition. Subversive activities

KE LAW OF CANADA KE

Criminal law
Particular offenses
Offenses against the state and public order
Political offenses -- Continued

9007	Terrorism
9009.A-Z	Other political offenses, A-Z
9012	Other
	Offenses against the public administration
9020	Corruption and bribery (Table KE5)
	For corrupt election practices see KE4648
9022	Violation of conflict-of-interest laws
	Offenses against the administration of justice
9028	Contempt of court (Table KE5)
	Judicial corruption see KE8293.J8
9033	Perjury. Subornation of perjury (Table KE5)
	Offenses against public safety
9041	Riot
	Traffic violations, drunk driving see KE2114
	Offenses against public health
9050	Illicit possession, use of, or traffic in narcotics (Table KE5)
	Offenses against public convenience and morality. Crimes without victims
9059	General works
9061	Adultery
9062	Bigamy
9066	Gambling. Lotteries (Table KE5)
9070	Obscenity (Table KE5)
9075	Prostitution. Procuring (Table KE5)
9078	Public intoxication. Drunkenness (Table KE5)
9080	Vagrancy
9083	Other
	Offenses against public property, public finance and currency
9088	Counterfeiting. Forgery
	Customs crimes, smuggling see KE6123
9090	Illicit liquor traffic
	Tax evasion see KE5728
	Offenses committed through the mail
9095	General. Postal offenses
9097.A-Z	Particular offenses, A-Z
	Gambling see KE9066
	Lotteries see KE9066
	Obscenity see KE9070
	Threats, extortion, blackmail see KE8980+
9112	Conspiracy (Table KE5)

Criminal procedure
For administration of criminal justice see KE8813+
9260 General (Table KE5)
Arrest and pre-trial detention. Rights of suspects. Criminal investigation
9265 General (Table KE5)
Habeas corpus see KE8569
9270 Searches and seizures (Table KE5)
9272 Bail (Table KE5)
9275 Extradition (Table KE5)
Right to speedy trial see KE8815
Indictment. Information. Public prosecutor
9280 General (Table KE5)
9282 Grand jury (Table KE5)
Preparation for trial. Arraignment. Pleas
9286 General (Table KE5)
9287 Arraignment
9289 Right to counsel. Public defenders
Pleas
9293 General (Table KE5)
9295 Special pleas (Table KE5)
9297 Procedure without trial. Plea bargaining. Pleas of guilty. Nolo contendere (Table KE5)
9300 Discovery (Table KE5)
Trial
9304 General works
9306 Trial practice. Trial tactics
Evidence. Burden of proof
9312 General (Table KE5)
Admission of evidence
9314 General works
9316 Confessions. Admissions (Table KE5)
9321 Self-incrimination. Entrapment (Table KE5)
9328 Wiretapping. Electronic listening and recording devices (Table KE5)
For wiretapping as a criminal offense see KE8940
9335 Witnesses
9337 Expert evidence. Expert witnesses (Table KE5)
9344 Corroboration
Jury
9348 General (Table KE5)
9350 Instructions to jury (Table KE5)
For individual instructions see KE448
Judgment. Sentence. Judicial discretion
9355 General (Table KE5)
9358 Costs (Table KE5)

Criminal procedure -- Continued

Proceedings before magistrates' courts and justices of the peace

Including magistrates' handbooks and manuals on criminal law and procedure

9365	General (Table KE5)
9368	Summary convictions
9375	Appeals. Apellate procedure
	Special proceedings, extraordinary remedies see KE8532+
9380	Pardon (Table KE5)
	Proceedings before juvenile courts see KE9445+
	Execution of sentence. Corrections
9410	General (Table KE5)
	Capital punishment see KE8824.C3
	Imprisonment
9415	Prison administration. Prison discipline (Table KE5)
9416	Prisoners (Table KE5)
	Particular types of penal or correctional institutions
9420	Penitentiaries. Prisons (Table KE5)
9422	Reformatories
	Juvenile detention homes see KE9450
	Preventive detention see KE8822
9429	Fines
9431	Forfeitures. Political disabilities (Table KE5)
9434	Probation. Parole (Table KE5)
9436	Community-based corrections (Table KE5)
9440	Judicial error. Compensation for judicial error
	Victims of crimes
9443	General (Table KE5)
	Compensation to victims of crimes see KE1312+
	Military criminal law and procedure see KE7146+
	Juvenile criminal law and procedure. Administration of juvenile justice
9445	General (Table KE5)
9446	Juvenile courts (Table KE5)
	Criminal procedure
9448	General (Table KE5)
	Execution of sentence
	Imprisonment
9450	Juvenile detention homes. Training schools (Table KE5)

KEA LAW OF CANADA (ALBERTA) KEA

1-599 Law of Canada (Alberta) (Table KEA-KEY)

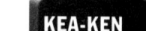

KEB LAW OF CANADA (BRITISH COLUMBIA) KEB

1-599 Law of Canada (British Columbia) (Table KEA-KEY)

KEM LAW OF CANADA (MANITOBA) KEM

1-599 Law of Canada (Manitoba) (Table KEA-KEY)

KEN LAW OF CANADA (NEW BRUNSWICK) KEN

1-599 Law of Canada (New Brunswick) (Table KEA-KEY)

1201-1799 Law of Canada (Newfoundland and Labrador) (Table KEA-KEY)

KEN LAW OF CANADA (NORTHWEST TERRITORIES) KEN

5401-5999 Law of Canada (Northwest Territories) (Table KEA-KEY)

7401-7999 Law of Canada (Nova Scotia) (Table KEA-KEY)

8001-8599 Law of Canada (Nunavut) (Table KEA-KEY)

KEO LAW OF CANADA (ONTARIO) KEO

Law of Canada (Ontario)

Law of the province of Ontario (1867-). Class here also materials relating to Upper Canada (1791-1867)

1	Bibliography
<5>	Periodicals
	For periodicals consisting primarily of informative material (Newsletters, bulletins, etc.) relating to particular subject, see subject and form division for periodicals
	For law reports, official bulletins or circulars, and official gazettes intended chiefly for the publication of laws and regulations, see appropriate entries in the text or form division tables
	For periodicals consisting predominantly of legal articles, regardless of subject matter, and jurisdiction see K1+
7	Monographic series
	Official gazettes see KEO83+
<17-33>	Legislative documents
	Including pre-Confederation publications see J101 (Upper Canada); J108 (Ontario)
	Legislative council
	Not reconstituted after Confederation
<17>	Journals
<21-28>	Legislative Assembly (Table KE13)
<33>	Bills
42	Other materials relative to legislative history
	e.g. Status tables
	Legislation
	For statutes, regulations, etc. on a particular subject, see the subject
	Statutes
	By period
	Upper Canada (1791-1841)
	Including the Province of Canada (1841-1867)
49	Session laws
52	Collections. Consolidations. "Revisions"
	By date of publication
	Including statutes passed in the Parliament of Great Britain and applying to Upper Canada
55	Indexes and tables
	By date of publication
	Province of Canada (1841-1867) see KEO49+
	1867-
	Sessional volumes and revised statutes
62	Sessional volumes to 1876
63	Revised statutes and sessional volumes, 1876-
	Arrange chronologically by date of revision, treating sessional volumes as supplements to the latest revision

KEO LAW OF CANADA (ONTARIO) KEO

Legislation
Statutes
By period
1867- -- Continued

67 Collections. Compilations
By date of publication
Including statutes passed in the Parliament of Great Britain and applying to Ontario

71 Abridgments and digests of statutes

72 Citators. Annotations

73 Indexes and tables to statutes
By date of publication

Subordinate [Delegated] legislation. Statutory orders and regulations. Statutory instruments
Official editions

83 Upper Canada Gazette

84 Ontario Gazette, 1868-1850

87 Consolidations and Ontario Gazette, 1950-
Arrange chronologically by date of consolidation, treating issues of the Ontario Gazette Parts I and II as supplements to the latest consolidation

91 Unofficial editions

95 Indexes and tables to regulations

Law reports and related materials
Including pre-Confederate materials
For reports on particular subjects, see the subject, e.g. KEO843, Reports of election cases

Law reports
Reports before 1881
Including report series begun before 1881 and continuing past that date

Particular courts

104 Court of [Error and] Appeal
By initial date of period covered

105 Court of Queen's (King's) Bench
By initial date of period covered

105.2 Cameron's Digest

106 Court of Common Pleas
By initial date of period covered

107 Court of Chancery
By initial date of period covered
For Chancery Chambers Reports see KEO108

108 "Practice" court. Chambers cases
By initial date of period covered
Class here Lefroy and Cassel's Practice Cases

Reports after 1881
Several courts

LAW OF CANADA (ONTARIO)

Law reports and related materials
Law reports
Reports after 1881
Several courts -- Continued

111	Ontario Weekly Reporter
113	Other Law Reports
115	Ontario Weekly Notes
115.2	Ontario Weekly Notes (New Series)
117	Ontario Reports
117.2	Ontario Law Reports
117.4	Ontario Law Reports (New Series)
117.6	Ontario appeal cases

Particular courts
Supreme Court

132	General works (Table KE9)
133	Court of Appeal (Table KE9)
134	High Court of Justice (Table KE9)
<140.A-Z>	Particular subjects, A-Z

This is an optional number provided for law libraries using this classification. Such libraries may wish to class the decisions of administrative boards on particular subjects here as well

142	Comprehensive digests and abridgments
144	Citators. Indexes. Tables

For citators, indexes, etc. relating to particular reports or digests and abridgments, see those works

Administrative decisions on a particular subject
see the subject

148	Encyclopedias
149	Law dictionaries. Words and phrases
150	Form books

General only
For form books on a particular subject, see the subject

151	Yearbooks

Class here only publications issued annually, containing information, statistics, etc., about the year just passed

Judicial statistics

152	General

Criminal statistics

153	General works
153.5	Juvenile crime
154.A-Z	Other. By subject, A-Z

Directories see KE213.A+

KEO LAW OF CANADA (ONTARIO) KEO

156	Legal research. Legal bibliography
	Methods of bibliographic research and how to find the law
	Class here provincial law only
	For general works (not limited to the province of Ontario) see KE250+
158	Law reporting
	Legal education see KE273+
	The legal profession. Practice of law
	General see KE330+
162	Admission to the bar
164	Legal ethics. Discipline. Disbarment (Table KE5)
166	Economics of law practice. Fees (Table KE5)
167	Law office management. Attorney and legal secretaries' handbooks
168.A-Z	Other topics, A-Z
168.L43	Legal assistants. Paralegal personnel (Table KE6)
	Paralegal personnel see KEO168.L43
	Law societies see KE361.A+
	Provincial bar associations see KE370.A+
	Local bar associations, lawyers' clubs, etc. see KE372.A+
	Community legal services. Legal aid. Legal assistance to the poor
	For collections of, and works on, substantive law see KEO190.P6
173	General (Table KE5)
174.A-Z	Local agencies and organizations. By place, A-Z
175.A-Z	Legal aid services to particular groups, A-Z
176	History
	Collective biography see KE396.A+
	Individual biography (To 1867) see KE406.A+
	Individual biography (1867-1931) see KE411.A+
	Individual biography (1931-) see KE416.A+
180	Law reform. Criticism. General administration of justice (Table KE5)
	Collected works (nonserial)
	For monographic series see KEO7
182	Several authors
183	Individual authors
	Under each:
	.x — *By date*
	.xA-.xZ — *By editor*
185	General works. Treatises
186	Compends, outlines. Examination aids. Popular works
188	Addresses, essays, lectures
	Including single essays, collected essays of several authors, festschriften, etc.
189.A-Z	Works for particular groups of users, A-Z

KEO LAW OF CANADA (ONTARIO) KEO

190.A-Z	Works on diverse aspects of a particular subject and falling within several branches of the law. By subject, A-Z
190.P6	Poverty. Legal protection of the poor. Handbooks for legal services (Table KE6)
192	Equity
194	Conflict of laws
197.A-Z	Concepts applying to several branches of law, A-Z
197.L56	Limitation of actions (Table KE6)
	Persons
202	General works
	Natural persons
203	General works
204	Civil status. Name (Table KE5)
	Capacity and disability
206	General works
207.A-Z	Particular groups of persons, A-Z
207.I5	Insane persons (Table KE6)
207.M5	Minors (Table KE6)
207.W6	Women (Table KE6)
209	Recording and registration (Table KE5)
	Including registers of births, marriages, deaths; birth and death certificates; vital statistics
	Corporations see KEO389+
	Domestic relations. Family law
213	General (Table KE5)
	Provincial courts (Family division)
	Including all predecessor courts
214	General. Collective (Table KE5)
	Local courts
214.5	Toronto (Table KE5)
	Marriage. Husband and wife
218	General (Table KE5)
220	Licenses. Premarital examinations (Table KE5)
222	Property relationships (Table KE5)
	Divorce. Separation
224	General (Table KE5)
225	Separate maintenance. Alimony (Table KE5)
225.5	Unmarried couples. Cohabitants
	Parent and child
	Cf. KEO1171.C45 Child abuse
226	General (Table KE5)
227	Legitimacy. Illegitimacy. Legitimation. Paternity (Table KE5)
228	Adoption (Table KE5)
230	Guardian and ward
	Property
234	General. Ownership (Table KE5)

Property -- Continued

Real property. Land law

236 General (Table KE5)

Land tenure

For seigneurial tenure see KEQ271+

237 General works

Estates and interests. Freehold. Fee simple

240 Housing condominium (Table KE5)

Future estates and interests

245 Rule against perpetuities (Table KE5)

Tenancy. Leaseholds. Landlord and tenant

251-260 General (Table KE4)

260.5 Rent. Rent control (Table KE5)

261.A-Z Particular kinds of leaseholds, A-Z

261.C65 Commercial leases

Rights and interests incident to ownership and possession. Interests less than estates

263 General works

265 Boundaries. Fences (Table KE5)

266 Riparian rights. Water rights of individuals

268 Right to dispose of land. Restraints on alienation

Rights as to the use and profits of another's land

269 General works

269.2 Easements

269.4 Covenants running with the land (Table KE5)

269.5.A-Z Special topics, A-Z

269.5.P7 Prescription

269.7 Other

Transfer of rights in land

Transfer inter vivos

Including vendor's liability

271 General. Vendor and purchaser. Real estate transactions (Table KE5)

Conveyances. Title investigation. Abstracts

272 General. Deeds (Table KE5)

Title investigation. Abstracts

273 General (Table KE5)

274 Registration. Land titles system (Table KE5)

275 Description of land. Surveying

277.A-Z Other modes of transfer, A-Z

Prescription see KEO269.5.P7

Mortgages

278 General (Table KE5)

278.5.A-Z Special topics, A-Z

278.5.F6 Foreclosure (Table KE6)

Personal property

280 General (Table KE5)

Property

Personal property -- Continued

280.5.A-Z — Special topics, A-Z

Trusts and trustees

282 — General (Table KE5)

284 — Trust companies (Table KE5)

284.5.A-Z — Special topics, A-Z

284.5.A3 — Accounting

284.5.M3 — Maintenance and advancement

Estate planning see KEO998

Succession upon death

286 — General (Table KE5)

287 — Testate succession. Wills (Table KE5)

289 — Probate law and practice. Surrogate courts (Table KE5)

291 — Intestate succession (Table KE5)

293 — Administration of decedents' estates. Execution of wills. Personal representatives (Table KE5)

295.A-Z — Special topics, A-Z

295.C4 — Claims against decedents' estates

295.F34 — Family provisions

Contracts

299 — General (Table KE5)

304 — Breach of contract. Remedies (Table KE5)

Particular contracts

306 — Comprehensive. Commercial law. Mercantile transactions (Table KE5)

Contract for work and labor (Contract for services). Independent contractors

308 — General works

308.3 — Mechanics' liens (Table KE5)

308.4 — Repairmen's liens (Table KE5)

Sale of goods

310 — General (Table KE5)

310.5.A-Z — Special topics, A-Z

310.5.C6 — Conditions and warranties. Implied warranties (Table KE6)

Contracts involving bailments

312 — General works

312.5.A-Z — Particular contracts, A-Z

Banking

314 — General (Table KE5)

Particular kinds of banks, A-Z

315.B8 — Building societies (Table KE6)

315.C7 — Credit unions (Table KE6)

Trust companies see KEO284

Loan of money. Interest. Usury

Including debtor and creditor in general

KEO LAW OF CANADA (ONTARIO) KEO

Contracts
Particular contracts
Loan of money. Interest. Usury -- Continued

317	General (Table KE5)
318	Consumer credit. Small loans. Finance charges (Table KE5)
321	Suretyship. Guaranty
	Secured transactions
322	General (Table KE5)
323	Chattel mortgages (Table KE5)
324	Conditional sale (Table KE5)
325	Other
	Investments
327	General (Table KE5)
	Securities. Stock exchange transactions
	For issuing and sale of securities see KEO407+
329	General (Table KE5)
	Particular stock exchanges
	Toronto Stock Exchange
330	Acts of incorporation. Bylaws
	By date of publication
330.5	General works. Treatises
332	Investment trusts. Investment companies. Mutual funds (Table KE5)
333.A-Z	Other topics, A-Z
333.S6	Speculation. "Blue sky" laws
334	Commodity exchanges. Produce exchanges
	Carriers. Carriage of goods and passengers
336	General works. Liability
	Carriage by sea. Maritime (commercial) law. Admiralty
339	General works
340	Admiralty proceedings. Maritime Court (Table KE5)
	Insurance
343	General. Insurance business. Agents. Brokers (Table KE5)
	Personal insurance
345	Life (Table KE5)
346	Disability insurance (Table KE5)
	Property insurance
348	General works
348.5.A-Z	Particular types, A-Z
348.5.F5	Fire (Table KE6)
	Casualty insurance
350	General liability (Table KE5)
	Automobile
351	General (Table KE5)
351.3.A-Z	Special topics, A-Z

Contracts
Particular contracts
Insurance
Casualty insurance
Automobile
Special topics, A-Z -- Continued

351.3.N6	No-fault
351.3.U5	Unsatisfied judgment funds
352.A-Z	Particular risks, A-Z
353.A-Z	Other, A-Z
353.S9	Suretyship. Guaranty. Bonding (Table KE6)
	Social insurance see KEO678+
	Municipal insurance see KEO875.5.I54
	Torts (Extracontractual liability)
358	General. Liability. Damages (Table KE5)
	Particular torts
	Torts in respect to the person
359	Personal injuries
361	Violation of privacy (Table KE5)
363	Torts in respect to reputation. Libel. Slander
364	Trespass to land (Table KE5)
364.5	Torts affecting chattels. Trespass to goods. Conversion. Trover (Table KE5)
	Negligence
365	General (Table KE5)
366	Malpractice (Table KE5)
367.A-Z	Particular types of accidents or cases of negligence, A-Z
367.A8	Automobile accidents (Table KE6)
367.L5	Liability for condition and use of the land. Occupiers' liability (Table KE6)
369.A-Z	Other torts, A-Z
(369.T74)	Trespass to land
	see KEO364
	Strict liability. Liability without fault
370	General (Table KE5)
371	Products liability (Table KE5)
371.5	Environmental damages (Table KE5)
372.A-Z	Parties to actions in torts, A-Z
	Liability for torts of others. Vicarious liability
374	General works
376	Employers' liability
	Cf. KEO681+ Workers' compensation
377	Government torts. Crown liability (Table KE5)
379	Compensation to victims of crimes. Reparation (Table KE5)
	Agency
382	General works
382.5	Power of attorney (Table KE5)

KEO LAW OF CANADA (ONTARIO) KEO

Associations

Including business enterprises in general, regardless of form of organization

385	General works
385.5.A-Z	Special topics, A-Z
385.5.B87	Business records. Record keeping and retention (Table KE6)
	Record keeping and retention see KEO385.5.B87
	Unincorporated associations
386	General works
387	Business associations. Partnership
	Corporations. Juristic persons
389	General (Table KE5)
389.5	Nonprofit corporations (Table KE2)
	Business corporations. Companies
391-400	General (Table KE4)
403	Incorporation (Table KE5)
404	Management. Board of directors. Officers (Table KE5)
	Corporate finance. Capital. Dividends
405	General (Table KE5)
	Issuing of securities and their sale
	For stock exchange transactions see KEO329+
407	General (Table KE5)
407.5	Ontario Securities Commission (Table KE5)
409	Accounting. Auditing. Financial statements (Table KE5)
	Shares and shareholders' rights. Stock transfers
410	General (Table KE5)
410.6	Minority stockholders
412.A-Z	Particular types of corporations, A-Z
412.C6	Cooperatives (Table KE6)
	Credit unions see KEO315.C7
412.3	Dissolution. Liquidation
412.5	Consolidation and merger (Table KE5)
	Insolvency and bankruptcy. Creditors' rights
417	General (Table KE5)
	Bankruptcy
418	General (Table KE5)
418.5.A-Z	Special topics, A-Z
418.5.F73	Fraudlent conveyances
	Debtors' relief
419	General works
419.3.A-Z	Particular forms of debt relief, A-Z
419.3.A8	Assignments for benefit of creditors (Table KE6)
419.3.B8	Bulk sales (Table KE6)
	Economic policy. Economic planning. Economic development
425	General (Table KE5)

Economic policy. Economic planning. Economic development -- Continued

425.5 Foreign investment (Table KE5)

Regulation of industry, trade, and commerce. Occupational law

430 General. Trade regulation. Control of trade practices. Consumer protection (Table KE5)

438 Small business

Primary production. Extractive industries

Agriculture. Forestry

441 General (Table KE5)
448 Marketing (Table KE5)

Dairy industry see KEO479

455 Forestry. Timber laws (Table KE5)

Game laws see KEO916

458 Fishing industry (Table KE5)

Mining. Quarrying

461 General (Table KE5)

Petroleum. Oil and gas

465 General (Table KE5)
469 Natural gas (Table KE5)

Manufacturing industries

472 General works
472.5.A-Z By industry or product, A-Z

Food processing industries

475 General works
479 Dairy industry. Dairy products industry. Milk production and distribution (Table KE5)

482 Construction and building industry. Contractors (Table KE5)

Trade and commerce

488 General (Table KE5)

Retail trade

495 General works
495.2 Sunday legislation (Table KE5)
495.4.A-Z Particular products, A-Z
495.4.A8 Automobiles (Table KE6)

Service trades

501 General works
502.A-Z Particular trades, A-Z
502.C6 Collection agencies (Table KE6)
502.D3 Day care centers. Nursery schools (Table KE6)

Funeral services see KEO502.U5

502.H6 Homemakers. Visiting nurses (Table KE6)

Insurance agents see KEO343+

Nursery schools see KEO502.D3

502.R43 Real estate agents (Table KE6)
502.T73 Travel agents (Table KE6)

Regulation of industry, trade, and commerce. Occupational law

Trade and commerce

Service trades

Particular trades, A-Z -- Continued

502.U5 Undertakers. Funeral services (Table KE6)

Cf. KEO715.B8 Burial and cemetery laws

Visiting nurses see KEO502.H6

Public utilities

512 General. Regulation. Finance (Table KE5)

Power supply

Including energy resources development in general

514 General (Table KE5)

515 Ontario Energy Board (Table KE5)

518 Electricity (Table KE5)

521 Gas (Table KE5)

524 Water (Table KE5)

Transportation and communication

Including government-owned and municipal services

528 General (Table KE5)

Road traffic. Automotive transportation

531 General. Motor vehicle laws (Table KE5)

532.A-Z Special topics, A-Z

532.D75 Drivers' licenses (Table KE6)

533.A-Z Particular vehicles, A-Z

533.S6 Snowmobiles. All-terrain vehicles (Table KE6)

Traffic regulation and enforcement. Traffic violations. Drunk driving

535 General (Table KE5)

535.3 Traffic courts (Table KE5)

Carriage of passengers and goods. Motor carriers

538 General (Table KE5)

541.A-Z Particular types of motor carriers, A-Z

541.T78 Trucks (Table KE6)

Railways

546 General. Regulation of industry (Table KE5)

561.A-Z Particular railways and railway companies, A-Z

Including litigation, decisions, rulings, etc.

563 Local transit. Street railways. Subways (Table KE5)

571 Water transportation. Navigation and shipping (Table KE5)

Communication

596 General works

601 Press law

Telecommunication

606 Telephone (Table KE5)

The professions

615 General. Licensing (Table KE5)

Regulation of industry, trade, and commerce. Occupational law

The professions -- Continued

The health professions

616	General. Physicians (Table KE5)
617.A-Z	Other, A-Z
	Chiropodists see KEO617.P6
617.D4	Dentists (Table KE6)
617.P4	Pharmacists (Table KE6)
617.P6	Podiatrists. Chiropodists (Table KE6)
617.P79	Psychologists. Psychiatrists. Psychotherapists (Table KE6)
618.A-Z	Other professions, A-Z
618.A7	Architects (Table KE6)
	Lawyers see KE330+; KEO162

Social law and legislation

628	General works
	Labor law
629	General (Table KE5)
	Management-labor relations
631-640	General (Table KE4)
641	Ontario Labour Relations Board (Table KE5, modified)
	Statutes. Regulations. Orders. Rules of practice, etc.
	Regulations. Orders. Rules of practice, etc.
641.A34	Rules of procedure. By date of publication
	Labor unions
643	General (Table KE5)
	Collective bargaining. Collective labor agreements
645	General (Table KE5)
647.A-Z	Particular industries, occupations, or groups of employees, A-Z
647.E5	Engineers (Table KE6)
647.P4	Public employees (Table KE6)
	Including provincial and municipal public service employees
	For particular occupations or groups of employees within the service, see the occupation or group
647.T4	Teachers (Table KE6)
	Labor disputes
649	General (Table KE5)
650	Arbitration. Conciliation (Table KE5)
	Strikes and lockouts. Boycotts. Picketing
651	General (Table KE5)
652	Labor injunctions (Table KE5)
653.A-Z	By industry, occupation, or group of employees, A-Z
653.H6	Hospitals (Table KE6)
653.M3	Manufacturing industry (Table KE6)

Social law and legislation
Labor law
Management-labor relations
Labor unions
Labor disputes
By industry, occupation, or group of employees, A-Z - - Continued

653.P7 Printing industry (Table KE6)
655.A-Z Particular industries, occupations, or groups of employees, A-Z
655.C6 Construction industry (Table KE6)
Labor standards
657 General. Labor conditions (Table KE5)
Employment and dismissal
658 General (Table KE5)
Discrimination in employment and its prevention
659 General. Racial discrimination (Table KE5)
660.A-Z Particular groups, A-Z
660.A4 Aged. Older people (Table KE6)
660.J4 Jews (Table KE6)
660.W6 Women (Table KE6)
663 Wages. Minimum wage
Nonwage payments. Fringe benefits
666 General (Table KE5)
666.2 Pension and retirement plans (Table KE5)
Protection of labor. Labor hygiene and safety
671 General (Table KE5)
Labor hygiene and safety. Hazardous occupations. Safety regulations
673 General (Table KE5)
673.5.A-Z By industry or type of labor, A-Z
Health facilities see KEO673.5.H66
673.5.H66 Hospitals. Health facilities (Table KE6)
673.5.L8 Lumbering (Table KE6)
676.A-Z Labor laws of particular industries, occupations, or types of employment, A-Z
Education see KEO676.T42
676.T42 Teachers. Education (Table KE6)
Social insurance
678 General (Table KE5)
679 Health. Medical care (Table KE5)
681-690 Workers' compensation (Table KE4)
693 Retirement pensions. Survivors' benefits (Table KE5)
Public welfare. Public assistance
703 General. Administration (Table KE5)
704.A-Z Special topics, A-Z
Particular groups

Social law and legislation
Public welfare. Public assistance
Particular groups -- Continued
Children. Child welfare. Youth services

706	General (Table KE5)
706.5	Mothers' allowances (Table KE5)
707	Older people (Table KE5)
708	People with disabilities. Vocational rehabilitation (Table KE5)
710	Other

Public health. Sanitation. Environmental pollution

713	General (Table KE5)

Particular public health hazards and measures
Contagious and infectious diseases

714	General works
714.5.A-Z	Particular diseases, A-Z
714.5.A54	AIDS (Table KE6)
714.5.V4	Venereal diseases (Table KE6)
715.A-Z	Other, A-Z
715.B8	Burial and cemetery laws (Table KE6)
715.R4	Refuse disposal (Table KE6)

Environmental pollution
Including abatement of public nuisances

717	General (Table KE5)

Water pollution

718	General (Table KE5)
719	Drainage (Table KE5)
720	Air pollution. Control of smoke, noxious gases, etc. (Table KE5)
721	Noise control (Table KE5)

Medical legislation

724	General (Table KE5)

Hospitals and other medical institutions

726	Hospitals (Table KE5)
727.A-Z	Other health services, A-Z
729	The mentally ill
730.A-Z	Special topics, A-Z

Hospital records see KEO730.R42

730.I53	Informed consent (Table KE3)
730.R42	Medical records. Hospital records. Records management (Table KE3)

Records management see KEO730.R42

Food. Drugs. Cosmetics

734	General (Table KE4)
736	Food (Table KE4)
738	Drug laws (Table KE4)

Alcohol. Alcoholic beverages. Prohibition. Liquor laws

Alcohol. Alcoholic beverages. Prohibition. Liquor laws -- Continued

741-750 General (Table KE4)

754.A-Z Special topics, A-Z

Public safety

759 General works

760 Hazardous articles and processes. Product safety (Table KE5)

Cf. KEO371 Products liability

764 Fire prevention and control (Table KE5)

Control of social activities

766 General (Table KE5)

766.5.A-Z Particular activities, A-Z

766.5.H65 Horse racing (Table KE6)

Education

Including public education

770 General (Table KE5)

771 Church and education. Denominational schools (Table KE5)

771.4 Other special aspects

School government and finance

773 General (Table KE5)

774 School districts. School boards (Table KE5)

Students. Compulsory education

778 General (Table KE5)

779.A-Z Special topics, A-Z

779.R4 Religious and patriotic observances. Bible reading. Religious instruction (Table KE6)

Teachers

781 General (Table KE5)

782.A-Z Special topics, A-Z

782.S3 Salaries, pensions, etc. (Table KE6)

Elementary and secondary education

784 General (Table KE5)

786 Elementary education. Public schools (Table KE5)

787 Secondary education. High schools (Table KE5)

Curricula. Courses of instruction

788 General works

788.4 Language training

Including bilingual instruction

788.7.A-Z Particular courses, A-Z

788.7.L3 Law

Higher education. Colleges and universities

793 General (Table KE5)

795.A-Z Particular colleges and universities. By name, A-Z

Science and the arts. Research

798 General works

The arts

KEO   LAW OF CANADA (ONTARIO)   KEO

   Science and the arts. Research
    The arts -- Continued
     Performing arts

800	General works
	Motion pictures
800.3	General works
800.5	Censorship
800.8	Other
800.9	Museums and galleries
802	Libraries (Table KE5)
	Constitutional law
804	Sources. By date of publication
	Cf. KE4136+ Constitutional law sources (General)
805	General works. History
806	Amending process
	Structure of government. Jurisdiction
808	General (Table KE5)
808.5.A-Z	Special topics, A-Z
	Boundary disputes see KE4285
	Individual and state
	Civil and political rights and liberties
811-820	General (Table KE4)
821	Linguistic and cultural rights. Bilingualism (Table KE5)
	Control of individuals
824	Aliens
	Church and state
831	General. Religious corporations
831.5.A-Z	Special topics, A-Z
831.5.C5	Clergy reserves (Table KE6)
	Organs of the government
834	General works
	The legislature
836	Legislative Council
	Not reconstituted after 1867
	Legislative Assembly
837	General works. History
	Election law
838	General (Table KE5)
839	Suffrage (Table KE5)
841	Campaign expenditures (Table KE5)
842	Corrupt practices. Illicit political activities
843	Contested elections (Table KE5)
	Organization. Legislative process
845	General (Table KE5)
846	Rules and procedure (Table KE5, modified)
	Statutes. Regulations. Orders. Rules of practice, etc.

Constitutional law
Organs of the government
The legislature
Legislative Assembly
Organization. Legislative process
Rules and procedure
Statutes. Regulations. Orders. Rules of practice, etc. -- Continued
Rules. Standing orders
Collections. Compilations

846.A33	Monographs. By date of publication
847	Committees
850.A-Z	Other topics, A-Z
850.C6	Conduct and discipline of legislators (Table KE6)
	Including individual cases
	The Crown and the Executive branch of the government
853	General works. Executive power
855	Attorney General
858	Commissions of inquiry, royal commissions, task forces, etc.
	Local government
860	General works
	Municipal government. Municipal services
	Including regional governments and rural municipalities and districts
861-870	General. Municipal corporations (Table KE4)
872	Ontario Municipal Board (Table KE5)
874	Municipal elections
	Municipal officials. Organs of government
875	General works
875.5.A-Z	Special topics, A-Z
875.5.C5	City councils (Table KE6)
875.5.C6	Conflict of interests (Table KE6)
875.5.I54	Insurance (Table KE6)
	Municipal public service see KEO884+
879	Special districts. Special authorities and boards
	Public service. Government officials and employees
	Provincial public service
881	General (Table KE5)
882.A-Z	Special topics, A-Z
882.P64	Political activities (Table KE6)
882.T4	Tenure and remuneration. Salaries. Pensions (Table KE6)
	Municipal public service
884	General (Table KE5)
885.A-Z	Special topics, A-Z

KEO LAW OF CANADA (ONTARIO) KEO

Public service. Government officials and employees
Municipal public service
Special topics, A-Z -- Continued

885.T4	Tenure and remuneration. Salaries. Pensions (Table KE6)
887	Police and power of the police (Table KE5)
	Administrative organization. Administrative law and procedure
889	General (Table KE5)
891	Judicial functions. Procedure. Administrative tribunals (Table KE5)
891.5	Judicial review of administrative acts (Table KE5)
892.A-Z	Special topics, A-Z
892.O4	Ombudsman (Table KE6)
	Public property. Public restraints on private property
895	General works
	Conservation and management of natural resources. Environmental planning
896	General (Table KE5)
896.7	Trees (Table KE5)
899	Roads. Highway law (Table KE5)
903	Water resources. Watersheds. Rivers. Lakes. Water courses (Table KE5)
	Expropriation
910	General (Table KE5)
910.5	Land Compensation Board (Table KE5, modified)
	Statutes. Regulations. Orders. Rules of practice, etc. Rules of practice
	Collections. Compilations
910.5.A33	Monographs. By date of publication
	Public land law
912	General. Crown lands (Table KE5)
	Reclamation. Irrigation. Drainage
913	General (Table KE2)
914.A-Z	Particular types of land, A-Z
	Marshes see KEO914.S9
914.S9	Swamps. Marshes. Wetlands
	Wetlands see KEO914.S9
	Provincial parks and forests. Wilderness preservation
915	General (Table KE5)
	Wildlife protection
	Including game, bird, and fish protection
	Cf. KEO458 Fishing industry
916	General. Game laws (Table KE5)
	Clergy reserves see KEO831.5.C5
	Regional and city planning. Zoning. Building
920	General (Table KE5)
	Land use. Zoning. Land subdivision

Public property. Public restraints on private property
Regional and city planning. Zoning. Building
Land use. Zoning. Land subdivision -- Continued

921	General (Table KE5)
921.2	Committees of adjustment (Table KE5)
921.3	Real estate development (Table KE5)
921.5	Solar access zoning (Table KE5)
921.7.A-Z	Particular types of land, A-Z
921.7.F3	Farms
	Building laws
923	General (Table KE5)
925.2	Electrical installations (Table KE5)
925.25	Plumbing (Table KE5)
925.3	Elevators (Table KE5)
	Housing. Slum clearance. City redevelopment
929	General (Table KE5)
931	Discrimination in housing (Table KE5)
933.A-Z	Particular types of accommodation, A-Z
933.M6	Mobile homes (Table KE6)
	Government property
936	General (Table KE5)
937	Access to public records. Freedom of information (Table KE5)
	Public finance
950	General (Table KE5)
	Provincial revenue
955	General works
	Taxation
961-970	General (Table KE4)
	Particular taxes
	Several. Collective see KEO961+
	Income tax
975	General. Personal income tax (Table KE5)
977.A-Z	Special topics, A-Z
	Income of business organizations
979	General works
	Corporation income tax
981	General (Table KE5)
983.A-Z	Particular lines of corporate business, A-Z
983.M5	Mining
	Property taxes. Taxation of capital
985	General works
	Provincial taxes affecting real property
	For ad valorem taxes upon real estate see KEO1025+
987	General (Table KE5)
989	Land transfer tax (Table KE5)

Public finance
Provincial revenue
Taxation
Particular taxes
Property taxes. Taxation of capital
Provincial taxes affecting real property -- Continued

990	Land speculation tax (Table KE5)
993	Business taxes
	Succession duties. Gift tax
997	General (Table KE5)
998	Estate planning. Estate tax planning (Table KE5)
1001	Gift tax (Table KE5)
	Excise taxes. Taxes on transactions
1004	General works
1005	Retail sales tax (Table KE5)
1005.5.A-Z	Particular commodities, services, transactions, A-Z
	Taxation of natural resources
1010	General works
1012.A-Z	Particular resources and resource industries, A-Z
1012.F6	Forestry (Table KE6)
1012.M5	Mining. Petroleum (Table KE6)
1014.A-Z	Other sources of revenue, A-Z
	Local finance
1017	General (Table KE5)
	Taxation
1022	General works. Tax powers of municipalities
	Property taxes
1024	General. Assessment (Table KE5)
1024.5	Assessment appeals. Review courts (Table KE5)
	Real property taxes
1025	General (Table KE5)
1025.5	Real property assessment. Land valuation (Table KE5)
	For assessment of particular kinds of land see KEO1025.7.A+
1025.7.A-Z	Particular kinds of land, tax-exempt lands, special modes of taxation, A-Z
1025.7.F3	Farm land (Table KE6)
1025.7.G6	Golf courses (Table KE6)
1027	Business taxes
1029.A-Z	Other sources of revenue, A-Z
1029.I54	Impact fees
	Indians
1044	General (Table KE5)
1045.A-Z	Special topics, A-Z
1045.C5	Civil rights (Table KE6)
1045.S63	Social legislation (Table KE6)

KEO LAW OF CANADA (ONTARIO) KEO

Indians -- Continued

1047.A-Z Particular groups or tribes, A-Z

Courts. Procedure

Administration of justice. Organization of the judiciary

History see KEO176

1054 General (Table KE5)

Court organization and procedure

For works on procedure in general, or before several courts see KEO1111+

1057 General (Table KE5)

1057.2 Congestion and delay. Case load (Table KE5)

1057.5 Administration and management (Table KE5)

Particular courts and procedure (General) before such courts

Prior to the Judicature Act of 1881

Superior courts

Common law courts

Original jurisdiction

1061 Court of Queen's (King's) Bench (Table KE5)

Class here works treating rules and practice of both the Court of Queen's Bench and the Court of Common Pleas

1062 Court of Common Pleas (Table KE5, modified)

1062.A54 Court records. By initial date of period covered

Appellate jurisdiction

1063 Court of [Error and] Appeal (Table KE5)

Equity courts

1064 Court of Chancery (Table KE5)

Intermediate courts: County courts. District courts

Including works on the Courts of General Sessions of the Peace

1067 General. Collective (Table KE5)

1068.A-Z Particular courts. By county or district, A-Z

Subarrange each by table KE6 modified as follows: .xA47 - Court records. By initial date of period covered

Lower courts

1072 Courts of requests. Division courts (Table KE5)

Magistrates' courts. Justices of the peace

General. Civil jurisdiction see KEO1099+

Criminal jurisdiction see KEO1188

Following the Judicature Act of 1881

Supreme Court

1075 General works. History

KEO **LAW OF CANADA (ONTARIO)** KEO

Courts. Procedure
Court organization and procedure
Particular courts and procedure (General) before such courts
Following the Judicature Act of 1881
Supreme Court -- Continued

1077 Procedure (Table KE5)
For editions of, and works on, the Judicature Act of 1881 and Supreme Court rules see KEO1111+

1079 Court of Appeal (Table KE5)
1081 High Court of Justice (Table KE5)
1085 Intermediate courts: County courts. District courts (Table KE5)
Lower courts
1090 Division courts. Small claims courts (Table KE5)
Magistrates' courts. Justices of the peace
General works. Civil jurisdiction see KEO1099+
Criminal jurisdiction see KEO1188
Courts of special jurisdiction
see the subject, e.g. Family courts, see KEO214+; Surrogate courts, see KEO289; Review courts, see KEO1024.5

Judicial officers. Court employees
1094 General (Table KE5)
Judges of superior and intermediate courts see KE8290+
1096 Constables (Table KE5)
Cf. KEO887 Police
Cf. KEO1165.5.P6 Criminal law
1097 Coroners. Medical examiners (Table KE5)
Justices of the peace. Magistrates
1099 General. Civil jurisdiction
For criminal jurisdiction see KEO1188
1099.5.A-Z Special topics, A-Z
1099.5.R4 Removal
Including individual cases
1101 Sheriffs
1102 Other
Civil procedure
Including common law and equity
Class here editions of, and works on, the Judicature Act of 1881 and Supreme Court rules
For works on procedure and practice in general before a particular court, see the court
1111-1120 General (Table KE4)
Equity practice and procedure see KEO1064+
1121 Jurisdiction. Venue

Courts. Procedure

Civil procedure -- Continued

1122	Actions
	Pleading and motions
1124	General works
	Defenses and objections (Exceptions)
1125	Lis pendens
	Parties
1128	General (Table KE5)
1129	Class action (Table KE5)
	Pretrial procedure
1130	General works. Deposition and discovery
1130.5.A-Z	Special topics, A-Z
	Settlement see KEO1159
	Trial. Trial practice. Trial tactics
1133	General works
	Evidence
1136	General (Table KE5)
	Particular kinds of evidence
	Witnesses. Testimony
1138	General (Table KE5)
1138.3	Oath and affirmation (Table KE5)
1139	Privileged (confidential) communications (Table KE5)
	Expert evidence. Expert witnesses
1140	General (Table KE5)
	Particular kinds
1141	Medical evidence. Medical witnesses (Table KE5)
1144	Jury and jurors (Table KE5)
	Judgment
1147	General works
	Costs. Fees
	Including works on costs under the Judicature Act
1148	General (Table KE5)
1148.4.A-Z	By particular court, A-Z
1148.4.C6	County courts
	Remedies and special proceedings
1151	General works
1152	Injunctions. Provisional remedies (Table KE5)
	For labor injunctions see KEO652
1152.5	Receivers (Table KE5)
	Execution of judgment. Attachment. Garnishment
1153	General (Table KE5)
1153.4	Attachment proceedings against property of absconding debtors

KEO LAW OF CANADA (ONTARIO) KEO

Courts. Procedure
Civil procedure -- Continued

1155	Appeals. Appellate proceedings
	For works on the appeal process in general see KE8585+
	Proceedings relating to particular branches of the law or special subjects, or governed by special rules.
	Noncontentious (ex-parte) jurisdiction
1157	General works
	Admiralty see KEO340
	Adoption see KEO228
	Mental incompetency proceedings see KEO207.I5
	Mortgage actions, foreclosures see KEO278.5.F6
	Probate see KEO289
1159	Negotiated settlement. Compromise
1160	Arbitration and award. Commercial arbitration
	Criminal law
	Cf. KEO1195+ Juvenile criminal law and procedure
1165	General works
1165.5.A-Z	Works for particular groups of users, A-Z
	Justices of the peace, magistrates see KEO1188
1165.5.P6	Police. Constables
	Administration of criminal justice. Reform of criminal law, enforcement, and procedure
1167	General (Table KE5)
1167.5	Special aspects
	e.g. Crime and publicity
1171.A-Z	Particular offenses, A-Z
1171.C45	Child abuse
1171.R3	Racketeering. Organized crime
	Criminal procedure
1175	General works (Table KE2)
1176	Arrest and commitment. Rights of suspects
1177	Searches and seizures (Table KE5)
1179	Preparation for trial. Arraignment. Right to counsel
1188	Proceedings before magistrates' courts and justices of the peace (Table KE5)
	Including magistrates' handbooks and manuals on criminal law and procedure
	Appeals. Appellate procedure
1190	General works
1190.5	Summary conviction appeals
	Proceedings before family courts see KEO214+
	Proceedings before juvenile courts see KEO1195+
	Execution of sentence. Corrections. Imprisonment
1192	General works
1193	Prisoners' rights (Table KE5)

Criminal procedure
Execution of sentence. Corrections. Imprisonment --
Continued
Particular types of penal or correctional institutions
Juvenile detention homes see KEO1196.2+
Juvenile criminal law and procedure. Administration of juvenile justice

1195	General (Table KE5)
1195.5	Juvenile courts (Table KE5)
	Criminal procedure
1196	General (Table KE5)
	Execution of sentence
	Imprisonment
1196.7	Juvenile detention homes. Training schools (Table KE5)
1199.A-Z	Law of particular counties, townships, regional municipalities (nonurban), etc. By county, etc., A-Z
	Subarrange each by Table KE3
<1199.5.A-Z>	Particular cities, A-Z
	see KEZ

KEP LAW OF CANADA (PRINCE EDWARD ISLAND) **KEP**

1-599 Law of Canada (Prince Edward Island) (Table KEA-KEY)

LAW OF CANADA (QUEBEC)

Law of Canada (Quebec)

Law of the province of Quebec (1867-). Class here also materials relating to Quebec under the French regime (New France), 1540-1759, and the English regime, 1760-1867

1	Bibliography
<5>	Periodicals
	For periodicals consisting primarily of informative material (Newsletters, bulletins, etc.) relating to particular subject, see subject and form division for periodicals
	For law reports, official bulletins or circulars, and official gazettes intended chiefly for the publication of laws and regulations, see appropriate entries in the text or form division tables
	For periodicals consisting predominantly of legal articles, regardless of subject matter, and jurisdiction see K1+
7	Monographic series
	Official gazettes see KEQ77+
<18-41>	Legislative documents
	Including pre-Confederation publications see J100, (Lower Canada); J107, (Quebec)
<18>	Both houses (Table KE14)
<21-28>	Legislative Council (Table KE13)
<31-38>	Legislative Assembly (Table KE13)
<41>	Bills
44	Other materials relative to legislative history
	Legislation
	For statutes, regulations, etc. on a particular subject, see the subject
	French regime (New France), 1540-1759
48	Royal edicts, ordinances, declarations, etc.
	By initial date of period covered
48.2	Abstracts. By date
49	Ordinances, regulations, etc. of the local governors and intendants
	By initial date of period covered
	Coutume de Paris
50	Abstracts
	By editor or compiler
	English regime, 1759-1867
53	Collections of acts of the British Parliament
	By date of publication
	Local ordinances, proclamations, statutes
	By period
55	1759-1764
	By initial date of period covered
56	1764-1791
	By initial date of period covered

KEQ LAW OF CANADA (QUEBEC) KEQ

Legislation
English regime, 1759-1867
Local ordinances, proclamations, statutes
By period -- Continued

57 1791-1838
By initial date of period covered

58 1838-1841
By date of publication

59 1841-1867
By date of publication
Class here works that, although published during the Province of Canada period, apply only to Lower Canada

61 Indexes and tables
By date of publication

1867-

/ Statutes
Official editions
Sessional volumes and revised statutes

63 Sessional volumes
Arrange chronologically

64 Revised statutes. Consolidations
Arrange chronologically

67 Unofficial editions
Including unofficial looseleaf editions

70 Statute revision commission acts and reports
By date of publication

72 Abridgments and digests of statutes

73 Citators to statutes

74 Indexes and tables to statutes
By date of publication

Subordinate [Delegated] legislation. Statutory orders and regulations. Statutory instruments
Official editions
Serials

77 Quebec Gazette, 1764-1874

78 Quebec Gazette, 1822-1848

79 Quebec Official Gazette, 1869-

83 Consolidations. By date

86 Unofficial editions

89 Indexes and tables to regulations

Law reports and related materials
For reports and materials on particular subjects, see the subject

Law reports and related materials -- Continued

Judicial decisions

Class reports spanning more than one period with the period of the earliest decision reported, e.g., Mathieu's reports (Rapports judiciares révisés de la Province de Québec) are classed with the reports of the French regime

Do not further subarrange courts represented by Cutter numbers

Reports of the French regime (New France), 1540-1759

100	Several courts (Table KE9)
	Particular courts
102	Conseil Souverain [Supérieur] (Table KE9)
104.A-Z	Other. By significant word in name, A-Z
107	19th century reports (i.e. reports issued prior to 1892 and not now current)
	Reports since 1892 (or series now current)
110	Several courts (Table KE9)
	Including Quebec practice courts
	Particular courts
112	Court of Queen's (King's) Bench (Table KE9)
113	Superior Court (Table KE9)
117.A-Z	Other
	By significant word in name, A-Z
<121.A-Z>	Particular subjects, A-Z
	This is an optional number provided for law libraries using this classification. Such libraries may wish to class the decisions of administrative boards on particular subjects here as well
124	Comprehensive digests and abridgments
126	Citators. Indexes. Tables
	For citators, indexes, etc. relating to particular reports or digests and abridgments, see those works
	Administrative decisions on a particular subject
	see the subject
131	Encyclopedias
132	Law dictionaries. Words and phrases
	Including bilingual Quebec law dictionaries
133	Legal maxims. Quotations
134	Form books
	General only
	For form books on a particular subject, see the subject
135	Yearbooks
	Class here only publications issued annually, containing information, statistics, etc., about the year just passed
	Judicial statistics
136	General works
	Criminal statistics

KEQ   LAW OF CANADA (QUEBEC)   KEQ

Judicial statistics
Criminal statistics -- Continued

137	General works
137.5	Juvenile crime
138.A-Z	Other. By subject, A-Z

Directories see KE213.A+
Legal research. Legal bibliography
Methods of bibliographic research and how to find the law
Class here provincial law only
For general works (not limited to the province of Quebec) see KE250+

140	General (Table KE5)
141	Electronic data processing. Information retrieval (Table KE5)
142	Systems of citation. Legal abbreviations
143	Legal composition and draftsmanship
144	Law reporting

Legal education see KE273+

149.A-Z	Law institutes, societies, etc., A-Z

For law societies incorporated to regulate the profession see KEQ159+

The legal profession
Lawyers
Including works on both lawyers and notaries
For works on notaries only see KEQ169+
Cf. KEQ656.L3 Collective bargaining

151	General
	Including works on law as a career
151.5	Special aspects
	e.g. The lawyer and society
152.A-Z	Particular classes of lawyers and types of careers, A-Z
152.G6	Government service
152.W65	Women lawyers

Practice of law

153	General (Table KE5)
153.5	Surveys of the legal profession

Biography of lawyers (Collective) see KE396.A+
Biography of lawyers (Individual - To 1867) see KE406.A+
Biography of lawyers (Individual - 1867-1931) see KE411.A+
Biography of lawyers (Individual - 1931-) see KE416.A+

153.8	Admission to the bar. Bar examinations

For examination questions and answers see KEQ202.7

Legal ethics and etiquette

154	General (Table KE5)

KEQ — LAW OF CANADA (QUEBEC) — KEQ

The legal profession
- Lawyers
  - Practice of law
    - Legal ethics and etiquette -- Continued

154.3 — Discipline. Unauthorized practice. Disbarment (Table KE5)

154.5.A-Z — Special topics, A-Z

- Attorney and client

155 — General (Table KE5)

155.5.A-Z — Special topics, A-Z

155.5.L4 — Liability

- Economics of law practice

156 — General (Table KE5)

156.5.A-Z — Special topics, A-Z

156.5.F4 — Fees (Table KE6)

- Law office management

157 — General (Table KE5)

157.3 — Attorneys' and legal secretaries' handbooks, manuals, desk-books, etc.

- Form books see KEQ134

157.5.A-Z — Special topics, A-Z

- The organized bar. Bar associations
  - *For monographs and other publications on a particular subject, see the subject*

159 — General works

- Bar of the Province of Quebec

160.A2 — Journals

- *Class here journals restricted to bar activities*
- *For journals devoted to legal subjects, either wholly or in part, see K1+*

160.A3 — Proceedings. Yearbooks

160.A4 — Presidents' reports

160.A5 — Incorporating statutes. By-laws. By date

160.A7-Z — Other documents

161 — General works. History

- *For collective biography see KE396.A+*
- *For individual biography (To 1867) see KE406.A+*
- *For individual biography (1867-1931) see KE411.A+*
- *For individual biography (1931-) see KE416.A+*

KEQ **LAW OF CANADA (QUEBEC)** KEQ

The legal profession
Lawyers
The organized bar. Bar associations
Bar of the Province of Quebec -- Continued

162.A-Z Subordinate sections. By section, A-Z
Under each:
Apply Table KEQ162/1

	Table for Quebec bar associations
.xA3-.xA39	*Proceedings*
.xA4	*Constitution and by-laws. By date*
.xA45-.xA459	*Other documents*
.xA7-.xZ	*General works. History*
	For collective biography, see KE396+; for individual biography (To 1867), see KE406; for individual biography (1867-1931), see KE411; for individual biography (1931-), see KE416

164.A-Z Other provincial associations. By name, A-Z
Apply Table KEQ162/1

	Table for Quebec bar associations
.xA3-.xA39	*Proceedings*
.xA4	*Constitution and by-laws. By date*
.xA45-.xA459	*Other documents*
.xA7-.xZ	*General works. History*
	For collective biography, see KE396+; for individual biography (To 1867), see KE406; for individual biography (1867-1931), see KE411; for individual biography (1931-), see KE416

166.A-Z Local associations, lawyers' clubs, etc. By place, A-Z
Notaries

169 General (Table KE5)

169.5 Directories
Board of Notaries of Quebec

172 By-laws. By date

173 General works

176.A-Z Special topics, A-Z
Collective bargaining see KEQ656.L3

176.F4 Fees

KEQ   LAW OF CANADA (QUEBEC)   KEQ

The legal profession
 Notaries
  Special topics, A-Z -- Continued
176.L4   Liability
 Community legal services. Legal aid. Legal assistance to the
  poor
   For collections of, and works on, substantive law see
    KEQ205.P6
180   General (Table KE5)
180.5   Directories of legal aid societies
181.A-Z   Local agencies and organizations. By place, A-Z
 History
   For collective biography see KE396.A+
   For individual biography (To 1867) see KE406.A+
   For individual biography (1867-1931) see KE411.A+
   For individual biography (1931-) see KE416.A+
185   General (Table KE5)
   By period
188   French regime (New France), 1540-1759
189   English regime, 1759-1867
190   1867-
192.A-Z   Special topics, A-Z
196   Law reform. Criticism. General administration of justice (Table
   KE5)
  Collected works (nonserial)
   For monographic series see KEQ7
198   Several authors
199   Individual authors
    Under each:
    .*x*   *By date*
    .*xA-.xZ*   *By editor*
200   Casebooks. Readings
   Class here general works only
   For casebooks on particular subjects, see the subject
202   General works. Treatises
202.3   Compends. Outlines, syllabi, etc.
202.7   Examination aids
203   Popular works
203.5   Addresses, essays, lectures
   Including single essays, collected essays of several authors,
    festschriften, etc.
205.A-Z   Works on diverse aspects of a particular subject and falling
   within several branches of the law. By subject, A-Z
205.C65   Computers (Table KE6)
205.P6   Poverty. Legal protection of the poor. Handbooks for legal
    services (Table KE6)
205.3   Common law (in Quebec)

KEQ   LAW OF CANADA (QUEBEC)   KEQ

205.6	Equity
205.9	Retroactive law
	General principles and concepts
	Comprehensive works see KEQ202
206.A-Z	Particular principles and concepts, A-Z
206.U8	Usage and custom
207.A-Z	Concepts applying to several branches of law, A-Z
	Cf. KEQ226.A+ Civil law
207.D3	Damages (Table KE6)
207.P8	Public policy (Table KE6)
	Conflict of laws. Private international law
208	General (Table KE5)
209.A-Z	Particular branches or subjects of the law, A-Z
209.A3	Adoption (Table KE6)
209.C64	Contracts. Obligations. Debtor and creditor (Table KE6)
	Creditor and debtor see KEQ209.C64
	Debtor and creditor see KEQ209.C64
	Divorce see KEQ209.M2
209.L3	Labor law (Table KE6)
209.M2	Marriage. Divorce. Matrimonial property (Table KE6)
(209.O2)	Obligations
	see KEQ209.C64
	Civil law
	Including works on the history of civil law in Quebec
211-220	General (Table KE4, modified)
	Statutes. Regulations. Orders. Rules of practice, etc.
	Statutes
214.5-.579	Civil Code
	Arrange chronologically by means of successive decimal numbers according to date of original enactment or revision of law
	Under each:
	.A15 *Legislative history. Compilations of documents. By date of publication*
	Unannotated texts
	Including official editions with or without annotations
	.A18 *Serials*
	.A19A-.A19Z *Looseleaf editions. By publisher*
	.A2 *Monographs. By date of publication*
	.A5-.Z *Annotated editions. Commentaries. By author of commentary or annotations*
	Code revision. Revision commissions
222	General (Table KE5)

Civil law
Code revision. Revision commissions -- Continued
Civil Code Revision Office

224	General (Table KE5)
<225.A-Z>	Committee reports. By subject, A-Z
226.A-Z	Concepts applying to several branches of civil law, A-Z
226.A25	Acte d'administration (Table KE6)
226.R4	Retention. Droit de rétention (Table KE6)

Persons

228	General (Table KE5)

Natural persons
Civil status

229	Domicile (Table KE5)
230	Name (Table KE5)
231	Absence. Missing persons. Presumption of death (Table KE5)

Capacity and disability

233	General (Table KE5)
234	Women (Table KE5)
	For civil status of married women see KEQ244
235.A-Z	Other groups of persons, A-Z
235.I5	Insane persons (Table KE6)
235.M5	Minors (Table KE6)
236	Recording and registration (Table KE5)
	Including registers of births, marriages, deaths; birth and death certificates (i.e. acts of civil status); vital statistics

Corporations see KEQ494+

Domestic relations. Family law

237	General (Table KE5)
238	Family courts and procedure (Table KE5)

Marriage. Husband and wife

240	General (Table KE5)
240.5	Special aspects
242	Performance of marriage. Civil and religious celebrations (Table KE5)
243	Void and voidable marriages. Nullity (Table KE5)

Rights and duties of husband and wife

244	Civil status of married women (Table KE5)

Matrimonial regimes. Property relationships.
Marriage contract

245	General (Table KE5)

Particular matrimonial regimes
Community property

246	General (Table KE5)
246.5.A-Z	Special topics, A-Z
246.5.R4	Reserved property. Biens réservés de la femme mariée (Table KE6)

KEQ LAW OF CANADA (QUEBEC) KEQ

Civil law
Persons
Domestic relations. Family law
Marriage. Husband and wife
Rights and duties of husband and wife
Matrimonial regimes. Property relationships.
Marriage contract
Particular matrimonial regimes -- Continued
247 Partnership of acquests (Table KE5)
248 Separate property (Table KE5)
Divorce. Separation
250 General (Table KE5)
251 Separation from bed and board (Table KE5)
252 Maintenance. Alimony (Table KE5)
253 Unmarried couples (Table KE5)
Parent and child
254 General (Table KE5)
255 Legitimacy. Legitimation. Paternity (Table KE5)
256 Natural children (Table KE5)
257 Adoption (Table KE5)
258 Parental rights and duties. Paternal authority
Tutorship and curatorship. Judicial advisors
260 General (Table KE5)
260.5.A-Z Special topics, A-Z
Agency see KEQ433
Property. Biens et propriété
264 General (Table KE5)
264.5 Distinction of things. Movable and immovable property
Ownership
267 General works
Real property. Land law
269 General (Table KE5)
Land tenure
270 General works
Seigneurial tenure
271 General (Table KE5)
274.A-Z Special topics, A-Z
274.B2 Banalité (Table KE6)
277.A-Z Special topics, A-Z
277.C6 Co-ownership of immovables (Table KE6)
277.C64 Condominium. Copropriété (Table KE6)
Accession rights
282 General (Table KE5)
283.A-Z Particular rights in relation to immovables, A-Z
283.R5 Riparian rights (Table KE6)
283.S86 Superficies. Building leases (Table KE6)
283.S87 Surface rights (Table KE6)

KEQ --- LAW OF CANADA (QUEBEC) --- KEQ

Civil law
- Property. Biens et propriété
  - Ownership
    - Accession rights -- Continued
      - 284.A-Z --- Particular rights in relation to movables, A-Z
    - 286 --- Possession
    - Limitations on rights of ownership and possession
      - Prescription
        - 290 --- General (Table KE5)
        - 290.5.A-Z --- Special topics, A-Z
      - 292 --- Usufruct. Use. Habitation (Table KE5)
      - Real servitudes
        - 295 --- General (Table KE5)
        - 296.A-Z --- Particular kinds, A-Z
          - 296.B7 --- Boundaries
          - 296.P3 --- Party walls
      - 298 --- Emphyteusis. Emphyteutic lease (Table KE5)
      - Personal and real surety. Sûretés personnelles et réelles
        - 302 --- General (Table KE5)
        - Personal surety
          - 304 --- Suretyship. Cautionement (Table KE5)
          - 305 --- Other
        - Real surety
          - 307 --- General works
          - Privileges and hypothecs
            - 309 --- General works
            - Privileges
              - 310 --- General (Table KE5)
              - 310.5 --- Special aspects
              - Privileges upon movable property
                - 311 --- General (Table KE5)
                - 312.A-Z --- Particular kinds, A-Z
              - Privileges upon immovables
                - 314 --- General (Table KE5)
                - 315.A-Z --- Particular kinds, A-Z
                  - 315.M4 --- Mechanics' liens
            - Hypothecs
              - 317 --- General (Table KE5)
              - 317.3 --- Legal hypothecs
              - 317.6 --- Judicial hypothecs
              - 317.9 --- Conventional hypothecs
            - Effects of privileges and hypothecs
              - 319 --- Hypothecary actions (Table KE5)
              - 321 --- Extinction of privileges and hypothecs
      - 323-327 --- Pledge. Natissement
        - 323 --- General works
        - 324 --- Pledge of immovables

KEQ LAW OF CANADA (QUEBEC) KEQ

Civil law
Property. Biens et propriété
Limitations on rights of ownership and possession
Personal and real surety. Sûretés personnelles et réelles
Real surety
Pledge. Natissement -- Continued

325	Pawn. Gage
326	Pledge of agricultural property
327	Commercial pledge
	Registration of real rights
332	General (Table KE5)
332.5	Special aspects
	Registry offices. Registers
334	General works
336.A-Z	Special topics, A-Z
336.C3	Cadastral plans (Table KE6)
340	Other topics
	Prescription see KEQ290+
342	Trusts and trustees (Table KE5)
	Successions and gifts. Successions et libéralités
345	General (Table KE5)
	Intestate successions
347	General (Table KE5)
348.A-Z	Special topics, A-Z
348.B5	Birthright (Table KE6)
	Gifts inter vivos and by will
350	General (Table KE5)
	Gifts inter vivos
351	General (Table KE5)
351.5.A-Z	Special topics, A-Z
	Wills. Testate successions
353	General (Table KE5)
354.A-Z	Special topics, A-Z
354.C3	Capacity to give and receive by will. Liberté testamentaire (Table KE6)
354.C66	Contracts to make wills (Table KE6)
354.F6	Forms of wills (Table KE6)
354.P7	Probate and proof of wills (Table KE6)
	Substitutions
356	General works
357	Fiduciary substitutions (Table KE5)
	Estate planning see KEQ1026
	Obligations
365	General (Table KE5)
	Modalities of obligations
368	General works
369.A-Z	Particular kinds, A-Z

KEQ LAW OF CANADA (QUEBEC) KEQ

Civil law
Obligations -- Continued
Protection of creditors' rights see KEQ404+
Voluntary fulfilment of obligations

372 General works
374 Payment. Tender. Payment with subrogation. Imputation of payments (Table KE5)

Non-fulfilment of obligations

377 General works
378 Damages (Table KE5)
379.A-Z Other types of recourse, A-Z

Breach of contract see KEQ411+

379.D4 Putting in default. Mise en demeure (Table KE6)
379.F6 Fortuitous event. Cas fortuit. Force majeure (Table KE6)

Extinction of obligations

382 General works
383 Compensation
384 Novation (Table KE5)
385 Confusion
386 Release. Remise
387.A-Z Other, A-Z

Contracts

390 General (Table KE5)
391 Contracts through correspondence, telephone, teletype, wire, computer, etc. (Table KE5)

Formation of contracts

392 General works
393.A-Z Special topics, A-Z
393.C6 Consent

Including works on contractual liberty, autonomy of the will

393.C65 Consideration. Cause

Void and voidable contracts

395 General works
396.A-Z Unlawful contracts, A-Z

Causes of nullity in contracts

397 General (Table KE5)
398.A-Z Particular causes, A-Z
398.E7 Error (Table KE6)

Fear see KEQ398.V5

398.F7 Fraud (Table KE6)
398.L4 Lesion (Table KE6)
398.V5 Violence and fear (Table KE6)
400 Interpretation of contracts

Parties to contract

402 Contracts in favor of third parties

KEQ LAW OF CANADA (QUEBEC) KEQ

Civil law
Obligations
Contracts
Parties to contract -- Continued
Creditors' rights
404 Subrogatory action. Action oblique (Table KE5)
405 Revocatory action. Action paulienne (Table KE5)
Discharge of contract
409 General works
409.5.A-Z Special topics, A-Z
Breach of contract. Remedies
411 General works
411.5.A-Z Particular remedies, A-Z
411.5.D36 Damages (Table KE6)
Government contracts see KEQ804
Particular contracts
For works on commercial law, mercantile transactions see KEQ477+
General see KEQ390
Sale. Vente
415 General (Table KE5)
416 Installment sale. Vente à tempérament
417 Sale of another's thing. Vente de la chose d'autrui
420.A-Z Special topics, A-Z
422 Exchange (Table KE5)
Lease and hire. Louage
424 General (Table KE5)
Lease of things
425 General (Table KE5)
Landlord and tenant
426 General (Table KE5)
427.A-Z Special topics, A-Z
427.R45 Rent. Rent control (Table KE6)
Lease and hire of work
428 General works
429 Contract of service. Master and servant (Table KE5)
For public service see KEQ837+
Contract for work and labor (Contract for services). Independent contractors
430 General (Table KE5)
Mechanics' liens see KEQ315.M4
431.A-Z Particular types, A-Z
431.B8 Building and construction. Engineering (Table KE6)
Carriers see KEQ587+

Civil law
Obligations
Contracts
Particular contracts -- Continued

433 Agency. Mandate. Representation (Table KE5)
Including power of attorney
Negotiable instruments see KEQ479+
Banking see KEQ481+
Loan. Prêt. Interest
For constitution of rent see KEQ441

435 General (Table KE5)

436 Consumer credit. Small loans. Finance charges (Table KE5)

439 Deposit. Sequestration
Including works on innkeeper and guest
Partnership see KEQ493

441 Life-rents. Constitution of rent

443 Transaction. Negotiated settlement. Compromise (Table KE5)

444 Gaming contracts and bets. Jeu et pari
For lotteries see KEQ919.L6

446.A-Z Other, A-Z
Insurance see KEQ487+
Pawn see KEQ325
Pledge see KEQ323+
Suretyship see KEQ304+

448 Quasi contracts. Unjust enrichment. Action in rem verso (Table KE5)
Delicts and quasi delicts. Civil responsibility. Torts
Including works dealing with both civil and contractual responsibility

451 General. Liability. Damages (Table KE5)

451.5.A-Z Special topics, A-Z

451.5.E9 Exoneration of liability clauses (Table KE6)
Particular torts
Torts in respect to the person

454 Personal injuries (Table KE5)

455 Death by wrongful act (Table KE5)
Violation of privacy

456 General (Table KE5)

456.3.A-Z Special aspects, A-Z

456.3.C6 Computers and privacy (Table KE6)

456.6.A-Z Special topics, A-Z

457 Torts in respect to reputation. Libel and slander (Table KE5)
Negligence

459 General (Table KE5)

KEQ LAW OF CANADA (QUEBEC) KEQ

Civil law
Obligations
Delicts and quasi delicts. Civil responsibility. Torts
Particular torts
Negligence -- Continued

460 Malpractice (Table KE5)
462.A-Z Particular types of accidents or cases of negligence, A-Z
462.A8 Automobile accidents (Table KE6)
464.A-Z Other torts, A-Z
Strict liability. Liability without fault
466 General works
467 Products liability (Table KE5)
467.5 Environmental damages (Table KE5)
468.A-Z Parties to actions in torts, A-Z
468.L32 Labor unions (Table KE6)
Liability for torts of others. Vicarious liability
470 Employer's liability (Table KE5)
Cf. KEQ705+ Workers' compensation
Government torts see KEQ811
473 Compensation to victims of crimes. Reparation (Table KE5)
Agency see KEQ433
Commercial law. Mercantile transactions
477 General (Table KE5)
477.5 Special aspects (Table KE5)
Negotiable instruments
479 General (Table KE5)
480 Bills of exchange (Table KE5)
480.5 Checks
480.8 Promissory notes
Banking
481 General (Table KE5)
482.A-Z Particular kinds of banks, A-Z
482.C7 Credit unions. Caisses populaires (Table KE6)
482.5.A-Z Particular banking transactions, A-Z
Loan of money see KEQ435+
Suretyship see KEQ304+
Investments
484 General (Table KE5)
Securities. Stock exchange transactions
For issuing and sale of securities see KEQ497
485 General (Table KE5)
485.4.A-Z Particular securities, A-Z
485.8.A-Z Special topics, A-Z
Carriers see KEQ587+
Insurance
487 General (Table KE5)

Insurance -- Continued

487.5	Insurance business. Agents. Brokers (Table KE5)
	Personal insurance
488	Life (Table KE5)
	Property insurance
489	General (Table KE5)
489.5.A-Z	Particular types, A-Z
489.5.F5	Fire (Table KE6)
	Casualty insurance
490	General liability (Table KE5)
490.3	Automobile (Table KE5)
490.7.A-Z	Particular risks, A-Z
490.9.A-Z	Other, A-Z
	Agency see KEQ433
	Associations
	Including business enterprises in general, regardless of form of organization
492	General (Table KE5)
	Unincorporated associations
492.5	General works
493	Business associations. Partnership (Table KE5)
	Including works on civil or commercial partnership
	Corporations. Juristic persons
494	General (Table KE5)
494.4	Nonprofit corporations
	Business corporations. Companies
495	General (Table KE5)
495.3	Incorporation. Corporate charters and bylaws. Promoters. Prospectus (Table KE5)
495.7	Management. Board of directors. Officers (Table KE5)
	Corporate finance. Capital. Dividends
496	General (Table KE5)
497	Issuing of securities and their sale in general (Table KE5)
	For stock exchange transactions see KEQ485+
498	Accounting. Auditing. Financial statements (Table KE5)
	Shares and shareholders' rights. Stock transfers
499	General works
499.5	Shareholders' meetings (Table KE5)
500.A-Z	Particular types of corporations, A-Z
	Close companies see KEQ500.P74
500.C6	Cooperatives (Table KE6)
	For agricultural cooperatives see KEQ526
	Credit unions see KEQ482.C7
	Family companies see KEQ500.P74

KEQ LAW OF CANADA (QUEBEC) KEQ

Associations
Corporations. Juristic persons
Business corporations. Companies
Particular types of corporations, A-Z -- Continued
500.P74 Private companies. Family companies. Close companies (Table KE6)
500.3 Dissolution. Liquidation
500.7 Consolidation and merger
Government-owned corporations see KEQ816
Insolvency and bankruptcy
For works on specific creditors' rights see KEQ404+
503 General (Table KE5)
503.3 Procedure (Table KE5)
503.7.A-Z Special topics, A-Z
Economic policy. Economic planning. Economic development
506 General (Table KE5)
506.5 Foreign investment (Table KE5)
Regulation of industry, trade, and commerce
For occupational law see KEQ980+
Trade regulation. Control of trade practices. Consumer protection
For consumer credit see KEQ436
510 General (Table KE5)
510.5 Special aspects
512 Advertising (Table KE5)
514 Labeling (Table KE5)
519 Small business (Table KE5)
Primary production. Extractive industries
Agriculture. Forestry
522 General (Table KE5)
524 Economic assistance. Rural development and rehabilitation (Table KE5)
526 Agricultural cooperatives. Agricultural societies (Table KE5)
Marketing
528 General (Table KE5)
529.A-Z Particular commodities, A-Z
529.F7 Fruit. Vegetables (Table KE6)
529.G7 Grain (Table KE6)
529.M4 Meat. Poultry (Table KE6)
529.T6 Tobacco (Table KE6)
Vegetables see KEQ529.F7
Dairy industry see KEQ549.D3
532 Forestry. Timber laws (Table KE5)
Game laws see KEQ859
534 Fishing industry (Table KE5)
Mining. Quarrying

Regulation of industry, trade, and commerce
Primary production. Extractive industries
Mining. Quarrying -- Continued

537	General (Table KE5)
540	Petroleum. Oil and gas (Table KE5)
	Manufacturing industries
544	General (Table KE5)
545.A-Z	Particular industries or products, A-Z
545.F4	Fertilizers (Table KE6)
	Food processing industries
548	General works
549.A-Z	Particular industries or products, A-Z
549.D3	Dairy industry. Dairy products industry. Milk production and distribution (Table KE6)
553	Construction and building industry. Contractors (Table KE5)
	For building laws see KEQ868+
	Trade and commerce
	For commercial law (General) see KEQ477+
	For trade regulation see KEQ510+
558	General (Table KE5)
	Retail trade
563	General (Table KE5)
564	Sunday legislation (Table KE5)
564.5.A-Z	Particular products, A-Z
564.5.A94	Automobiles (Table KE6)
	Service trades
567	General works. Licensing
568.A-Z	Particular trades, A-Z
568.E5	Employment agencies (Table KE6)
568.H6	Hotels. Restaurants (Table KE6)
	Cf. KEQ439 Innkeeper and guest
568.T73	Travel agents (Table KE6)
	Public utilities
	Including both privately and publicly owned utilities
575	General. Regulation. Finance (Table KE5)
	Power supply
	Including energy resources and development in general
577	General (Table KE5)
578	Electricity (Table KE5)
579	Gas (Table KE5)
580	Water (Table KE5)
	Including water supply
	For water power development see KEQ850+
	Transportation and communication. Carriers
	Including government-owned and municipal services
585	General (Table KE5)
	Carriers. Contract of carriage

KEQ LAW OF CANADA (QUEBEC) KEQ

Regulation of industry, trade, and commerce
Transportation and communication. Carriers
Carriers. Contract of carriage -- Continued

587	General (Table KE5)
588	Carriage by land (Table KE5)
	For motor carriers see KEQ597+
	For railways see KEQ602+
	Carriage by sea see KEQ620
	Road traffic. Automotive transportation
590	General. Motor vehicle laws (Table KE5)
591.A-Z	Special topics, A-Z
592.A-Z	Particular vehicles, A-Z
592.S6	Snowmobiles (Table KE6)
594	Traffic regulation and enforcement. Traffic violations.
	Drunk driving (Table KE5)
	Carriage of passengers and goods. Motor carriers
597	General (Table KE5)
597.5.A-Z	Particular types of motor carriers, A-Z
597.5.T38	Taxicabs
	Railways
602	General (Table KE5)
608.A-Z	Particular railways and railway companies, A-Z
	Including litigation, decisions, rulings, etc.
610	Local transit. Street railways. Subways
	Water transportation. Navigation and shipping. Carriage by sea
618	General (Table KE5)
620	Carriage by sea. Maritime law. Admiralty (Table KE5)
622.A-Z	Special topics, A-Z
622.I56	Insurance, Marine (Table KE6)
622.M3	Maritime labor law. Merchant mariners (Table KE6)
	Communication
628	General (Table KE5)
629	Press law (Table KE5)
	For freedom of the press see KEQ757
	Telecommunication
632	General (Table KE5)
635	Radio communication (Table KE5)
	Including radio and television combined
	The professions see KEQ980+
637	Intellectual and industrial property. Patents and trademarks (Table KE5)
	Social law and legislation
640	General (Table KE5)
	Labor law
642	General (Table KE5)

Social law and legislation -- Continued

643 Administration. Department of Labor and Manpower (Table KE5)

Management-labor relations

645 General (Table KE5)

Labor relations boards

647 General (Table KE5)

648 Investigation commissioners (Table KE5)

Formerly Quebec Labour Relations Board

Labor unions

650 General (Table KE5)

651 Professional syndicates (Table KE5)

652 Union security. Union shop

653 Union organization

Collective bargaining. Collective labor agreements

655 General (Table KE5)

656.A-Z Particular industries, occupations, or groups of employees, A-Z

656.A3 Accountants (Table KE6)

656.A4 Agronomists (Table KE6)

656.C4 Chemical industries (Table KE6)

656.C6 Clothing industry (Table KE6)

656.C65 Construction industry (Table KE6)

656.D4 Dentists (Table KE6)

656.E53 Engineers (Table KE6)

656.G35 Game wardens (Table KE6)

Government employees see KEQ656.P8

656.H6 Hospital workers. Nurses (Table KE6)

656.L3 Lawyers. Notaries (Table KE6)

656.M3 Machine industry (Table KE6)

656.M4 Metal products industry (Table KE6)

656.M5 Mining industry (Table KE6)

Notaries see KEQ656.L3

Nurses see KEQ656.H6

656.P5 Physicians (Table KE6)

656.P64 Police (Table KE6)

656.P7 Printing industry (Table KE6)

656.P8 Public employees (Table KE6)

Including provincial and municipal public service employees

For particular occupations or groups of employees within the service, see the occupation or group

656.T42 Teachers (Table KE6)

656.T48 Textile industry (Table KE6)

656.T73 Transportation (Table KE6)

656.W6 Wood-using industries (Table KE6)

Labor disputes

KEQ LAW OF CANADA (QUEBEC) KEQ

Social law and legislation
Labor law
Management-labor relations
Labor unions
Labor disputes -- Continued

658	General (Table KE5)
659	Arbitration. Conciliation (Table KE5)
	Strikes and lockouts. Boycotts. Picketing
660	General (Table KE5)
661	Labor injunctions (Table KE5)
663.A-Z	By industry, occupation, or group of employees, A-Z
663.C6	Construction industry (Table KE6)
663.H6	Hospitals (Table KE6)
663.P8	Public employees (Table KE6)
	Including provincial and municipal public service employees
666.A-Z	Particular industries, occupations, or groups of employees, A-Z
666.C6	Construction industry (Table KE6)
666.H6	Hospitals (Table KE6)
	Labor standards
668	General. Labor conditions (Table KE5)
	Employment and dismissal
	For contract of service, master and servant see KEQ429
670	General (Table KE5)
	Preferential employment
670.2	General (Table KE5)
670.3	Seniority (Table KE5)
	Discrimination in employment and its prevention
671	General. Racial discrimination (Table KE5)
672.A-Z	Particular groups, A-Z
672.W65	Women (Table KE6)
675	Wages. Minimum wage
	Nonwage payments. Fringe benefits
678	General (Table KE5)
679	Pension and retirement plans (Table KE5)
681	Hours of labor. Night work (Table KE5)
682	Vacations. Holidays. Leaves of absence (Table KE5)
	Labor discipline. Work rules
683	General works
684	Grievances. Grievance procedure (Table KE5)
686	Labor supply. Manpower controls (Table KE5)
	Protection of labor. Labor hygiene and safety
689	General (Table KE5)
690	Woman labor (Table KE5)

Social law and legislation
Labor law
Protection of labor. Labor hygiene and safety -- Continued
Labor hygiene and safety. Hazardous occupations.
Safety regulations

692	General (Table KE5)
693	Factory inspection (Table KE5)
694.A-Z	By industry or type of labor, A-Z
694.C6	Construction industry (Table KE6)
694.M56	Mining (Table KE6)
694.T8	Tunneling (Table KE6)
696.A-Z	Labor laws of particular industries, occupations, or types of employment, A-Z
696.C6	Construction industry (Table KE6)
	Education see KEQ696.T4
696.P8	Public employees (Table KE6)
	Including provincial and municipal public service employees
696.T4	Teachers. Education (Table KE6)
	Social insurance. Social security
700	General (Table KE5)
700.5	Special aspects
702	Health insurance. Medical care (Table KE5)
	For works on health and social services combined see KEQ718
	Workers' compensation
705	General (Table KE5)
706	Workmen's Compensation Commission (Table KE5)
	Retirement pension. Survivors' benefits. Quebec pension plan
709	General (Table KE5)
710	Quebec Pension Board (Table KE5)
	Public welfare. Public assistance
715	General. Administration (Table KE5)
718	Health and social services (Table KE5)
	For health insurance see KEQ702
720.A-Z	Special topics, A-Z
	Particular groups
722	General (Table KE5)
723	Children. Child welfare. Youth services (Table KE5)
725	Older people (Table KE5)
727	People with disabilities. Vocational rehabilitation (Table KE5)
728	Other
735	Public law in general
	Constitutional law
738	Sources. By date of publication
	Cf. KE4136+ Constitutional law sources (General)

KEQ LAW OF CANADA (QUEBEC) KEQ

Constitutional law -- Continued

740	General. History (Table KE5)
	Structure of government. Federal-provincial relations.
	Jurisdiction
744	General (Table KE5)
746.A-Z	Special topics, A-Z
746.B6	Boundaries. Territory (Table KE6)
	For boundary disputes see KE4285+
746.F6	Foreign relations (Table KE6)
	Individual and state
	Civil and political rights and liberties
749	General (Table KE5)
752	Linguistic and cultural rights. Bilingualism (Table KE5)
	Freedom of expression
755	General works
757	Freedom of the press and of information (Table KE5)
	For press law see KEQ629
759	Freedom of religion and of conscience (Table KE5)
	Control of individuals see KEQ913.92+
	Church and state
762	General (Table KE5)
763.A-Z	Special topics, A-Z
	Jesuit estates see KE4508
	Parishes see KEQ834
764.A-Z	Particular denominations, A-Z
	Organs of the government
766	General works
	The people
767	Initiative and referendum (Table KE5)
	The legislature
	Legislative Council
	Abolished December 31, 1968
768	General works. History
769	Rules and procedure
	By date of publication
	Legislative Assembly. National Assembly
772	General works. History
	Election law
774	General (Table KE5)
775.A-Z	Special topics, A-Z
775.C35	Campaign expenditures (Table KE6)
775.E5	Election districts (Table KE6)
776	Contested elections (Table KE5)
	Organization. Legislative process
778	General works
779	Rules and procedure (Table KE5, modified)

KEQ LAW OF CANADA (QUEBEC) KEQ

Constitutional law
Organs of the government
The legislature
Legislative Assembly. National Assembly
Organization. Legislative process
Rules and procedure -- Continued
Statutes. Regulations. Orders. Rules of practice, etc.
Rules. Standing orders
Collections. Compilations

779.A33 Monographs. By date of publication
780 Committees (Table KE5)
782 Private bill procedure (Table KE5)
783.A-Z Other topics, A-Z
783.B54 Bill drafting
The Crown and the Executive branch of government
785 General works. Executive power
787 Department of Justice (Table KE5)
Administrative law
798 General (Table KE5)
Administrative functions
800 Legislative functions. Rulemaking power. Regulations (Table KE5)
802 Administrative acts
804 Government contracts. Public contracts (Table KE5)
806 Judicial functions. Procedure. Administrative tribunals (Table KE5)
Abuse of administrative power
808 General (Table KE5)
808.3 Ombudsman. Protecteur du citoyen (Table KE5)
809 Judicial review of administrative acts. Appeals (Table KE5)
811 Government tort liability (Table KE5)
Administrative organization
814 General (Table KE5)
816 Government agencies. Crown corporations. Government-owned corporations and business organizations (Table KE5)
Local government
818 General (Table KE5)
Municipal government. Municipal services
820 General. Municipal corporations (Table KE5)
822 Rural municipalities. Municipal Code (Table KE5)
824 Cities and towns (Table KE5)
826 Urban and regional communities (Table KE5)
828 Charters and ordinances. Local laws (Collections) Including model ordinances and drafting manuals

KEQ LAW OF CANADA (QUEBEC) KEQ

Administrative law
Administrative organization
Local government
Municipal government. Municipal services -- Continued

830.A-Z	Special topics, A-Z
830.A5	Annexation (Table KE6)
830.E43	Elections (Table KE6)
	Municipal officials. Organs of government
832	General (Table KE5)
832.5.A-Z	Particular officers or organs, A-Z
	Municipal public service see KEQ840+
	Municipal finance see KEQ1034+
834	Parishes. Fabriques (Table KE5)
	School boards see KEQ926
	Public service. Government officials and employees
	Provincial public service
837	General (Table KE5)
838.A-Z	Special topics, A-Z
	Collective bargaining. Collective labor agreements see KEQ656.P8
	Labor disputes see KEQ663.P8
	Labor law (General) see KEQ696.P8
838.T4	Tenure and remuneration. Salaries. Pensions (Table KE6)
	Municipal public service
840	General (Table KE5)
840.5.A-Z	Special topics, A-Z
842	Police and power of the police (Table KE5)
	Public property. Public restraints on private property
844	General (Table KE5)
846	Conservation and management of natural resources. Environmental planning (Table KE5)
848	Roads. Highway law (Table KE5)
	Water resources. Watersheds. Rivers. Lakes. Water courses
850	General. Conservation and management. Water resources development (Table KE5)
850.5	Special aspects
	Riparian rights see KEQ283.R5
	Water pollution see KEQ886
853	Expropriation
	Public land law
856	General. Crown lands
	Provincial parks and forests. Wilderness preservation
858	General (Table KE5)
859	Wildlife protection. Game laws (Table KE5)
862	Land grants (Table KE5)

Administrative law
Public property. Public restraints on private property --
Continued
Regional and city planning. Building

865	General (Table KE5)
	Land use. Zoning. Land subdivision
867	General (Table KE5)
867.5.A-Z	Particular land uses and zoning controls, A-Z
867.5.S48	Sex-oriented businesses
	Building laws
868	General (Table KE5)
869	Electrical installations (Table KE5)
870	Plumbing (Table KE5)
	Housing. Slum clearance. City redevelopment
872	General (Table KE5)
873.A-Z	Particular types of accommodation, A-Z
875	Government property (Table KE5)
876	Access to public records. Freedom of information (Table KE5)
878	Public works (Table KE5)
	Public welfare. Public assistance see KEQ715+
	Public health. Sanitation. Environmental pollution
882	General (Table KE5)
	Particular public health hazards and measures
	Contagious and infectious diseases
882.5	General works (Table KE5)
882.7.A-Z	Particular diseases, A-Z
882.7.A35	AIDS (Table KE6)
883.A-Z	Other, A-Z
883.B8	Burial and cemetery laws (Table KE6)
	Environmental pollution
	Including abatement of public nuisance
885	General (Table KE5)
886	Water pollution. Drainage (Table KE5)
	Air pollution. Control of smoke, noxious gases, etc.
888	General (Table KE5)
888.5	Tobacco smoking (Table KE5)
890	Noise control (Table KE5)
	Medical legislation
	For works on health and social services combined see KEQ718
	For physicians and related professions see KEQ982+
893	General (Table KE5)
	Hospitals and other medical institutions
895	Hospitals (Table KE5)
896.A-Z	Other health services, A-Z
	Subarrange each by Table KE5

KEQ LAW OF CANADA (QUEBEC) KEQ

Administrative law
Medical legislation -- Continued
Pharmacies see KEQ983.P5

898 The mentally ill (Table KE5)
Including psychiatric hospitals and mental health facilities
For civil status of insane persons see KEQ235.I5

Food. Drugs. Cosmetics
For regulation of the food processing industries see KEQ548+

900 General (Table KE5)
902 Food law (Table KE5)
Alcohol. Alcoholic beverages. Prohibition. Liquor laws
906 General (Table KE5)
906.5.A-Z Special topics, A-Z
Public safety
Hazardous articles and processes
909 General works
910.A-Z Particular products and processes, A-Z
910.E9 Explosives (Table KE6)
Herbicides see KEQ910.P47
910.P47 Pesticides. Herbicides (Table KE6)
Control of individuals
Aliens
914 Immigration (Table KE5)
Control of social activities. Recreation
918 General (Table KE5)
919.A-Z Particular activities, A-Z
919.H67 Horse racing (Table KE6)
919.L6 Lotteries (Table KE6)
Education
Including public education
922 General (Table KE5)
923 Church and education. Denominational schools (Table KE5)
923.5 Other special aspects
School government and finance
925 General (Table KE5)
926 School districts. School boards (Table KE5)
928.A-Z Special topics, A-Z
928.T7 Transportation of students (Table KE6)
Students. Compulsory education
930 General (Table KE5)
931.A-Z Special topics, A-Z
Teachers
933 General (Table KE5)
934.A-Z Special topics, A-Z
Pensions see KEQ934.S25

Administrative law
Education
Teachers
Special topics, A-Z -- Continued

934.S25	Salaries, pensions, etc. (Table KE6)
	Elementary and secondary education
936	General (Table KE5)
938	Secondary education (Table KE5)
	Curricula. Courses of instruction
940	General works
942.A-Z	Special topics, A-Z
942.V6	Vocational and technical education (Table KE6)
944	Private education. Private schools (Table KE5)
	Higher education. Colleges and universities
946	General (Table KE5)
	Finances
948	General works
949	Student aid. Scholarships (Table KE5)
951	Faculties. Legal status of academic teachers. Academic freedom (Table KE5)
954	Colleges. Collèges d'enseignement générale et professionnel (Table KE5)
959.A-Z	Particular universities, A-Z
959.M3	McGill University (Table KE6)
959.S5	Université de Sherbrooke (Table KE6)
962	Adult education
	Science and the arts. Research
968	General works
	The arts
	Performing arts
970	General works
	Motion pictures
971	General works
971.5	Censorship
973	Museums and galleries
975	Libraries (Table KE5)
	The professions
	Including occupations
980	General. Professional corporations (Table KE5)
	Particular professions
	The health professions
982	General. Physicians (Table KE5)
983.A-Z	Other, A-Z
983.M53	Midwives (Table KE6)
983.P5	Pharmacists (Table KE6)
	Engineering and construction
985	General (Table KE5)

Administrative law
The professions
Particular professions
Engineering and construction -- Continued
986 Architects (Table KE5)
987 Engineers (Table KE5)
Building contractors see KEQ431.B8
988.A-Z Other professions, A-Z
988.C4 Chemists
988.F6 Forest engineers (Table KE6)
Lawyers see KEQ151+
Notaries see KEQ169+
Teachers see KEQ933+
988.V4 Veterinarians (Table KE6)
Public finance
995 General (Table KE5)
997 Budget. Expenditure control. Auditing and accounting (Table KE5)
998 Public debts. Loans. Bond issues (Table KE5)
Provincial revenue
1000 General (Table KE5)
Taxation
1002 General (Table KE5)
Tax administration and procedure
1004 General (Table KE5)
1006.A-Z Special topics, A-Z
1006.E9 Exemption (Table KE6)
General only
For exemptions under particular taxes, see the relevant tax
Particular taxes
Several. Collective see KEQ1002
Income tax
1008 General. Personal income tax (Table KE5)
1009.A-Z Special topics, A-Z
1011 Income of nonprofit organizations, corporations, foundations, endowments, etc. (Table KE5)
Income of business organizations
1013 General works
Corporation income tax
1014 General (Table KE5)
1016.A-Z Particular lines of corporate business, A-Z
1016.B3 Banks (Table KE6)
Property taxes. Taxation of capital
1018 General works
Provincial taxes affecting real property
For real property assessment see KEQ1043

Public finance
Provincial revenue
Taxation
Particular taxes
Property taxes. Taxation of capital
Provincial taxes affecting real property -- Continued

1019	General works
1020.A-Z	Particular taxes affecting real property, A-Z
1020.R43	Real estate transactions (Table KE6)
1022	Business taxes. Licenses (Table KE5)
	Succession duties. Gift tax
1025	General (Table KE5)
1026	Estate planning. Estate tax planning (Table KE5)
	Excise taxes. Taxes on transactions
1028	General works
1029	Retail sales tax (Table KE5)
1030.A-Z	Particular commodities, services, transactions, A-Z
1030.A3	Admission. Amusements (Table KE6)
1030.G3	Gasoline (Table KE6)
	Hotels see KEQ1030.M4
1030.M4	Meals and hotels (Table KE6)
1030.T4	Telecommunication facilities (Table KE6)
1030.T6	Tobacco (Table KE6)
1032.A-Z	Other sources of revenue, A-Z
	Local finance
1034	General (Table KE5)
1036	Local government debts. Municipal bonds (Table KE5)
	Taxation
1038	General. Tax powers of municipalities (Table KE5)
	Property taxes
1040	General. Assessment (Table KE5)
	Real property taxes
1042	General (Table KE5)
1043	Real property assessment. Land valuation (Table KE5)
1045	Business taxes
1048.A-Z	Other sources of revenue, A-Z
	Military law
1052	General (Table KE5)
1053	Militia (Table KE5)
	Military criminal law and procedure. Courts-martial
1055	General
1056.A-Z	Particular trials. By defendant, A-Z
	Native peoples. Indians. Inuit
1060	General (Table KE5 modified)
1060.A17	Treaties. By date of publication
1062.A-Z	Special topics, A-Z

Native peoples. Indians. Inuit
Special topics, A-Z -- Continued
Fishing rights see KEQ1062.H85
1062.H85 Hunting and fishing rights (Table KE6)
1062.L35 Land tenure (Table KE6)
Courts. Procedure
Administration of justice. Organization of the judiciary
History see KEQ185+
1068 General (Table KE5)
Court organization and procedure
For works on procedure in general, or before several courts see KEQ1101+
1070 General (Table KE5)
1070.5.A-Z Special aspects, A-Z
Bilingualism see KEQ1070.5.C65
1070.5.C65 Conduct of court proceedings. Decorum
Including bilingualism
Decorum see KEQ1070.5.C65
Particular courts and procedure (General) before such courts
Class works dealing with the rules of two different courts with the higher court
Prior to the Code of Civil Procedure of 1965
1072 Court of appeals. Court of Queen's (King's) Bench (Table KE5)
1074 Superior Court (Table KE5)
1076.A-Z Other courts. By significant word in name, A-Z
Subarrange each by Table KE6
1076.C6 Commissioners' court (Table KE6)
1076.M8 Municipal courts (Table KE6)
1076.P7 Prévôté de Québec (Table KE6)
Following the Code of Civil Procedure of 1965
Superior courts
1079 Court of Appeal (Table KE5)
1082 Superior Court (Table KE5)
Lower courts. Local courts
Provincial Court
1086 General (Table KE5)
1087 Small Claims Court (Table KE5)
1090 Municipal courts (Table KE5)
Courts of special jurisdiction
see the subject, e.g. Social welfare courts, see KEQ238
Judicial officers. Court employees
1093 General (Table KE5)
Judges of superior courts see KE8290+
Justices of the peace. Magistrates
1095 General (Table KE5)

Courts. Procedure
Court organization and procedure
Judicial officers. Court employees
Justices of the peace. Magistrates -- Continued

1096.A-Z	Special topics, A-Z
1096.R4	Removal
	Including individual cases
1098.A-Z	Others, A-Z
1098.B3	Bailiffs. Huissiers (Table KE6)
1098.C6	Coroners. Medical examiners (Table KE6)
1098.P7	Prothonotaries (Table KE6)
1098.S5	Sheriffs (Table KE6)

Civil procedure

For works on procedure and practice in general before a particular court, see the court

1101-1110	General (Table KE4 modified)
	Statutes. Regulations. Orders. Rules of practice, etc.
	Statutes
1104.5-.579	Code of Civil Procedure
	Arrange chronologically by means of successive decimal numbers according to date of original enactment or revision of law
	Under each:
	.A15 — *Legislative history. Compilations of documents. By date of publication*
	Unannotated texts
	Including official editions with or without annotations
	.A18 — *Serials*
	.A2 — *Monographs. By date of publication*
	.A5-.Z — *Annotated editions. Commentaries. By author of commentary or annotations*
	Including looseleaf editions
1112	Code revision commission acts and reports
	By date of publication
1115	Jurisdiction. Venue (Table KE5)
1117	Actions (Table KE5)
1119	Pleading and motions (Table KE5)
	Parties
1121	General (Table KE5)
1122	Class action (Table KE5)
	Trial. Trial practice. Trial tactics
1124	General (Table KE5)
	Evidence

Courts. Procedure
Civil procedure
Trial. Trial practice. Trial tactics
Evidence -- Continued

1126	General (Table KE5)
	Particular kinds of evidence
1128	Proof by writings
1129	Commencement of proof in writing
	Witnesses. Testimony
1130	General (Table KE5)
	Privileged (confidential) communications
1131	General (Table KE5)
1131.5.A-Z	Particular relationships, A-Z
1131.5.P4	Physician and patient (Table KE6)
1131.5.P74	Press (Table KE6)
	Expert evidence. Expert witnesses
1132	General
	Particular kinds
1133	Medical evidence. Medical witnesses (Table KE5)
1135	Presumptions. Res judicata (Table KE5)
1137	Admissions (Table KE5)
	Admissibility and exclusion of evidence
1138	General (Table KE5)
1139	Hearsay (Table KE5)
1141	Jury and jurors (Table KE5)
	Judgment
1143	General (Table KE5)
	Res judicata see KEQ1135
	Costs. Fees
1144	General (Table KE5)
1144.5.A-Z	By particular court, A-Z
1145.A-Z	Particular types of judgments, A-Z
1145.D42	Declaratory judgments (Table KE6)
	Remedies and special proceedings
1146	General works
1147	Habeas corpus (Table KE5)
	Execution of judgment
1149	General works
	Seizure
1150	General (Table KE5)
	Garnishment
1151	General works
1152	Voluntary deposit of salary or wages (Table KE5)
1152.5.A-Z	Other topics, A-Z
1152.5.I5	Imprisonment for debt. Coercive imprisonment (Table KE6)

Courts. Procedure
Civil procedure
Remedies and special proceedings -- Continued
Extraordinary remedies

1154	General works
1155.A-Z	Particular remedies, A-Z
	Habeas corpus see KEQ1147
1157	Appeals. Appellate procedure (Table KE5)
	For works on the appeal process in general see KE8585+
	Proceedings relating to particular branches of the law or special subjects, or governed by special rules.
	Noncontentious (ex-parte) jurisdiction
1159	General works
	Admiralty see KEQ620
	Adoption see KEQ257
	Divorce see KEQ250+
	Hypothecary actions see KEQ319+
	Probate see KEQ354.P7
1162	Arbitration and award. Commercial arbitration (Table KE5)
	Negotiated settlement. Compromise see KEQ443
	Criminal law
1168	General. History (Table KE5)
	Administration of criminal justice. Reform of criminal law, enforcement, and procedure
1170	General (Table KE5)
1170.5	Special aspects
1172.A-Z	Particular offenses, A-Z
1172.F6	Forgery (Table KE6)
	Criminal procedure
1174	General (Table KE5)
1175	Arrest and commitment. Rights of suspects (Table KE5)
	Indictment. Information. Public prosecutor
1178	General (Table KE5)
1179	Grand jury (Table KE5)
	Trial
1184	General works
	Evidence. Burden of proof
1186	General (Table KE5)
	Admission of evidence
1186.2	General (Table KE5)
1186.5	Wiretapping. Electronic listening and recording devices (Table KE5)
1187	Jury
	Proceedings before magistrates' courts and justices of the peace
1191	General (Table KE5)

KEQ LAW OF CANADA (QUEBEC) KEQ

Criminal procedure
Proceedings before magistrates' courts and justices of the peace -- Continued

1191.5	Summary convictions (Table KE5)
	Proceedings before social welfare courts see KEQ238
	Execution of sentence. Corrections. Imprisonment
1193	General (Table KE5)
	Particular types of penal or correctional institutions
1195	Common jails (Table KE5)
1197	Probation. Parole (Table KE5)
1199.A-Z	Law of particular counties, townships, regional municipalities (nonurban), etc. By county, etc., A-Z
	Subarrange each by Table KE3
<1199.5.A-Z>	Particular cities, A-Z
	see KEZ

KES LAW OF CANADA (SASKATCHEWAN) KES

1-599 Law of Canada (Saskatchewan) (Table KEA-KEY)

KEY LAW OF CANADA (YUKON TERRITORY) KEY

1-599 Law of Canada (Yukon Territory) (Table KEA-KEY)

Law of Canada (Cities, towns, etc.)

Number	Description
1001	A
	Subarrange each by Table KE3
1053	B
	Subarrange each by Table KE3
1103	Calgary, Alberta (Table KE2)
1203	Calgary to Charlottetown
	Subarrange each by Table KE3
1302	Charlottetown, Prince Edward Island (Table KE2)
1401	Charlottetown to Edmonton
	Subarrange each by Table KE3
1504	Edmonton, Alberta (Table KE2)
1602	Edmonton to Fredericton
	Subarrange each by Table KE3
1703	Fredericton, New Brunswick (Table KE2)
1802	Fredericton to Halifax
	Subarrange each by Table KE3
1904	Halifax, Nova Scotia (Table KE2)
2003	Halifax to Hamilton
	Subarrange each by Table KE3
2101	Hamilton, Ontario (Table KE2)
2203	Hamilton to Kingston
	Subarrange each by Table KE3
2304	Kingston, Ontario (Table KE2)
2402	Kingston to London
	Subarrange each by Table KE3
2501	London, Ontario (Table KE2)
2603	London to Montreal
	Subarrange each by Table KE3
2701-2720	Montreal, Quebec (Table KE1)
2804	Montreal to Ottawa
	Subarrange each by Table KE3
2902	Ottawa, Ontario (Table KE2)
3003	Ottawa to Quebec
	Subarrange each by Table KE3
3104	Quebec, Quebec (Table KE2)
3201	Quebec to Regina
	Subarrange each by Table KE3
3302	Regina, Saskatchewan (Table KE2)
3403	Regina to St. John
	Subarrange each by Table KE3
3501	St. John, New Brunswick (Table KE2)
3602	St. John to Saskatoon
	Subarrange each by Table KE3
3703	Saskatoon, Saskatchewan (Table KE2)
3804	Saskatoon to Toronto
	Subarrange each by Table KE3

KEZ LAW OF CANADA (CITIES, TOWNS, ETC.) KEZ

Code	Description
3901-3920	Metropolitan Toronto, Ontario (Table KE1)
4001-4020	Toronto, Ontario (Table KE1)
4105	Toronto to Vancouver
	Subarrange each by Table KE3
4201-4220	Vancouver, British Columbia (Table KE1)
4304	Vancouver to Victoria
	Subarrange each by Table KE3
4402	Victoria, British Columbia (Table KE2)
4501	Victoria to Windsor
	Subarrange each by Table KE3
4603	Windsor, Ontario (Table KE2)
4704	Windsor to Winnipeg
	Subarrange each by Table KE3
4801-4820	Greater Winnipeg, Manitoba (Table KE1)
4901-4920	Winnipeg, Manitoba (Table KE1)
5002	Winnipeg to Z
	Subarrange each by Table KE3

KE1 LAW OF CANADA -- DIVISIONS UNDER CITIES, ETC. KE1 (20 NOS.)

1.A1	Bibliography
<1.A2>	Periodicals
	For periodicals consisting predominantly of legal articles, regardless of subject matter and jurisdiction, see K1+
	For periodicals consisting primarily of informative material (Newsletters, bulletins, etc.) relating to a particular subject, see subject and form division for periodicals
	For law reports, official bulletins or circulars, and official gazettes intended chiefly for the publication of laws and regulations, see appropriate entries in the text or form division tables
	Legislative documents
	For documents relating to a particular subject, see the subject
1.A3	Serials
1.A35	Monographs
	By agency and date of publication
1.A38	Statutes (Federal and/or provincial) affecting cities, etc.
	By date of publication
	Ordinances and local laws. Charters
1.A4	Serials
1.A45	Collections
	By date of publication
1.A5	Charters. Acts of incorporation
	By date of publication
	Local law reports. Collections of decisions and rulings affecting a particular city
	For decisions and ruling relative to a particular subject, see the subject
2	Serials
2.2	Monographs
	By date of publication
	Yearbooks. Judicial statistics. Surveys of local administration of justice
3	Serials
3.2	Monographs
	By date of publication
	Directories
	see KE214
	Legal profession, local practice of law in general
	see KE330+
	Local bar associations, lawyers' clubs, etc.
	see KE372
	Legal aid
	see KEO174 ; KEQ181 ; KEA-KEY 162
4.5	General works. Local legal history
	For biography, see KE397, Collective; KE406, KE411, KE416, Individual

KE1 LAW OF CANADA -- DIVISIONS UNDER CITIES, ETC. KE1 (20 NOS.)

Particular subjects

Government

5	General (Table KE7)
5.2	Legislative functions. City Council (Table KE7)
5.5	Executive functions. Mayor (Table KE7)
	Judicial functions. City court organization and procedure
5.7	General (Table KE7)
5.75.A-Z	Particular courts, A-Z
5.75.C7	Criminal courts (Table KE7)
5.75.P6	Police courts (Table KE7)
5.85	Real property (Table KE7)
	Including tenure, landlord and tenant, etc.
	Municipal services. Municipal police power. Regulation of industry, trade, and individuals
6	General (Table KE7)
6.2	Police (Table KE7)
	Municipal franchises. Licensing. Control of industry, trade, professions
6.4	General (Table KE7)
6.5.A-Z	Particular industries, groups, etc., A-Z
	Transportation. Local transit
8	General (Table KE7)
8.2.A-Z	Particular types of carriers, A-Z
8.4	Road traffic. Traffic regulations. Parking (Table KE7)
	Social legislation. Labor relations. Public welfare
10	General (Table KE7)
10.1.A-Z	Particular groups, A-Z
10.3.A-Z	Special topics, A-Z
	Public health. Sanitation
10.7	General (Table KE7)
10.8.A-Z	Special topics, A-Z
10.8.E5	Environmental law
	Public safety
12	General (Table KE7)
12.3.A-Z	Special topics, A-Z
12.3.F5	Fire prevention and control
13	Education (Table KE7)
	Public property
14	General (Table KE7)
14.3	Expropriation. Condemnation procedures (Table KE7)
14.4	Public land law. Parks (Table KE7)
	City planning and redevelopment. Building
14.6	General (Table KE7)
14.7	Zoning (Table KE7)
14.8	Building (Table KE7)
	Housing

KE1 LAW OF CANADA -- DIVISIONS UNDER CITIES, ETC. KE1
(20 NOS.)

Particular subjects
Public property
Housing -- Continued

15	General (Table KE7)
15.1.A-Z	Special topics, A-Z
15.1.R4	Rent. Rent control
	Public finance
16	General (Table KE7)
	Taxation
16.3	General (Table KE7)
16.5.A-Z	Particular taxes, A-Z
16.5.P7	Property taxes. Assessment
	Local offenses (Violations of local ordinances) and local administration of criminal justice
17	General (Table KE7)
17.3.A-Z	Particular offenses and special topics, A-Z
18.A-Z	Other subjects, A-Z
19.A-Z	Particular boroughs, wards, districts, etc., A-Z

KE2 LAW OF CANADA -- DIVISIONS UNDER CITIES, ETC. KE2 (1 NO.)

.A1	Bibliography
<.A2>	Periodicals
	For periodicals consisting predominantly of legal articles, regardless of subject matter and jurisdiction, see K1+
	For periodicals consisting primarily of informative material (Newsletters, bulletins, etc.) relating to a particular subject, see subject and form division for periodicals
	For law reports, official bulletins or circulars, and official gazettes intended chiefly for the publication of laws and regulations, see appropriate entries in the text or form division tables
	Legislative documents
	For documents relating to a particular subject, see the subject
.A3	Serials
.A35	Monographs
	By agency and date of publication
.A38	Statutes (Federal and/or provincial) affecting cities, etc.
	By date of publication
	Ordinances and local laws. Charters
.A4	Serials
.A45	Collections
	By date of publication
.A5	Charters. Acts of incorporation
	By date of publication
	Local law reports. Collections of decisions and rulings affecting a particular city
	For decisions and ruling relative to a particular subject, see the subject
.A6	Serials
.A65	Monographs
	By date of publication
	Yearbooks. Judicial statistics. Surveys of local administration of justice
.A7	Serials
.A75	Monographs
	By date of publication
	Directories
	see KE214
	Legal profession, local practice of law in general
	see KE330+
	Local bar associations, lawyers' clubs, etc.
	see KE372
	Legal aid
	see KEO174 ; KEQ181 ; KEA-KEY 162
.A85	General works. Local legal history
	For biography, see KE397, Collective; KE406, KE411, KE416, Individual

KE2 LAW OF CANADA -- DIVISIONS UNDER CITIES, ETC. KE2 (1 NO.)

Particular subjects

.15	Government (Table KE7)
.18	Real property (Table KE7)
	Including tenure, landlord and tenant, etc.
	Municipal services. Municipal police power. Regulation of industry, trade, and individuals
.2	General (Table KE7)
.23	Police (Table KE7)
.25	Municipal franchises. Licensing. Control of industry, trade, professions (Table KE7)
.27	Transportation. Local transit (Table KE7)
.4	Social legislation. Labor relations. Public welfare (Table KE7)
.45	Public health. Sanitation (Table KE7)
.5	Public safety (Table KE7)
.55	Education (Table KE7)
	Public property
.6	General (Table KE7)
	City planning and redevelopment. Building
.63	General (Table KE7)
.64	Zoning (Table KE7)
.65	Building (Table KE7)
.68	Housing (Table KE7)
	Public finance
.7	General (Table KE7)
.73	Taxation (Table KE7)
.8	Local offenses (Violations of local ordinances) and local administration of criminal justice (Table KE7)
.85.A-Z	Other subjects, A-Z
.9.A-Z	Particular boroughs, wards, districts, etc., A-Z

KE3 LAW OF CANADA -- DIVISIONS UNDER CITIES, ETC. (CUTTER NOS.) KE3

.xA15-.xA159	Bibliography
<.xA2-.xA25>	Periodicals

For periodicals consisting predominantly of legal articles, regardless of subject matter and jurisdiction, see K1+

For periodicals consisting primarily of informative material (Newsletters, bulletins, etc.) relating to a particular subject, see subject and form division for periodicals

For law reports, official bulletins or circulars, and official gazettes intended chiefly for the publication of laws and regulations, see appropriate entries in the text or form division tables

Legislative documents

For documents relating to a particular subject, see the subject

.xA3-.xA34	Serials
.xA35-.xA39	Monographs
	By agency and date of publication
.xA4	Statutes (Federal and/or provincial) affecting cities, etc.
	By date of publication
	Ordinances and local laws. Charters
.xA44-.xA49	Serials
.xA5	Collections
	By date of publication
.xA55	Charters. Acts of incorporation
	By date of publication
	Local law reports. Collections of decisions and rulings affecting a particular city
	For decisions and rulings relative to a particular subject, see the subject
.xA7-.xA74	Serials
.xA75	Monographs
	By date of publication
.xA8-.xZ	General works. Local legal history
.x2	Particular subjects
	Building see KE3 .x2Z6
	City government see KE3 .x2G6
	City planning and redevelopment see KE3 .x2Z6
	County government see KE3 .x2G6
.x2C7	Criminal offenses (Violations of local law) and local administration of justice
.x2E4	Education. Teachers. Schools
.x2F5	Finance. Taxation
.x2G6	Government
.x2H4	Health regulations
	Local transit see KE3 .x2T7
.x2M8	Municipal services
.x2P6	Police
	Public finance see KE3 .x2F5

TABLES

KE3 LAW OF CANADA -- DIVISIONS UNDER CITIES, ETC. KE3 (CUTTER NOS.)

Particular subjects -- Continued

Public health see KE3 .x2H4

.x2P9 Public safety

Public welfare see KE3 .x2S6

Schools see KE3 .x2E4

.x2S6 Social legislation. Public welfare

Taxation see KE3 .x2F5

Teachers see KE3 .x2E4

.x2T6 Traffic regulation

.x2T7 Transportation. Local transit

.x2Z6 Zoning. Building. City planning and redevelopment

.x4A-.x4Z Particular boroughs, wards, districts, etc., A-Z

KE4 LAW OF CANADA -- FORM DIVISIONS (10 NOS.) KE4

1	Bibliography
2	Periodicals
	Class here periodicals consisting primarily of informative materials (newsletters, bulletins, yearbooks, etc.) relating to a particular subject, and monographic series
	For periodicals consisting predominantly of legal articles, regardless of subject matter or jurisdiction, see K1+
(2.4)	Monographic series
	The Library of Congress discontinued use of this form subdivision in 2008
	see KE4 2
	Legislative documents
	Committee minutes of proceedings and evidence, reports, etc.
3.A-Z	Joint committees. By committee, A-Z
3.2.A-Z	Upper house. By committee, A-Z
3.3.A-Z	Lower house. [Provincial legislature]. By committee, A-Z
3.5	Other miscellaneous documents. By date
	Including staff reports, research reports, memoranda, bills, etc.
(3.7)	Bills. By date
	The Library of Congress discontinued use of this form subdivision in 2008
	see KE4 3.5
	Statutes. Regulations. Orders. Rules of practice, etc.
	Class federal legislation passed in respect of a particular province or territory with the province or territory in the appropriate form divisions that follow
	Statutes
	Collections. Compilations
	Including annotated editions, and including collections of both statutes and regulations, collections of both federal and provincial statutes, and collections of provincial statutes
3.9	Serials
4	Monographs. By date of publication
(4.5-.579)	Particular acts (or groups of acts adopted as a whole)
	The Library of Congress discontinued use of this span of numbers in 2008
	see KE4 4.58<date>

TABLES

Statutes. Regulations. Orders. Rules of practice, etc.

Statutes -- Continued

4.58<date> Particular acts (or groups of acts adopted as a whole)

Arrange chronologically by appending the date of original enactment or total revision of the law to this number and deleting any trailing zeros. If more than one law is enacted in a single year, append a lowercase letter to the year (b, c, d, etc.) for each subsequent law

Under each:

.A15 *Legislative history. Compilations of documents. Treatises. By date of publication*

Texts

Including official editions, with or without annotations, and annotated editions and commentaries

(.A18) *Serials*

Serial editions are classed in the number for Serials under "Collections. Compilations," above

.A2 *Monographs. By date of publication*

(.A6-.Z) *Annotated editions.*

Commentaries. By author of commentary or annotations see .A2, above

Including collections consisting of an individual act and its associated regulations

Regulations. Orders. Rules of practice, etc.

Collections. Compilations

Including annotated editions

For collections consisting of both statutes and regulations see KE4 3.9+

For collections consisting of an individual act and its associated regulations see KE4 4.58<date>

4.599 Serials

Including serial editions of individual regulations

4.6 Monographs. By date of publication

(4.7-.729) Particular regulations, orders, rules of practice, etc. (or groups of regulations, etc., adopted as a whole)

The Library of Congress discontinued use of this span of numbers in 2008

see KE4 4.73

Statutes. Regulations. Orders. Rules of practice, etc.
Regulations. Orders. Rules of practice, etc. -- Continued

4.73 Particular regulations, orders, rules of practice, etc. (or groups of regulations, etc., adopted as a whole). By date of adoption or promulgation

Including official editions, annotated editions, and commentaries

For rules of practice before a separately classed agency, see the issuing agency

For serials see KE4 4.599

(4.74) Digests of statutes and regulations

The Library of Congress discontinued use of this form subdivision in 2008

see KE4 4.8

(4.75) Citators to statutes and regulations

The Library of Congress discontinued use of this form subdivision in 2008

see KE4 4.8

Indexes

(4.76) Serials

The Library of Congress discontinued use of this form subdivision in 2008

see KE4 4.8

(4.77) Monographs. By date

The Library of Congress discontinued use of this form subdivision in 2008

see KE4 4.8

(4.78) Collections of summaries of legislation

The Library of Congress discontinued use of this form subdivision in 2008

see KE4 4.8

4.8 Finding aids for statutes and regulations

Including digests, citators, indexes, and summaries

Class citators for both cases and legislation with citators for court decisions or decisions of regulatory agencies

Comparative and uniform provincial legislation

Collections. Selections

Including annotated editions

For collections of both federal and provincial legislation and collections of provincial legislation see KE4 3.9+

4.9 Serials

5 Monographs. By date of publication

Particular uniform provincial laws

(5.2) Drafts. By date

The Library of Congress discontinued use of this form subdivision in 2008

see KE4 5.6

KE4 LAW OF CANADA -- FORM DIVISIONS (10 NOS.) KE4

Statutes. Regulations. Orders. Rules of practice, etc.
Comparative and uniform provincial legislation
Particular uniform provincial laws -- Continued

(5.4) Unannotated texts. By date of publication
The Library of Congress discontinued use of this form subdivision in 2008
see KE4 5.6

5.5 Annotated editions. Commentaries. By author of commentary or annotations
The Library of Congress discontinued use of this form subdivision in 2008
see KE4 5.6

5.6 Particular uniform provincial laws. By date of adoption
Including drafts, amendments, annotated texts, unannotated texts, and commentaries
For serials see KE4 4.9

Court decisions
Reports

5.8 Serials
6 Monographic collections
6.22 Digests of reports
6.24 Citators
Including citators to both cases and statutes
6.26 Indexes

Decisions of regulatory agencies. Orders. Rulings
Reports

6.4 Serials
6.5 Monographic collections
6.7 Digests of reports
6.8 Citators. Indexes
(6.9.A-Z) Collections of summaries ("Digests") of cases decided by courts or regulatory agencies. By editor or title, A-Z
The Library of Congress discontinued use of this form subdivision in 2008
see KE4 6.22 or KE4 6.7

(7.2.A-Z) Encyclopedias. By editor or title, A-Z
The Library of Congress discontinued use of this form subdivision in 2008
see KE4 7.3

7.3.A-Z Dictionaries. Encyclopedias
7.5.A-Z Looseleaf services
Not further subarranged by date of publication
7.6.A-Z Formbooks
(7.7.A-Z) Yearbooks
see KE4 2
8 Congresses. Conferences. By date of the congress
Collected works (nonserial)

KE4 LAW OF CANADA -- FORM DIVISIONS (10 NOS.) KE4

Collected works (nonserial) -- Continued

(8.2) Several authors

The Library of Congress discontinued use of this form subdivision in 2008

see KE4 2 or KE4 9.A7+

(8.4) Individual authors

The Library of Congress discontinued use of this form subdivision in 2008

see KE4 9.A7+

(8.5) Casebooks. Readings

The Library of Congress discontinued use of this form subdivision in 2008

see KE4 9.A7+

Official reports (Serial and nonserial)

(9.A2A-.A2Z) General. Alphabetically by significant word in heading

Class here publications of the executive and judicial branches of government

The Library of Congress discontinued use of this form subdivision in 1995. After 1995, official reports are classed as periodicals or general works

(9.A3-.A49) Commissions, committees of inquiry, task forces, etc.

Arranged chronologically by means of successive Cutter numbers, according to date (estimated) of final report of commission, etc.

Under each:

.xA15	*Reports. By date of publication Including preliminary reports, recommendations, etc.*
.xA4-.xZ	*Studies, submissions, briefs, hearings, etc.*

The Library of Congress discontinued use of this form subdivision in 1995. After 1995, official reports are classed as periodicals or general works

9.A7-Z General works. Treatises

9.2 Compends. Outlines, syllabi, etc. Examination aids. Popular works

(9.5) Addresses, essays, lectures

The Library of Congress discontinued use of this form subdivision in 2008

see KE4 9.A7+

<10.Z9-.Z99> Law of individual provinces or territories, arranged alphabetically by province

Optional arrangement for law libraries using this classification

<10.Z91> Alberta

<10.Z92> British Columbia

<10.Z93> Manitoba

<10.Z94> New Brunswick

KE4 LAW OF CANADA -- FORM DIVISIONS (10 NOS.) KE4

Law of individual provinces or territories, arranged alphabetically by province -- Continued

Code	Province/Territory
<10.Z942>	Newfoundland
<10.Z944>	Northwest Territories
<10.Z946>	Nova Scotia
<10.Z95>	Ontario
<10.Z96>	Prince Edward Island
<10.Z97>	Quebec
<10.Z98>	Saskatchewan
<10.Z99>	Yukon Territory

KE5 LAW OF CANADA -- FORM DIVISIONS (1 NO.) KE5

Call Number	Description
0.A1	Bibliography
0.A13	Periodicals
	Class here periodicals consisting primarily of informative materials (newsletters, bulletins, yearbooks, etc.) relating to a particular subject, and monographic series
	For periodicals consisting predominantly of legal articles, regardless of subject matter or jurisdiction, see K1+
(0.A15)	Monographic series
	The Library of Congress discontinued the use of this form subdivision in 2008
	see KE5 0.A13
	Legislative documents
	Committee minutes of proceedings and evidence, reports, etc.
0.A2A-.A2Z	Joint committees. By committee, A-Z
0.A22A-.A22Z	Upper house. By committee, A-Z
0.A23A-.A23Z	Lower house. [Provincial legislature]. By committee, A-Z
0.A25	Other miscellaneous documents. By date
	Including staff reports, research reports, memoranda, bills, etc.
(0.A27)	Bills. By date
	The Library of Congress discontinued the use of this form subdivision in 2008
	see KE5 0.A25
	Statutes. Regulations. Orders. Rules of practice, etc.
	Class federal legislation passed in respect of a particular province or territory with the province or territory in the appropriate form divisions that follow
	Statutes
	Collections. Compilations
	Including annotated editions, and including collections of both statutes and regulations, collections of both federal and provincial statutes, and collections of provincial statutes
0.A29	Serials
0.A3	Monographs. By date of publication
0.A31-.A328	Particular acts (or groups of acts adopted as a whole)
	The Library of Congress discontinued the use of this span of numbers in 2008
	see KE5 0.A328<date>

KE5 LAW OF CANADA -- FORM DIVISIONS (1 NO.) KE5

Statutes. Regulations. Orders. Rules of practice, etc.
Statutes -- Continued

0.A328<date> Particular acts (or groups of acts adopted as a whole)
Arrange chronologically by appending the date of original enactment or total revision of the law to this number and deleting any trailing zeros. If more than one law is enacted in a single year, append a lowercase letter to the year (b, c, d, etc.) for each subsequent law

Under each:

.xA15 *Legislative history. Compilations of documents. Treatises. By date of publication*
Texts
Including official editions, with or without annotations, and annotated editions and commentaries

(.xA18-.xA19) *Serials*
Serial editions are classed in the number for Serials under "Collections. Compilations," above

.xA2 *Monographs. By date of publication*

(.xA5-.xZ) *Annotated editions. Commentaries. By author of commentary or annotations see .xA2, above*

Including collections consisting of an individual act and its associated regulations

Regulations. Orders. Rules of practice, etc.
Collections. Compilations
Including annotated editions
For collections consisting of both statutes and regulations see KE5 0.A29+

0.A329 Serials
Including serial editions of individual regulations

0.A33 Monographs. By date of publication

(0.A35-.A369) Particular regulations, orders, rules of practice, etc. (or groups of regulations, etc., adopted as a whole)
The Library of Congress discontinued use of this span of numbers in 2008
see KE5 0.A37

Statutes. Regulations. Orders. Rules of practice, etc.
Regulations. Orders. Rules of practice, etc. -- Continued

0.A37 Particular regulations, orders, rules of practice, etc. (or groups of regulations, etc., adopted as a whole). By date of adoption or promulgation
Including official editions, annotated editions, and commentaries
For rules of practice before a separately classed agency, see the issuing agency
For serials see KE5 0.A329

(0.A375) Digests of statutes and regulations
The Library of Congress discontinued the use of this form subdivision in 2008
see KE5 0.A386
Indexes

(0.A377) Serials
The Library of Congress discontinued the use of this form subdivision in 2008
see KE5 0.A386

(0.A38) Monographs. By date
The Library of Congress discontinued the use of this form subdivision in 2008
see KE5 0.A386

(0.A385) Collections of summaries of legislation
The Library of Congress discontinued the use of this form subdivision in 2008
see KE5 0.A386

0.A386 Finding aids for statutes and regulations
Including digests, citators, indexes, and summaries
Class citators for both cases and legislation with citators for court decisions or decisions of regulatory agencies
Comparative and uniform provincial legislation
Collections. Selections
Including annotated editions
For collections of both federal and provincial legislation and collections of provincial legislation see KE5 0.A29+
For collections consisting of an individual act and its associated regulations see KE5 0.A328<date>

0.A39 Serials

0.A4 Monographs. By date of publication
Particular uniform provincial laws

(0.A42) Drafts. By date
The Library of Congress discontinued the use of this form subdivision in 2008
see KE5 0.A445

KE5 LAW OF CANADA -- FORM DIVISIONS (1 NO.) KE5

Statutes. Regulations. Orders. Rules of practice, etc.
Comparative and uniform provincial legislation
Particular uniform provincial laws -- Continued

(0.A43) Unannotated texts. By date of publication
The Library of Congress discontinued the use of this form subdivision in 2008
see KE5 0.A445

(0.A44) Annotated editions. Commentaries. By author of commentary or annotations
The Library of Congress discontinued the use of this form subdivision in 2008
see KE5 0.A445

0.A445 Particular uniform provincial laws. By date of adoption
Including drafts, amendments, annotated texts, unannotated texts, and commentaries
For serials see KE5 0.A39

Court decisions
Reports

0.A45 Serials
0.A47 Monographic collections
0.A48 Digests of reports
0.A485 Indexes

Decisions of regulatory agencies. Orders. Rulings
Reports

0.A49 Serials
0.A5 Monographic collections
0.A52 Digests of reports
0.A53 Citators. Indexes

(0.A54) Collections of summaries ("Digests") of cases decided by courts or regulatory agencies
The Library of Congress discontinued the use of this form subdivision in 2008
see KE5 0.A48 or KE5 0.A52

(0.A55) Encyclopedias
The Library of Congress discontinued the use of this form subdivision in 2008
see KE5 0.A57

0.A57 Dictionaries. Encyclopedias
0.A6 Looseleaf services
Not further subarranged by date of publication
0.A62 Formbooks
(0.A64) Yearbooks
see KE5 0.A13
0.A66 Congresses. Conferences. By date of the congress

KE5 LAW OF CANADA -- FORM DIVISIONS (1 NO.) KE5

(0.A7)	Casebooks. Readings
	The Library of Congress discontinued the use of this form subdivision in 2008
	see KE5 0.A76+
	Official reports (Serial and nonserial)
(0.A72A-.A72Z)	General. Alphabetically by significant word in heading
	Class here publications of the executive and judicial branches of government
	The Library of Congress discontinued use of this form subdivision in 1995. After 1995, official reports are classed as periodicals or general works
(0.A73-.A749)	Commissions, committees of inquiry, task forces, etc.
	Arranged chronologically by means of successive Cutter numbers, according to date (estimated) of final report of commission, etc.
	Under each:
	.xA15 Reports. *By date of publication*
	Including preliminary reports, recommendations, etc.
	.xA4-.xZ *Studies, submissions, briefs, hearings, etc.*
	The Library of Congress discontinued use of this form subdivision in 1995. After 1995, official reports are classed as periodicals or general works
0.A76-.Z8	General works. Treatises
(0.Z82)	Compends. Outlines, syllabi, etc. Examination aids. Popular works
	The Library of Congress discontinued the use of this form subdivision in 2008
	see KE5 0.A76+
(0.Z85)	Addresses, essays, lectures
	The Library of Congress discontinued the use of this form subdivision in 2008
	see KE5 0.A76+
<0.Z9-.Z99>	Law of individual provinces or territories, arranged alphabetically by province
	Optional arrangement for law libraries using this classification
<0.Z91>	Alberta
<0.Z92>	British Columbia
<0.Z93>	Manitoba
<0.Z94>	New Brunswick
<0.Z942>	Newfoundland
<0.Z944>	Northwest Territories
<0.Z946>	Nova Scotia
<0.Z95>	Ontario
<0.Z96>	Prince Edward Island
<0.Z97>	Quebec

KE5 LAW OF CANADA -- FORM DIVISIONS (1 NO.) KE5

Law of individual provinces or territories, arranged alphabetically by province -- Continued

<0.Z98> Saskatchewan
<0.Z99> Yukon Territory

KE6 LAW OF CANADA -- FORM DIVISIONS (CUTTER NO.) KE6

Call Number	Description
.xA15-.xA199	Periodicals
	Including gazettes, bulletins, circulars, etc.
.xA2	Legislative documents. By date
.xA3	Treaties. Statutes. Statutory orders (Collective or individual). By date
.xA52	Cases. Decisions (Collective or individual). By date
.xA7-.xZ9	General works. Treatises

KE7 LAW OF CANADA -- SUBARRANGEMENT OF PARTICULAR SUBJECTS UNDER CITIES KE7

.A2-.A29	Legislative documents
.A3	Legislation. By date
.A5-.A59	Decisions. By court, agency, etc.
.A7-.A79	Miscellaneous documents
.A8-.Z	General works. Treatises

KE8 LAW OF CANADA -- SUBARRANGEMENT OF CANADIAN LAW REPORTS KE8

	Reports
0.A2-.A29	Serials
	Arrange chronologically by beginning date of coverage
0.A3	Monographs. By date
0.1	Reasons for judgment. By initial date of period covered
0.2	Digests. Summaries
0.3	Citators
0.5	Indexes
	For indexes and other finding aids relating to a particular publication, see that publication
(0.6)	Summaries of judgments
	see KE8 0.2
0.8	Records and briefs. Factums

KE9 LAW OF CANADA - SUBARRANGEMENT OF PROVINCIAL LAW REPORTS KE9

	Reports
0.A2-.A29	Serials
	Arrange chronologically by beginning date of coverage
0.A3	Monographs
0.2	Digests. Summaries
0.3	Citators
0.5	Indexes
	For indexes and other finding aids relating to a particular publication, see that publication
(0.6)	Summaries of judgments
	see 0.2

KE10 LAW OF CANADA -- SUBARRANGEMENT OF PARTICULAR LAW SCHOOLS KE10

This table is provided as an optional subarrangement for libraries using this classification. The table is not applied by the Library of Congress

Catalogs, bulletins
see KE286

Classification	Description
<.xA2-.xA29>	Outlines of study, teachers' manuals, etc.
<.xA3>	Registers. By date
<.xA4-.xA49>	Yearbooks
	Alumni associations
<.xA7-.xA79>	Periodicals (official organs)
<.xA8>	Yearbooks
<.xA83-.xA839>	Directories
<.xA84>	Reports. By date
<.xA85-.xZ>	History and general works
<.x25A-.x25Z>	Faculty
<.x3A3>	Class yearbooks
<.x3A4-.x3A49>	Law clubs, societies
	Administration
	Including organization and policy
<.x3A5-.x3A59>	General works
	Governing body. Council
	Including minutes of meetings, etc.
<.x3A6-.x3A69>	General works
	Committees
<.x3A7-.x3A79>	General works
<.x3A8-.x3Z5>	Particular committees, A-Z
	Deans' reports
<.x4A2-.x4A29>	Serials
<.x4A3>	Individual reports. By date
<.x4A5-.x4Z49>	Special topics, A-Z
<.x4C8>	Curricula
	Including student course evaluations
	For study and teaching of particular subjects, see KE298
	History. General works
<.x4Z5-.x4Z9>	Periodicals (i.e. official organs or student newspapers)
	For law journals, see K1+
<.x5A5-.x5Z6>	Treatises
<.x5Z7-.x5Z79>	Addresses, essays, lectures
<.x6A2-.x6A29>	Anniversaries, special celebrations, etc.
<.x6A3-.x6A39>	Convocations

KE11 LAW OF CANADA -- SUBARRANGEMENT OF INDIVIDUAL BIOGRAPHY KE11

.xA3	Autobiography. By date
	Letters. Correspondence
.xA4	General collections. By date of publication
.xA41-.xA49	Collections of letters to particular individuals. By correspondent, alphabetically
	For correspondence on a particular subject, see the subject
.xA8-.xZ	Biography and criticism

KE12 TABLE FOR EMERGENCY ECONOMIC LEGISLATION KE12

1	General (Table KE5)
1.4	Control of unemployment (Table KE5)
	Alien property. Enemy property
	see KE621
	Rationing
2	General (Table KE5)
2.1.A-Z	By commodity or service, A-Z
	Foreign exchange regulation
	see KE5612
	Price control. Profiteering
2.5	General (Table KE5)
2.6.A-Z	By commodity or service, A-Z
	Rent
	see KE692
	Wage control
	see KE3277 (1939-1945)
	Industrial priorities and allocations
3	General (Table KE5)
3.1.A-Z	By industry or commodity, A-Z
3.5	War damage compensation. Foreign claims settlement (Table KE5)
4	Other

KE13 TABLE FOR PARLIAMENTARY PUBLICATIONS OR KE13 LEGISLATIVE DOUCMENTS (8 NOS.)

<1>	Indexes (General). Guides
<1.2>	Collections. Selections
<2>	Order of business and notices (formerly Routine proceedings and order of the day)
<3>	Minutes of the proceedings. Votes and proceedings
	Journals
<4>	Texts
<4.2>	Indexes
	Sessional papers
<5>	Texts
<5.2>	Indexes
	Debates
<6>	Texts
<6.2>	Indexes
<7>	Committee proceedings, reports, etc. By committee and date
	Class committee proceedings, reports, etc., on particular topics with the topic in classes A-Z
	Bills
	see (KE65), (KE68), (KEO33), (KEQ41), (KEA27), etc., as applicable
<8>	Other, miscellaneous

KE14 TABLE FOR PARLIAMENTARY PUBLICATIONS OR LEGISLATIVE DOUCMENTS (1 NO.) KE14

Code	Description
<0>	Indexes (General). Guides
<0.12>	Collections. Selections
<0.2>	Order of business and notices (formerly Routine proceedings and order of the day)
<0.3>	Minutes of the proceedings. Votes and proceedings
	Journals
<0.4>	Texts
<0.42>	Indexes
	Sessional papers
<0.5>	Texts
<0.52>	Indexes
	Debates
<0.6>	Texts
<0.62>	Indexes
<0.7>	Committee proceedings, reports, etc. By committee and date
	Class committee proceedings, reports, etc., on particular topics with the topic in classes A-Z
	Bills
	see (KE65), (KE68), (KEO33), (KEQ41), (KEA27), etc., as applicable
<0.8>	Other, miscellaneous

KEA-KEY LAW OF CANADA (PROVINCES AND TERRITORIES) KEA-KEY

Each province or territory (except Ontario and Quebec) is subdivided by this provincial table

1	Bibliography
<4>	Periodicals
	For periodicals consisting predominantly of legal articles, regardless of subject matter and jurisdiction, see K1+
	For periodicals consisting primarily of informative material (Newsletters, bulletins, etc.) relating to a particular subject, see subject and form division for periodicals
	For law reports, official bulletins or circulars, and official gazettes intended chiefly for the publication of laws and regulations, see appropriate entries in the text or form division tables
7	Monographic series
	Official gazettes see KEA-KEY 71+
	Legislative documents
	Including pre-Confederation publications see J104+
	Class materials relating to the Colony of Vancouver Island (1849-1866) with the province of British Columbia
<16>	Both Houses (Table KE14)
<19>	Legislative Council (Table KE14)
<22>	Legislative Assembly (Table KE14)
<27>	Bills
32	Other materials relating to legislative history
	Including Status tables
	Legislation
	Class materials relating to Assiniboia (1862-1869) with the province of Manitoba
	Statutes. Ordinances
	Including pre-Confederation publications
	Class materials relating to the Colony of Vancouver Island (1849-1866) with the province of British Columbia
	Class ordinances of the North-West Territories which apply to the provinces of Alberta or Saskatchewan with those provinces
	Public general acts
	Sessional volumes and revised statutes
39.A2-.A29	Serial sessional volumes
	Arranged chronologically
40	Monographic sessional volumes to date of first revision
41	Revised statutes with sessional volumes from date of first revision
	Arranged chronologically with date of revision, treating sessional volumes as supplements to the latest revision
42	Gazettes, Part III
44	Codifications. "Consolidations."
	By date of publication

KEA-KEY LAW OF CANADA (PROVINCES AND TERRITORIES) KEA-KEY

Legislation
Statutes. Ordinances
Public general acts -- Continued

51	Statute revision commission acts and reports
	By date of publication
54	Local and private acts
	By date of publication
58	Abridgments and digests of statutes
60	Citators to statutes
62	Indexes and tables to statutes
	Subordinate [Delegated] legislation. Statutory orders and regulations. Statutory instruments
	Official editions
71.A2-.A29	Serial official gazettes, Parts I and II
	Arranged chronologically
72	Monographic official gazettes, Parts I and II, to date of first consolidation
74	Consolidations and official gazettes, Parts I and II, from date of first consolidation
	Arrange chronologically by date of consolidation, treating issues of the gazette as supplements to the latest consolidation
78	Other
	Including looseleaf editions, etc.
83	Unofficial editions
87	Digests, summaries of regulations
89	Indexes and tables to regulations
	Law reports and related materials
	For reports and materials on particular subjects, see the subject
	Law reports
104	Several courts (Table KE9)
	Particular courts
118	Superior courts (Table KE9)
	Class here reports of single superior courts which include cases covering both original and appellate jurisdiction, or cases from both such divisions of the court
119	Courts of appeal, or appeal divisions (Table KE9)
121	Trial courts, or trial divisions (Table KE9)
	Including Supreme Court, Court of Queen's Bench, Queen's Bench Division
123	Courts of chancery (Table KE9)
	Including equity reports in general
<130.A-Z>	Particular subjects, A-Z
	This is an optional number provided for law libraries using this classification. Such libraries may wish to class the decisions of administrative boards on particular subjects here as well

Law reports and related materials -- Continued

132 Comprehensive abridgments and digests

134 Citators. Indexes. Tables

For citators, indexes, etc. relating to particular reports or digests and abridgments, see those works

Administrative decisions on a particular subject see the subject

138 Encyclopedias

139 Law dictionaries. Words and phrases

140 Form books

Class here general works only For form books on a particular subject, see the subject

141 Yearbooks

Class here only publications issued annually, containing information, statistics, etc., about the year just passed For other publications appearing yearly, see K1+

Judicial statistics

142 General works

Criminal statistics

143 General works

143.5 Juvenile crime

144.A-Z Other. By subject, A-Z

144.F57 Fisheries and wildlife cases

Wildlife cases see KEA-KEY 144.F57

Directories see KE213

146 Legal research. Legal bibliography

Including methods of bibliographic research and how to find the law Class here provincial law only For general works, see KE250

Legal education see KE273+

149.A-Z Law institutes, Law societies, etc. A-Z

For law societies incorporated to regulate the profession, see KE361

The legal profession. Practice of law

General see KE330+

153 Legal ethics. Discipline. Disbarment

154 Economics of law practice. Fees (Table KE5)

155 Law office management. Attorneys' and legal secretaries' handbooks, manuals, etc., of provincial law

157.A-Z Other topics, A-Z

157.M34 Malpractice

The organized bar, law societies, bar associations see KE361

Community legal services. Legal aid. Legal assistance to the poor

For collections of, and works on, substantive law see KEA-KEY 178.P6

160	General (Table KE5, modified)
160.A65	Directories of legal aid agencies
162.A-Z	Local agencies and organizations. By place, A-Z
163.A-Z	Legal aid services to particular groups, A-Z
163.I53	Indians (Table KE6)
165	History
	For biography (Collective), see KE396+; for biography (Individual), see KE406, KE411, KE416
168	Law reform. Criticism. General administration of justice (Table KE5)
170	Congresses. Conferences
171	Collected works (nonserial)
	For monographic series see KEA-KEY 7
173	General works. Treatises
174	Compends, outlines. Examination aids. Popular works
176	Addresses, essays, lectures
	Including single essays, collected essays of several authors, festschriften, etc.
177.A-Z	Works for particular groups of users, A-Z
177.A34	Aged persons. Older people. Retired persons
177.F37	Farmers
	Older people see KEA-KEY 177.A34
	Retired persons see KEA-KEY 177.A34
177.W6	Women
178.A-Z	Works on diverse aspects of a particular subject and falling within several branches of the law
	By subject, A-Z
178.P6	Poverty. Legal protection of the poor. Handbooks for legal services
180	Equity
182	Conflict of laws (Table KE5)
184.A-Z	Concepts applying to several branches of law, A-Z
	Affidavits see KEA-KEY 184.O2
184.A77	Artificial insemination, Human
184.D3	Damages
	Depositions see KEA-KEY 184.O2
	Legal advertising see KEA-KEY 184.N66
184.L55	Limitation of actions
184.N66	Notice. Legal advertising (Table KE5)
184.O2	Oaths. Affidavits. Depositions
	Persons
186	General works
	Natural persons

Persons

Natural persons -- Continued

187	General works
188	Civil status. Name (Table KE5)
	Capacity and disability
190	General works
190.3.A-Z	Particular groups of persons, A-Z
190.3.I5	Insane persons (Table KE6)
190.3.M5	Minors (Table KE6)
190.3.W6	Women (Table KE6)
	Conservatorship see KEA-KEY 208
192	Recording and registration
	Including registers of birth, marriages, deaths; birth and death certificates; vital statistics
	Corporations see KEA-KEY 305+
	Domestic relations. Family law
194	General (Table KE5)
195	Family courts (Table KE5)
	Cf. KEA-KEY 593 Juvenile courts
	Marriage. Husband and wife
196	General (Table KE5)
	Inter-spousal immunity in tort see KEA-KEY 296.H8
198	Matrimonial property relationships (Table KE5)
	Divorce. Separation
201	General (Table KE5)
203	Separate maintenance. Alimony (Table KE5)
	Parent and child
206	General (Table KE5)
206.4	Illegitimate children (Table KE5)
206.5	Adoption (Table KE5)
	Parental rights and duties. Property of minors. Custody
206.7	General (Table KE5)
206.8	Support. Desertion and nonsupport (Table KE5)
208	Guardian and ward. Conservatorship (Table KE5)
	Property
212	General. Ownership (Table KE5)
	Real property. Land law
214	General (Table KE5)
214.5	Alien landownership (Table KE5)
	Land tenure
215	General (Table KE5)
	Estates and interests. Freehold. Fee simple
217	Housing condominium (Table KE5)
	Future estates and interests
221	Rule against perpetuities (Table KE5)
	Estates and interests arising from marriage
223	Dower. Curtesy. Homestead rights (Table KE5)

Property

Real property. Land law

Land tenure -- Continued

Tenancy. Leaseholds. Landlord and tenant

224	General (Table KE5)
224.5	Rent. Rent control (Table KE5)
225.A-Z	Particular kinds of leaseholds, A-Z
225.C6	Commercial leases (Table KE6)
225.F35	Farm tenancy (Table KE6)
227.A-Z	Other topics, A-Z
227.D58	Distress (Table KE6)
227.F59	Fixtures. Improvements (Table KE6)
	Improvements see KEA-KEY 227.F59
227.P37	Partition (Table KE6)
227.P7	Prescription (Table KE6)
227.R54	Rights as to the use and profits of another's land (Table KE6)
227.R57	Riparian rights (Table KE6)
	Transfer of rights in land
	Including vendor's liability
230	General. Vendor and purchaser. Real estate transactions (Table KE5)
231	Conveyances. Title investigation. Deeds. Registration (Table KE5)
233.A-Z	Other modes of transfer, A-Z
	Prescription see KEA-KEY 227.P7
	Mortgages
235	General (Table KE5)
235.5.A-Z	Special topics, A-Z
235.5.F67	Foreclosure (Table KE6)
	Personal property
238	General (Table KE5)
238.5.A-Z	Special topics, A-Z
238.5.R44	Replevin (Table KE6)
	Trusts and trustees
240	General (Table KE5)
241	Trust companies (Table KE5)
242.A-Z	Special topics, A-Z
242.M3	Maintenance and advancement (Table KE6)
	Estate planning see KEA-KEY 515.3
	Succession upon death
244	General (Table KE5)
245	Testate succession. Wills (Table KE5)
246	Probate law and practice. Surrogate courts (Table KE5)
247	Intestate succession (Table KE5)
248	Administration of decedents' estates. Execution of wills. Personal representatives (Table KE5)

Succession upon death -- Continued

248.5.A-Z Special topics, A-Z

248.5.F34 Family provisions (Table KE6)

Contracts

250 General (Table KE5)

250.5 Formation of contracts (Table KE5)

Including consideration, conditions, formalities, etc.

251 Parties to contract (Table KE5)

252 Void and voidable contracts. Unlawful contracts. Unconscionable transactions. Mistake. Duress. Fraud (Table KE5)

254 Discharge of contract. Impossibility of performance (Table KE5)

Breach of contract. Remedies

255 General works (Table KE5)

Particular remedies

255.2 Damages. Quantum meruit (Table KE5)

255.5 Other

Particular contracts

257 Comprehensive. Commercial law. Mercantile transactions (Table KE5)

Contract for work and labor (Contract for services). Independent contractors

259 General (Table KE5)

259.5 Mechanics' liens (Table KE5)

259.8.A-Z Particular types of contracts, A-Z

259.8.B8 Building and construction (Table KE6)

Sale of goods

261 General (Table KE5)

261.5.A-Z Special topics, A-Z

261.5.C6 Conditions and warranties. Implied warranties (Table KE6)

Banking

264 General works

265.A-Z Particular kinds of banks, A-Z

265.C7 Credit unions (Table KE6)

Trust companies see KEA-KEY 241

Particular banking transactions

266 Collections of accounts. Collection law (Table KE5)

For collection agencies see KEA-KEY 373.C6

Loan of money. Interest. Usury

Including debtor and creditor in general

Cf. KEA-KEY 252 Unconscionable transactions

267 General (Table KE5)

268 Consumer credit. Small loans. Finance charges (Table KE5)

270 Suretyship. Guaranty (Table KE5)

Contracts

Particular contracts -- Continued

Secured transactions

271	General (Table KE5)
271.5.A-Z	Particular transactions, A-Z
271.5.L54	Liens (Table KE6)

Investments

273	General (Table KE5)

Securities. Stock exchange transactions

For issuing and sale of securities see KEA-KEY 318

274	General (Table KE5)
274.5.A-Z	Particular stock exchanges, A-Z
275.A-Z	Other topics, A-Z
275.L43	Legal investments. Trust investments

Trust investments see KEA-KEY 275.L43

Carriers. Carriage of goods and passengers

278	General works

Carriage by sea. Maritime (Commercial) law. Admiralty

279	General works
280	Admiralty proceedings. Admiralty courts (Table KE5)
280.5.A-Z	Special topics, A-Z
280.5.B6	Bottomry and respondentia. Ship mortgages. Maritime liens

Insurance

Including schemes operated by the government

282	General. Insurance business. Agents. Brokers (Table KE5)

Personal insurance

Life

283	General works
283.3	Life insurance companies. Finance. Investment of funds (Table KE5)

Property insurance

284	General works
284.5.A-Z	Particular types of insurance, A-Z
284.5.F5	Fire (Table KE6)
284.8.A-Z	Particular kinds of property, A-Z
284.8.C7	Crops

Casualty insurance

285	General liability (Table KE5)
285.4	Automobile (Table KE5)

Including unsatisfied judgment fund

285.6.A-Z	Particular risks, A-Z
286	Suretyship. Guaranty. Title insurance. Bonding

Social insurance see KEA-KEY 411+

Torts (Extracontractual liability)

290	General. Liability. Damages (Table KE5)

Torts (Extracontractual liability) -- Continued
Particular torts
Torts in respect to the person

291	Personal injuries. Death by wrongful act (Table KE5)
	Violation of privacy
292	General (Table KE5)
292.5.A-Z	Special topics, A-Z
293	Torts in respect to reputation. Libel. Slander (Table KE5)
293.5	Torts in respect to domestic relations (Table KE5)
	Negligence
	Including contributory negligence
294	General (Table KE5)
294.3.A-Z	Particular types of accidents or cases of negligence, A-Z
294.3.A8	Automobile accidents (Table KE6)
294.3.L5	Liability for condition and use of land. Occupiers' liability (Table KE6)
294.3.S66	Sports accidents (Table KE6)
294.5.A-Z	Other torts, A-Z
	Strict liability. Liability without fault
295	General (Table KE5)
295.2	Damage caused by animals (Table KE5)
295.3	Products liability (Table KE5)
295.5	Environmental damages (Table KE5)
296.A-Z	Parties to actions in torts, A-Z
296.H8	Husband and wife. Inter-spousal immunity (Table KE6)
296.M8	Municipalities (Table KE6)
296.P8	Public officers (Table KE6)
296.5.A-Z	Special topics, A-Z
296.5.G6	Government liability (Table KE6)
297	Compensation to victims of crimes. Reparation (Table KE5)
298	Assistance in emergencies. Good Samaritan laws (Table KE5)
	Agency
299	General works (Table KE5)
299.3	Power of attorney (Table KE5)
	Associations
	Including business enterprises in general, regardless of form of organization
302	General (Table KE5)
	Unincorporated associations
303	General works
304	Business associations. Partnership
	Corporations. Juristic persons
305	General (Table KE5)
305.4	Nonprofit corporations (Table KE5)
	Business corporations. Companies
306-315	General (Table KE4)
316	Incorporation (Table KE5)

Associations
Corporations. Juristic persons
Business corporations. Companies -- Continued

316.5	Management. Board of directors. Officers (Table KE5)
	Corporate finance. Capital. Dividends
317	General (Table KE5)
318	Issuing of securities and their sale in general (Table KE5)
	For stock exchange transactions see KEA-KEY 274+
319	Accounting. Auditing. Financial statements (Table KE5)
320	Shares and shareholders' rights. Stock transfers (Table KE5)
321.A-Z	Particular types of corporations, A-Z
	Close companies see KEA-KEY 321.P74
	Family companies see KEA-KEY 321.P74
321.P74	Private companies. Family companies. Close companies (Table KE6)
321.3	Dissolution. Liquidation (Table KE5)
321.5	Consolidation and merger (Table KE5)
	Insolvency and bankruptcy. Creditors' rights
322	General (Table KE5)
	Bankruptcy
323	General (Table KE5)
323.5.A-Z	Special topics, A-Z
323.5.P74	Priority of claims (Table KE6)
323.5.R43	Receivers in bankruptcy (Table KE6)
	Debtors' relief
324	General (Table KE5)
324.5.A-Z	Particular forms of relief, A-Z
324.5.A8	Assignments for benefit of creditors (Table KE6)
324.5.B84	Bulk transfers. Bulk sales (Table KE6)
324.5.M6	Moratorium (Table KE6)
	Economic policy. Economic planning. Economic development
328	General (Table KE5)
328.5	Foreign investment (Table KE5)
	Regulation of industry, trade, and commerce. Occupational law
330	General. Trade regulation. Control of trade practices. Consumer protection (Table KE5)
	Advertising
331	General (Table KE5)
331.3.A-Z	By industry or product, A-Z
331.3.A4	Alcoholic beverages (Table KE6)
334	Small business (Table KE5)
	Primary production. Extractive industries
	Agriculture. Forestry
338	General (Table KE5)
339	Conservation of agricultural forest lands. Soil conservation (Table KE5)

Regulation of industry, trade, and commerce. Occupational law
Primary production. Extractive industries
Agriculture. Forestry -- Continued

340	Economic assistance. Rural development and rehabilitation (Table KE5)
340.5	Farm corporations (Table KE5)
341	Marketing (Table KE5)
345	Forestry. Timber laws (Table KE5)
	Game laws see KEA-KEY 499.6
347	Fishing industry (Table KE5)
	Mining. Quarrying
349	General (Table KE5)
349.3	Coal (Table KE5)
	Nonferrous metals
350	General works
350.3.A-Z	Particular metals, A-Z
350.3.C6	Copper (Table KE6)
350.3.G6	Gold (Table KE6)
	Petroleum. Oil and gas
351	General (Table KE5)
352	Conservation (Table KE5)
353.A-Z	Special topics, A-Z
353.L4	Leases (Table KE6)
353.O36	Oil sands (Table KE6)
353.S92	Submerged land legislation. Tidal oil (Table KE6)
	Tidal oil see KEA-KEY 353.S92
	Manufacturing industries
356	General (Table KE5)
356.3.A-Z	Particular industries or products, A-Z
	Food processing industries
359	General (Table KE5)
359.3.A-Z	Particular industries or products, A-Z
359.3.D3	Dairy industry. Dairy products industry. Milk production and distribution (Table KE6)
362	Construction and building industry. Contractors (Table KE5)
	Trade and commerce
368	General (Table KE5)
	Export trade
369	General works
369.5.A-Z	Particular commodities, A-Z
369.5.F8	Furs
	Retail trade
371	General works
371.3	Sunday legislation (Table KE5)
371.4	Franchises (Table KE5)
371.5.A-Z	Particular products, A-Z
371.5.G3	Gasoline

Regulation of industry, trade, and commerce. Occupational law
Trade and commerce -- Continued
Service trades

372	General. Licensing (Table KE5)
373.A-Z	Particular trades, A-Z
373.C6	Collection agencies (Table KE6)
373.C7	Credit bureaus (Table KE6)
	Funeral services see KEA-KEY 373.U5
373.H67	Hotels. Restaurants (Table KE6)
	Insurance agents see KEA-KEY 282
373.R4	Real estate agents (Table KE6)
	Restaurants see KEA-KEY 373.H67
373.U5	Undertakers. Funeral services (Table KE6)
	Public utilities
375	General. Regulation. Finance (Table KE5)
	Power supply
	Including energy resources and development in general
376	General (Table KE5)
376.3	Electricity (Table KE5)
376.4	Gas (Table KE5)
376.5	Water (Table KE5)
	For waterpower development see KEA-KEY 493+
	Transportation and communication
379	General (Table KE5)
	Road traffic. Automotive transportation
381	General. Motor vehicle laws (Table KE5)
381.5	Safety responsibility laws. Compulsory insurance (Table KE5)
	Cf. KEA-KEY 285.4 Unsatisfied judgment fund
381.7.A-Z	Particular vehicles, A-Z
	All-terrain vehicles see KEA-KEY 381.7.S66
381.7.S66	Snowmobiles. All-terrain vehicles (Table KE6)
	Traffic regulation and enforcement. Traffic violations.
	Drunk driving
382	General (Table KE5)
382.2	Traffic courts (Table KE5)
	Carriage of passengers and goods. Motor carriers
382.5	General (Table KE5)
382.7.A-Z	Particular types of motor carriers, A-Z
382.7.S3	School buses
382.7.T76	Trucks
	Railways
383	General (Table KE5)
383.5.A-Z	Special topics, A-Z
384.A-Z	Particular railways and railway companies, A-Z
	Including litigation, decisions, rulings, etc.
	Water transportation. Navigation and shipping

Regulation of industry, trade, and commerce. Occupational law
Transportation and communication
Water transportation. Navigation and shipping -- Continued

387	General works
388.A-Z	Special topics, A-Z
388.H3	Harbors and ports
	Communication
390	General (Table KE5)
	Telecommunication
393	Telephone (Table KE5)
	The professions
395	General. Licensing (Table KE5)
395.4.A-Z	Particular professions, A-Z
395.4.A3	Accountants. Auditors (Table KE6)
395.4.A7	Architects (Table KE6)
	Building contractors see KEA-KEY 362
	Lawyers see KEA-KEY 153
395.4.P5	Physicians. Health professions (General) (Table KE6)
	Teachers see KEA-KEY 441+
396	Intellectual and industrial property. Patents and trademarks (Table KE5)
	Social law and legislation
398	General (Table KE5)
	Labor law
399	General (Table KE5)
	Management-labor relations
400	General (Table KE5)
400.3	Labor relations boards (Table KE5)
	Labor unions
401	General (Table KE5)
	Collective bargaining. Collective labor agreements
402	General (Table KE5)
403.A-Z	Particular industries, occupations, or groups of employees, A-Z
403.E5	Engineers (Table KE6)
403.F6	Forestry (Table KE6)
	Government employees see KEA-KEY 403.P8
403.M4	Medical personnel (Table KE6)
403.N85	Nurses (Table KE6)
403.P8	Public employees (Table KE6)
	Including provincial and municipal public service employees
	Class particular occupations or groups of employees within the services with the occupation or group above
403.S6	Social workers (Table KE6)
403.T4	Teachers (Table KE6)

Social law and legislation
Labor law
Management-labor relations
Labor unions -- Continued
Labor disputes

404	General (Table KE5)
404.3	Arbitration. Conciliation (Table KE5)
404.5	Strikes and lockouts. Boycotts. Labor injunctions (Table KE5)
404.7.A-Z	By industry, occupation or group of employees, A-Z
405.A-Z	Particular industries, occupations, or groups of employees, A-Z

Labor standards

406	General. Labor conditions (Table KE5)

Employment and dismissal

406.2	General (Table KE5)

Discrimination in employment and its prevention

406.4	General (Table KE5)
406.5.A-Z	Particular groups, A-Z
406.5.P46	People with disabilities

Wages. Minimum wage

407	General (Table KE5)
407.7.A-Z	Particular industries, occupations or groups of employees, A-Z
407.7.F5	Fishing industry (Table KE6)
408	Hours of labor. Night work (Table KE5)
408.5.A-Z	Other topics, A-Z

Fringe benefits see KEA-KEY 408.5.N65
Grievance procedure see KEA-KEY 408.5.G7

408.5.G7	Grievances. Grievance procedures (Table KE6)
408.5.N65	Nonwage payments. Fringe benefits (Table KE6)

Protection of labor. Labor hygiene and safety

409	General (Table KE5)

Labor hygiene and safety. Hazardous occupations. Safety regulations

409.4	General (Table KE5)
409.5	Factory inspection (Table KE5)
409.7.A-Z	By industry or type of labor, A-Z
409.7.A35	Agricultural laborers (Table KE6)
409.7.F5	Fishing (Table KE6)
409.7.M5	Mining (Table KE6)

Social insurance

411	General (Table KE5)
412	Health insurance. Medical care (Table KE5)
413	Workmen's compensation (Table KE5)
415	Retirement pensions. Survivors' benefits (Table KE5)

Public welfare. Public assistance. Poor laws

Social law and legislation

Public welfare. Public assistance. Poor laws -- Continued

418	General (Table KE5)
418.3.A-Z	Special topics, A-Z
418.5.A-Z	Particular groups, A-Z
	Child welfare see KEA-KEY 418.5.C55
418.5.C55	Children. Child welfare. Youth services (Table KE6)
	Youth services see KEA-KEY 418.5.C55
	Public health. Sanitation. Environmental pollution
420	General (Table KE5)
420.5.A-Z	Particular public health hazards and measures, A-Z
	Environmental pollution
421	General (Table KE5)
422.A-Z	Particular types of pollution, A-Z
422.W3	Water pollution (Table KE6)
	Medical legislation
423	General (Table KE5)
423.2	Hospitals and other medical institutions (Table KE5)
424	The mentally ill (Table KE5)
424.5	Eugenics. Sterilization (Table KE5)
424.8.A-Z	Special topics, A-Z
424.8.D43	Death, Definition of (Table KE6)
424.8.D65	Donation of organs, tissues, etc. (Table KE6)
424.8.E88	Euthanasia. Right to die. Living wills (Table KE6)
424.8.I5	Informed consent (Table KE6)
	Living wills see KEA-KEY 424.8.E88
	Right to die see KEA-KEY 424.8.E88
426	Veterinary laws. Veterinary hygiene (Table KE5)
	Food. Drugs. Cosmetics
427	General (Table KE5)
	Drug laws
427.5	General (Table KE5)
427.8	Drugs of abuse (Table KE5)
	Including narcotics
	Alcohol. Alcoholic beverages. Prohibition. Liquor laws
428	General (Table KE5)
428.5.A-Z	Special topics, A-Z
	Advertising see KEA-KEY 331.3.A4
	Public safety
430	General (Table KE5)
	Hazardous articles and processes. Product safety
	Cf. KEA-KEY 295.3 Products liability
431	General (Table KE5)
431.5.A-Z	Particular products and processes, A-Z
431.5.W37	Wastes (Table KE6)
	Accident control
432	General works

Public safety

Accident control -- Continued

432.5.A-Z — Special topics, A-Z
432.5.G3 — Gas containers and equipment (Table KE6)
432.5.S7 — Steam boilers (Table KE6)
433 — Fire prevention and control

Control of social activities

434 — General (Table KE5)
434.3.A-Z — Particular activities, A-Z
434.3.B5 — Billiards and pool (Table KE6)
— Gambling see KEA-KEY 434.3.L67
— Games of chance see KEA-KEY 434.3.L67
434.3.H6 — Horse racing (Table KE6)
434.3.L67 — Lotteries. Games of chance. Gambling (Table KE6)

Education

Including public education

438 — General (Table KE5)
438.5 — Church and education. Denominational schools (Table KE5)

School government and finance

439 — General (Table KE5)
439.3 — School districts. School boards (Table KE5)
439.6.A-Z — Special topics, A-Z
439.6.T7 — Transportation of students. School safety patrols (Table KE6)
— For school bus regulations see KEA-KEY 382.7.S3

Students. Compulsory education

440 — General (Table KE5)
440.5.A-Z — Special topics, A-Z
440.5.R4 — Religious instruction. Religious and patriotic observances. Bible reading (Table KE6)

Teachers

441 — General (Table KE5)
441.5.A-Z — Special topics, A-Z
441.5.S3 — Salaries, pensions, etc. (Table KE6)
441.5.T4 — Tenure (Table KE6)

Nonteaching school personnel

442 — General works
442.5.A-Z — Particular classes of employees, A-Z
442.5.G8 — Guidance workers. Student counselors (Table KE6)

Elementary and secondary education

444 — General (Table KE5)

Curricula. Courses of instruction

445 — General (Table KE5)
445.7.A-Z — Particular courses, A-Z
445.7.L37 — Law (Table KE6)
445.8 — Educational services for particular classes or types of students (Table KE5)

Education -- Continued

Higher education. Colleges and universities

446 General (Table KE5)

446.5.A-Z Particular colleges and universities. By name, A-Z

Science and the arts. Research

448 General (Table KE5)

Performing arts

448.4 General works

Motion pictures

448.6 General. Censorship (Table KE5)

448.8 Other

448.9 Historical buildings and monuments. Architectural landmarks (Table KE5)

Including preservation of cultural property

449 Libraries (Table KE5)

Constitutional law

452 Sources. By date of publication

Cf. KE4136+, Constitutional law sources (General)

454 General. History (Table KE5)

455 Conflict of interests (Table KE5)

Structure of government. Jurisdiction

456 General (Table KE5)

456.5.A-Z Special topics, A-Z

Boundary disputes

see KE4285

456.5.D5 Disallowance and reservation of provincial legislation

Individual and state

Civil and political rights and liberties

458 General

458.3.A-Z Particular groups, A-Z

458.5.A-Z Particular rights and freedoms, A-Z

458.5.A7 Freedom of assembly and association (Table KE6)

Bilingualism see KEA-KEY 458.5.L56

458.5.E94 Freedom of expression (Table KE6)

458.5.L56 Linguistic and cultural rights. Bilingualism (Table KE6)

Control of individuals

460 General. Aliens

460.5.A-Z Particular ethnic groups, A-Z

460.5.C4 Chinese

Church and state

462 General. Religious corporations

462.5.A-Z Special topics, A-Z

Organs of the government

464 General works

The legislature

466 Legislative Council (Table KE5)

Legislative Assembly

Constitutional law
Organs of the government
The legislature
Legislative Assembly -- Continued
467 General works. History
Election law
468 General (Table KE5)
468.5.A-Z Special topics, A-Z
468.5.A6 Apportionment. Election districts (Table KE6)
468.5.C3 Campaign expenditures (Table KE6)
Election districts see KEA-KEY 468.5.A6
Enumeration see KEA-KEY 468.5.R4
Expenditures, Campaign see KEA-KEY 468.5.C3
Qualification see KEA-KEY 468.5.R4
468.5.R4 Registration. Qualification. Enumeration (Table KE6)
468.8 Contested elections
Organization. Legislative process
469 General (Table KE5)
470 Rules and procedure (Table KE5, modified)
Statutes. Regulations. Orders. Rules of practice, etc.
Rules. Standing orders. Speaker's decisions
Collections. Compilations
470.A329 Serials
470.A33 Monographs. By date of publication
471.A-Z Special topics, A-Z
471.C6 Conflict of interests (Table KE6)
471.L4 Legislative reporting (Table KE6)
471.P85 Private bill procedure (Table KE6)
The Crown and Executive branch
473 General. Executive power (Table KE5)
474 Lieutenant-Governor
475 Department of Justice (Table KE5)
476 Commissions of inquiry, royal commissions, task forces, etc. (Table KE5)
Local government
477 General (Table KE5)
Municipal government. Municipal services
478 General. Municipal corporations (Table KE5)
478.5.A-Z Special topics, A-Z
478.5.A55 Annexation (Table KE6)
478.5.E43 Elections (Table KE6)
Municipal officials. Organs of government
479 General (Table KE5)
479.5.A-Z Special topics, A-Z
479.5.C6 Conflict of interests (Table KE6)
481 County government

Public service. Government officials and employees

Provincial public services

483	General (Table KE5)
483.5.A-Z	Special topics, A-Z
	Collective bargaining see KEA-KEY 403.P8
483.5.P6	Political activities (Table KE6)
483.5.T4	Tenure and remuneration. Salaries. Pensions (Table KE6)
484	Municipal public service (Table KE5)
486	Police and power of the police (Table KE5)

Administrative organization. Administrative law and procedure

487	General (Table KE5)
	The administrative process. Regulatory agencies
	For particular agencies, see the appropriate subject
488	General (Table KE5)
488.2	Legislative functions. Rulemaking power. Delegated legislation (Table KE5)
488.4	Judicial functions. Procedure. Administrative tribunals (Table KE5)
	For particular tribunals, see relevant subject
488.5	Judicial review of administrative acts (Table KE5)
488.6	Abuse of administrative power. Ombudsman (Table KE5)

Public property. Public restraints on private property

490	General (Table KE5)
491	Conservation and management of natural resources. Environmental planning (Table KE5)

Water resources. Watersheds. Rivers. Lakes. Water courses

493	General. Conservation and management. Water resources development (Table KE5)
493.5.A-Z	Particular inland waterways and channels, A-Z
495	Expropriation (Table KE5)

Public land law

497	General. Crown lands (Table KE5)

Reclamation. Irrigation. Drainage

498	General (Table KE5)
498.5.A-Z	Particular types of land, A-Z
	Marshes see KEA-KEY 498.5.S9
498.5.S9	Swamps. Marshes. Wetlands (Table KE6)
	Wetlands see KEA-KEY 498.5.S9

Provincial parks and forests. Wilderness preservation

499	General (Table KE5)
499.3	Grazing lands (Table KE5)
499.6	Wildlife protection. Game laws (Table KE5)

Regional and city planning. Zoning. Building

502	General (Table KE5)
503	Land use. Zoning. Land subdivision (Table KE5)

Building laws

504	General (Table KE5)

Public property. Public restraints on private property
Regional and city planning. Zoning. Building
Building laws -- Continued

Code	Description
504.4.A-Z	Particular types of buildings, A-Z
504.4.S35	School buildings (Table KE6)
504.4.T4	Theaters (Table KE6)
504.55	Gas installations (Table KE5)
504.57	Electrical installations (Table KE5)
504.7	Access for people with disabilities (Table KE5)

Housing. Slum clearance. City redevelopment

Code	Description
505	General (Table KE5)
505.4.A-Z	Special topics, A-Z
505.4.M63	Mobile homes (Table KE5)

Government property

Code	Description
505.6	General (Table KE5)
505.62	Access to public records. Freedom of information (Table KE5)
505.8	Public works

Public finance

Code	Description
508	General (Table KE5)
508.3	Budget. Government expenditures (Table KE5)

Provincial revenue

Code	Description
509	General (Table KE5)

Taxation

Code	Description
510	General (Table KE5)
510.5.A-Z	Special topics, A-Z

Particular taxes
Several. Collective see KEA-KEY 510
Income tax

Code	Description
511	General. Personal income tax (Table KE5)
511.5.A-Z	Special topics, A-Z
511.5.D36	Damages. Settlements

Settlements see KEA-KEY 511.5.D36
Income of business organizations

Code	Description
512	General works

Corporation income tax

Code	Description
513	General (Table KE5)
513.5.A-Z	Particular lines of corporate business, A-Z
513.5.P83	Public utilities (Table KE6)

Property taxes. Taxation of capital

Code	Description
514	General (Table KE5)
514.5.A-Z	Particular taxes, A-Z

Succession duties. Gift tax

Code	Description
515	General (Table KE5)
515.3	Estate planning. Estate tax planning (Table KE5)

Excise taxes. Taxes on transactions

Code	Description
516	General (Table KE5)

Public finance
Provincial revenue
Taxation
Particular taxes
Excise taxes. Taxes on transactions -- Continued

516.4	Retail sales tax (Table KE5)
516.5	Use tax (Table KE5)
516.7.A-Z	Particular commodities, services, transactions, A-Z

Taxation of natural resources

518	General (Table KE5)
518.5.A-Z	Particular resources and resource industries, A-Z
518.5.F6	Forestry. Logging (Table KE6)
518.5.M5	Mining. Petroleum (Table KE6)
519.A-Z	Other sources of revenue, A-Z
519.C8	Customs duties. Smuggling (Table KE6)

Local finance

For works on both provincial and local finance see KEA-KEY 508+

520	General (Table KE5)

Taxation

521	General. Tax powers of municipalities (Table KE5)

Property taxes

522	General. Assessment (Table KE5)
522.2	Assessment appeals. Courts of revision (Table KE5)

Real property taxes

523	General (Table KE5)
523.4	Real property assessment. Land valuation (Table KE5)
523.6.A-Z	Particular kinds of land, tax-exempt lands, special modes of taxation, A-Z
523.6.F3	Farm land (Table KE6)

Personal property taxes

524	General works
524.3.A-Z	Particular kinds of personal property, A-Z
524.3.S5	Ships
525	Business taxes. Licenses
525.5.A-Z	Other taxes, A-Z
525.7.A-Z	Other sources of revenue, A-Z

Military law

527	General works
527.2	Militia (Table KE5)
527.5.A-Z	Special topics, A-Z

Native peoples. Indians. Inuit

529	General (Table KE5)
529.4	Claims (Table KE5)
529.5.A-Z	Other special topics, A-Z
529.5.C45	Children (Table KE6)
529.5.C6	Courts. Procedure (Table KE6)

Native peoples. Indians. Inuit
Special topics, A-Z -- Continued

529.5.C75	Criminal law (Table KE6)
529.5.E38	Education (Table KE6)
529.5.H8	Hunting and fishing rights (Table KE6)
529.5.L3	Land tenure (Table KE6)
529.7.A-Z	Particular groups or tribes, A-Z

Courts. Procedure

Administration of justice. Organization of the judiciary History see KEA-KEY 165

532	General (Table KE5)
532.3	Judicial districts (Table KE5)

Court organization and procedure

For works on procedure in general, or before several courts see KEA-KEY 541+

533	General (Table KE5)
533.3.A-Z	Special aspects, A-Z
533.3.F67	Foreign judgments (Table KE6)

Particular courts and procedure (General) before such courts

For particular subjects, e.g. actions, special pleading, trial evidence, see the relevant subject

535	Superior courts (Table KE5)
	Class here works on single superior courts with both original and appellate jurisdiction, or with two such divisions
535.2	Courts of appeal, or appeal division (Table KE5)
535.4	Trial courts, or trial divisions (Table KE5)
	Including Supreme Court, Court of Queen's (King's) Bench, Queen's Bench Division
535.6	Courts of chancery (Table KE5)
536	Intermediate courts: County courts. District courts (Table KE5)

Lower courts. Local courts

538	Small claims courts (Table KE5)
	Magistrates' courts. Justices of the peace
	General. Civil jurisdiction see KEA-KEY 541+
	Criminal jurisdiction see KEA-KEY 583
538.6	Other

Courts of special jurisdiction

see subject, e.g., Surrogate courts, see 246

Judicial officers. Court employees

539	General (Table KE5)
	Judges of superior and intermediate courts
	see KE8290+
	Justices of the peace. Magistrates
540	General. Civil jurisdiction (Table KE5)
	For criminal jurisdiction see KEA-KEY 583
540.5.A-Z	Special topics, A-Z

Courts. Procedure

Court organization and procedure

Judicial officers. Court employees

Justices of the peace. Magistrates

Special topics, A-Z -- Continued

540.5.R4 Removal (Table KE6)

Including individual cases

540.7.A-Z Others, A-Z

540.7.C6 Constables (Table KE6)

Cf. KEA-KEY 486 Police

Cf. KEA-KEY 569.3.P6 Criminal law

540.7.C67 Coroners. Medical examiners (Table KE6)

540.7.N67 Notaries (Table KE6)

540.7.R43 Registrars (Table KE6)

540.7.S53 Sheriffs (Table KE6)

Civil procedure

Including common law and equity

For works on practice and procedure in general before a particular court, see the court

541-550 General (Table KE4)

Equity practice and procedure see KEA-KEY 535.6

Pleading and motions

555 General (Table KE5)

556.A-Z Special topics, A-Z

556.L56 Limitation of actions (Table KE6)

Parties

557 General (Table KE5)

557.8 Citizen suits (Table KE5)

Trial. Trial practice. Trial tactics

558 General (Table KE5)

Evidence

559 General (Table KE5)

560.A-Z Particular kinds of evidence, A-Z

560.D63 Documentary evidence (Table KE6)

560.E8 Expert evidence. Expert witnesses. Medical evidence (Table KE6)

560.W5 Witnesses. Oath. Subpoena (Table KE6)

561 Jury and jurors (Table KE5)

561.5 Referees (Table KE5)

Judgment

562 General (Table KE5)

562.3 Costs. Fees (Table KE5)

Remedies and special proceedings

563 General (Table KE5)

563.5 Injunctions. Provisional remedies (Table KE5)

564 Execution of judgment. Attachment. Garnishment (Table KE5)

Courts. Procedure
Civil procedure
Remedies and special proceedings -- Continued

565	Appeals. Appellate procedure (Table KE5)
	For works on the appeal process in general, see KE8585
	Proceedings relating to particular branches of the law or special subjects, or governed by special rules. Non-contentious (ex-parte) jurisdiction
567	General works
	Admiralty see KEA-KEY 280
	Divorce and matrimonial causes see KEA-KEY 201+
	Probate see KEA-KEY 246
567.5	Negotiated settlement. Compromise (Table KE5)
567.6	Arbitration and award. Commercial arbitration (Table KE5)
	Criminal law
	Cf. KEA-KEY 592+ Juvenile criminal law and procedure
569	General (Table KE5)
569.3.A-Z	Works for particular groups of users, A-Z
	Justices of the peace, magistrates see KEA-KEY 583
569.3.P6	Police. Constables
570	Administration of criminal justice (Table KE5)
570.5	Criminal liability (Table KE5)
570.7.A-Z	Particular offenses, A-Z
570.7.P47	Offenses against the person (Table KE6)
570.7.R3	Racketeering. Organized crime (Table KE6)
	Criminal procedure
572	General (Table KE5)
572.3	Arrest and commitment. Rights of suspects (Table KE5)
572.5	Searches and seizures (Table KE5)
572.7	Bail (Table KE5)
	Indictment. Information. Public prosecutor
573	General (Table KE5)
573.4	Grand jury (Table KE5)
	Preparation for trial. Arraignment. Pleas
574	General (Table KE5)
574.2	Right to counsel
	Pleas
575	General works
575.3	Special pleas (Table KE5)
575.5	Procedure without trial. Plea bargaining. Pleas of guilty. Nolo contendere (Table KE5)
	Trial
576	General works
577	Trial practice. Trial tactics (Table KE5)
	Evidence. Burden of proof
578	General (Table KE5)
	Admission of evidence

Criminal procedure
Trial
Evidence. Burden of proof
Admission of evidence -- Continued

578.2	General (Table KE5)
578.5	Wiretapping. Electronic listening and recording devices (Table KE5)
579	Witnesses (Table KE5)
583	Proceedings before magistrates' courts and justices of the peace (Table KE5)
	Including magistrates' handbooks and manuals on criminal law and procedure
584	Appeals. Appellate procedure (Table KE5)
	Proceedings before juvenile courts see KEA-KEY 592+
	Execution of sentence. Corrections. Imprisonment
588	General (Table KE5)
	Particular types of penal or correctional institutions
590.5	Common jails (Table KE5)
591	Criminal registration (Table KE5)
	Juvenile criminal law and procedure. Administration of juvenile justice
592	General (Table KE5)
593	Juvenile courts (Table KE5)
	Cf. KEA-KEY 195 Family courts
599.A-Z	Law of particular counties, townships, regional districts, etc. By county, etc., A-Z
	Subarrange each by Table KE3
<599.5.A-Z>	Particular cities, A-Z
	see KEZ

INDEX

A

Abatement of public nuisance:
KE3611+
Ontario: KEO717+
Quebec: KEQ885+

Abbreviations, Legal: KE259
Quebec: KEQ142

Abduction: KE8935

Aboriginal title
Land tenure: KE7739.L3

Abortion
Criminal law: KE8920
Trials: KE226.A2

Absence
Natural persons: KE503
Quebec: KEQ231

Absentee voting
House of Commons: KE4636

Abstracts
Land transfer: KE731+
Ontario: KEO272+

Abuse of administrative power: KE5034
Quebec: KEQ808+

Abuse of power
Municipal officials: KE4923.A2

Academic freedom: KE3917
Quebec: KEQ951

Access for people with disabilities
KE provincial table: KEA-KEY 504.7

Access to children: KE600+

Accession rights
Quebec: KEQ282+

Accident control
Public safety: KE3773+
KE provincial table: KEA-KEY 432+

Accord and satisfaction
Contracts: KE884

Accountants
Collective bargaining
Quebec: KEQ656.A3
Legal works for: KE450.A3
Regulation: KE2722
KE provincial table: KEA-KEY 395.4.A3
Works about income tax for:
KE5759.8.A3

Accounting
Associations: KE1347
Corporations: KE1430
KE provincial table: KEA-KEY 319
Ontario: KEO409
Quebec: KEQ498
Law office management: KE355.A3
Succession upon death: KE833.A3
Trusts and trustees: KE798.A3
Ontario: KEO284.5.A3

Acquisition of property: KE770+

Acte d'administration
Civil law
Quebec: KEQ226.A25

Action in rem verso
Quebec: KEQ448

Action oblique
Obligations
Quebec: KEQ404

Action paulienne
Quebec: KEQ405

Actions
Civil procedure: KE8370+
Ontario: KEO1122
Quebec: KEQ1117

Actuarial evidence
Civil procedure: KE8478.A28

Actuaries
Collective bargaining: KE3196.A25

Administration of courts
Ontario: KEO1057.5

Administration of criminal justice
KE provincial table: KEA-KEY 570
Ontario: KEO1167+
Quebec: KEQ1170+

Administration of government contracts
Quebec: KEQ804

Administration of justice: KE8199.2+
KE provincial table: KEA-KEY 531.2+
Ontario: KEO1053.2+
Quebec: KEQ1067.2+

Administration of juvenile justice:
KE9445+
KE provincial table: KEA-KEY 592+
Ontario: KEO1195+

Administration of labor law
Quebec: KEQ643

INDEX

Administration of native peoples: KE7742
Administration of public welfare
  Quebec: KEQ715+
Administration of taxation: KE5688+
Administrative law: KE5015
  KE provincial table: KEA-KEY 487+
  Ontario: KEO889+
  Quebec: KEQ798+
Administrative organization and procedure: KE5015+
  KE provincial table: KEA-KEY 487+
  Ontario: KEO889+
  Quebec: KEQ814+
Administrative tribunals: KE5029
  KE provincial table: KEA-KEY 488.4
  Ontario: KEO891
  Quebec: KEQ806
Admiralty
  Contracts
    Ontario: KEO339+
  KE provincial table: KEA-KEY 279+
  Quebec: KEQ620
Admiralty courts
  KE provincial table: KEA-KEY 280
Admiralty proceedings: KE1112
  KE provincial table: KEA-KEY 280
  Ontario: KEO340
Admission of evidence
  Civil procedure: KE8485+
    Quebec: KEQ1137, KEQ1138+
  Criminal procedure
    Canada: KE9314+
    KE provincial table: KEA-KEY 578.2+
  Quebec: KEQ1186.2+
Admission to events
  Excise taxes
    Quebec: KEQ1030.A3
Admission to the bar: KE337
  Ontario: KEO162
  Quebec: KEQ153.8
Admissions
  Criminal procedure
    Canada: KE9316
Adoption: KE598
Adoption
  Conflict of laws
    Quebec: KEQ209.A3
  KE provincial table: KEA-KEY 206.5
  Ontario: KEO228
  Quebec: KEQ257
Adult education
  Quebec: KEQ962
Adulteration of food: KE3705
Adultery: KE9061
Advertising: KE1610+
  KE provincial table: KEA-KEY 331+
  Legal ethics: KE344.A38
  Quebec: KEQ512
Advertising, Restrictions on roadside: KE5134
Affidavits
  KE provincial table: KEA-KEY 184.O2
Affiliation of children: KE596
Agency: KE1328+
  KE provincial table: KEA-KEY 299+
  Ontario: KEO382+
  Quebec: KEQ433
Agents, Real estate: KE1987.R4
Agricultural cooperatives
  Quebec: KEQ526
Agricultural laborers
  Safety regulations
    KE provincial table: KEA-KEY 409.7.A35
Agricultural products: KE1870+
Agricultural property, Pledge of
  Quebec: KEQ326
Agricultural societies
  Quebec: KEQ526
Agriculture: KE1671+
  Collective bargaining: KE3196.A37
  KE provincial table: KEA-KEY 338+
  Ontario: KEO441+
  Quebec: KEQ522+
Agronomists
  Collective bargaining
    Quebec: KEQ656.A4
AIDS (Disease): KE3593.A54
  Ontario: KEO714.5.A54
  Quebec: KEQ882.7.A35
Air Canada: KE2287.A4

INDEX

Air Force: KE7057+
Air navigation orders: KE2244.73
Air pollution: KE3630+
- Ontario: KEO720
- Quebec: KEQ888+

Air traffic controllers
- Collective bargaining: KE3196.A4

Airlines: KE2273+
Airports: KE2265
Airspace: KE634
Alberta, Law of: KEA1+
Alcohol: KE3734+
- KE provincial table: KEA-KEY 428+
- Ontario: KEO741+
- Quebec: KEQ906+

Alcoholic beverages
- Advertising: KE1612.A4
  - KE provincial table: KEA-KEY 331.3.A4
- Taxation: KE6009.A43

Alcoholism
- Medical legislation: KE3660.A4

Aleatory contracts: KE1225+
Alien landownership: KE626
- KE provincial table: KEA-KEY 214.5

Alien property: KE621
Alienation, Restraints on: KE711
- Ontario: KEO268

Aliens: KE518.A4
- Control of
  - KE provincial table: KEA-KEY 460
- Taxation: KE5864.N6

Alimony: KE589
- Divorce
  - KE provincial table: KEA-KEY 203
  - Ontario: KEO225
  - Quebec: KEQ252
- Income tax: KE5799.A44

All-terrain vehicles: KE2107.S6
- KE provincial table: KEA-KEY 381.7.S66
- Ontario: KEO533.S6

Allocation of taxing power: KE5661+
Allocations, Industrial: KE12 3+
Allowances
- Air Force: KE7070+
- Armed Forces: KE6880+

Allowances
- Army: KE6940+
- Income tax: KE5808+
- Navy: KE7010+
- War veterans: KE7230+

Amateur radio stations: KE2607
Amending process, Constitutional: KE4228
- Ontario: KEO806

Amusements
- Excise taxes
  - Quebec: KEQ1030.A3

Anesthesiologists: KE2714.A5
Animal protection: KE3676
Animal rights: KE3676
Animal welfare: KE3676
Animals, Damages caused by: KE1279
- KE provincial table: KEA-KEY 295.2

Animals, Legal works on: KE452.A5
Annexation
- KE provincial table: KEA-KEY 478.5.A55
- Quebec: KEQ830.A5

Annuities
- Income tax: KE5799.P4

Annulment: KE561+
Antenuptial contracts: KE559
- Quebec: KEQ244

Antidumping duties: KE6129
Apiculture: KE1745
Appeal division
- KE provincial table: KEA-KEY 535.2

Appeals
- Civil procedure
  - KE provincial table: KEA-KEY 565
  - Ontario: KEO1155
  - Quebec: KEQ1157
- Criminal procedure: KE9375
  - KE provincial table: KEA-KEY 584
  - Ontario: KEO1190+
- Judicial review of administrative acts
  - Quebec: KEQ809

Appellate procedure
- Civil procedure: KE8585+
  - KE provincial table: KEA-KEY 565
  - Ontario: KEO1155
  - Quebec: KEQ1157

INDEX

Appellate procedure
- Criminal procedure: KE9375
  - KE provincial table: KEA-KEY 584
  - Ontario: KEO1190+
- Military justice: KE7185+

Appointments
- Air Force officers: KE7092
- Army officers: KE6962
- Judges: KE8293.A6
- Military officers: KE6902
- Navy officers: KE7032

Apportionment
- House of Commons: KE4640
- Legislative Assembly
  - KE provincial table: KEA-KEY 468.5.A6

Arbitration
- Labor disputes: KE3206
  - KE provincial table: KEA-KEY 404.3
  - Ontario: KEO650
  - Quebec: KEQ659

Arbitration and award: KE8618
- KE provincial table: KEA-KEY 567.6
- Ontario: KEO1160
- Quebec: KEQ1162

Architects: KE2727
- KE provincial table: KEA-KEY 395.4.A7
- Ontario: KEO618.A7
- Quebec: KEQ986

Architectural landmarks: KE3995
- KE provincial table: KEA-KEY 448.9

Architecture and town planning
- Collective bargaining: KE3196.A7

Archives: KE4010

Armed Forces: KE6859.2+

Armed Forces electors: KE4629

Arms transfers
- Export regulation: KE1952.W43

Army: KE6928+

Arraignment: KE9287
- Criminal procedure
  - KE provincial table: KEA-KEY 574+
  - Ontario: KEO1179

Arrest and commitment: KE9265+
- Criminal procedure
  - KE provincial table: KEA-KEY 572.3

Arrest and commitment
- Ontario: KEO1176
- Quebec: KEQ1175

Arson: KE8986

Art works
- Copyright: KE2868+

Artificial insemination, Human
- KE provincial table: KEA-KEY 184.A77

Artificial satellites in telecommunication: KE2565

Arts, The: KE3968+
- Ontario: KEO799.92+
- Quebec: KEQ969.92+

Assassination
- Trials: KE226.M8

Assault and battery: KE8925

Assessment
- Local property taxes: KE6280
  - KE provincial table: KEA-KEY 522
  - Ontario: KEO1024
  - Quebec: KEQ1040

Assessment appeals
- Local property taxes
  - KE provincial table: KEA-KEY 522.2
  - Ontario: KEO1024.5

Assignments for benefit of creditors: KE1518.A8
- KE provincial table: KEA-KEY 324.5.A8
- Ontario: KEO419.3.A8

Assistance in emergencies: KE1314
- KE provincial table: KEA-KEY 298

Associations: KE1345+
- KE provincial table: KEA-KEY 302+
- Ontario: KEO385+
- Quebec: KEQ492+

Atomic power
- Regulation: KE2056

Attachment
- Civil procedure: KE8552+
  - KE provincial table: KEA-KEY 564
  - Ontario: KEO1153+

Attorney and client: KE346+
- Quebec: KEQ155+

Attorney General
- Ontario: KEO855

INDEX

Attorneys
- Handbooks
  - KE provincial table: KEA-KEY 155
  - Ontario: KEO167
- Attornment clause: KE754.D5
- Auction sales: KE951

Auditing
- Associations: KE1347
- Corporations: KE1430
  - KE provincial table: KEA-KEY 319
  - Ontario: KEO409
  - Quebec: KEQ498
- Local finance: KE6267
- Provincial finance: KE6178
- Public finance
  - Quebec: KEQ997

Auditors
- Collective bargaining: KE3196.A9
- Regulation: KE2722
  - KE provincial table: KEA-KEY 395.4.A3

Author and publisher: KE2900

Authorship
- Copyright: KE2825

Automation
- Law office management: KE355.A96

Automobile accidents
- Torts: KE1274.A8
  - KE provincial table: KEA-KEY 294.3.A8
  - Ontario: KEO367.A8
  - Quebec: KEQ462.A8

Automobile expenses
- Income tax: KE5822.A9

Automobile insurance: KE1202+

Automobile trade
- Ontario: KEO495.4.A8
- Quebec: KEQ564.5.A94

Automobiles: KE1980.A3

Automotive transportation: KE2095+
- KE provincial table: KEA-KEY 381+
- Ontario: KEO531+
- Quebec: KEQ590+

Autonomy of the will
- Contracts
  - Quebec: KEQ393.C6

Aviation
- Collective bargaining: KE3196.A34
- Regulation: KE2241+

Aviation accidents
- Torts: KE1274.A9

Aviation insurance: KE1184.A9

B

Bad faith
- Insurance contracts: KE1163.B33

Bail
- Criminal procedure: KE9272
  - KE provincial table: KEA-KEY 572.7

Bailiffs
- Quebec: KEQ1098.B3

Bailment
- Contracts involving bailment: KE970+
  - Ontario: KEO312+
- Personal property: KE779

Banalité
- Land tenure
  - Quebec: KEQ274.B2

Bank secrets: KE1024.R42

Banking: KE991+
- Collective bargaining: KE3196.B36
- KE provincial table: KEA-KEY 264+
- Ontario: KEO314+
- Quebec: KEQ481+

Banks
- Income tax
  - Quebec: KEQ1016.B3

Bar associations: KE363+
- Quebec: KEQ159+

Bar examinations: KE337
- Quebec: KEQ153.8

Bar of the Province of Quebec: KEQ160+

Barley
- Marketing: KE1714.G7
- Price supports: KE1694.G7
- Standards, grading, and inspection: KE1719.G7

Beekeeping: KE1745

Behavior modification
- Medical legislation: KE3663.B44

INDEX

Benefits
- Air Force: KE7070+
- Armed Forces: KE6880+
- Army: KE6940+
- Navy: KE7010+

Bets
- Contracts
  - Quebec: KEQ444

Beverages: KE1906.A+

Bible reading
- Educational law: KE3839.R4
  - KE provincial table: KEA-KEY 440.5.R4
  - Ontario: KEO779.R4

Bicycles: KE2107.B5

Biens et propriété
- Quebec: KEQ264+

Biens réservés de la femme mariée
- Marriage law
  - Quebec: KEQ246.5.R4

Bigamy: KE9062

Bilingual instruction
- Elementary and secondary education: KE3878
  - Ontario: KEO788.4

Bilingualism: KE4413
- Court procedure: KE8227
  - Quebec: KEQ1070.5.C65
  - KE provincial table: KEA-KEY 458.5.L56
  - Ontario: KEO821
  - Quebec: KEQ752

Bill drafting: KE4560
- Quebec: KEQ783.B54

Billards and pool
- KE provincial table: KEA-KEY 434.3.B5

Bills of exchange: KE981
- Quebec: KEQ480

Bills of lading: KE956

Biotechnology industries: KE1858.B56

Bird protection: KE5210+
- Ontario: KEO916+

Birth certificates: KE521
- KE provincial table: KEA-KEY 192
  - Ontario: KEO209
  - Quebec: KEQ236

Birth registration: KE521
- KE provincial table: KEA-KEY 192
  - Ontario: KEO209
  - Quebec: KEQ236

Birthright
- Quebec: KEQ348.B5

Blackmail: KE8980+

Blind
- Public welfare: KE3534

Blindness: KE516.B5

Blue sky laws
- Ontario: KEO333.S6

Board of directors: KE1402
- KE provincial table: KEA-KEY 316.5
  - Ontario: KEO404
  - Quebec: KEQ495.7

Board of Notaries of Quebec: KEQ172+

Boards of education: KE3814

Bond issues: KE5627
- Quebec: KEQ998

Bonded warehouses: KE1999

Bonding: KE1213
- KE provincial table: KEA-KEY 286
  - Ontario: KEO353.S9

Bonds
- Provincial finance: KE6182

Bottomry: KE1114.B6
- KE provincial table: KEA-KEY 280.5.B6

Boundaries
- Jurisdiction
  - Quebec: KEQ746.B6
- Real property: KE705
  - Ontario: KEO265
  - Quebec: KEQ296.B7

Boundary disputes: KE4285

Boycotts
- Labor disputes: KE3213+
  - KE provincial table: KEA-KEY 404.5
  - Ontario: KEO651+
  - Quebec: KEQ660+

Breach of contract: KE890+
- KE provincial table: KEA-KEY 255+
  - Ontario: KEO304
  - Quebec: KEQ411+

Breach of trust
- Trusts and trustees: KE798.L5

INDEX

Bridges: KE5142
British North America Act of 1867: KE4165+
Brokers
   Agency: KE1332.B7
Budget
   Local finance: KE6267
   Public finance: KE5617
      KE provincial table: KEA-KEY 508.3
      Quebec: KEQ997
Building
   KE provincial table: KEA-KEY 502+
   Ontario: KEO920+
   Quebec: KEQ865+
Building contractors
   Taxation: KE5669.8.B8
Building laws: KE5268+
   KE provincial table: KEA-KEY 504+
   Ontario: KEO923+
   Quebec: KEQ868+
Building leases: KE695.G7
   Quebec: KEQ283.S86
Building materials
   Taxation: KE6009.B85
Building societies: KE1012.B8
   Ontario: KEO315.B8
Bulk sales
   Debt relief
      KE provincial table: KEA-KEY 324.5.B84
      Ontario: KEO419.3.B8
Bulk transfers
   Debt relief
      KE provincial table: KEA-KEY 324.5.B84
Burden of proof
   Civil procedure: KE8445+
   Criminal procedure: KE9312+
      KE provincial table: KEA-KEY 578+
      Quebec: KEQ1186+
Burial and cemetery laws: KE3581
   Ontario: KEO715.B8
   Quebec: KEQ883.B8
Business associations, Unincorporated: KE1356+
   KE provincial table: KEA-KEY 304
   Ontario: KEO387

Business associations, Unincorporated
   Quebec: KEQ493
Business corporations: KE1381+
   KE provincial table: KEA-KEY 306+
   Ontario: KEO391+
   Quebec: KEQ495+
Business enterprises: KE1345+
   KE provincial table: KEA-KEY 302+
   Ontario: KEO385+
   Quebec: KEQ492+
Business interruption insurance: KE1184.B87
Business organizations
   Income tax: KE5875+
      KE provincial table: KEA-KEY 512+
Business property taxes
   Local finance: KE6310
      KE provincial table: KEA-KEY 525
      Ontario: KEO1027
      Quebec: KEQ1045
   Provincial finance: KE6214
      Ontario: KEO993
      Quebec: KEQ1022
Business records
   Ontario: KEO385.5.B87
Businesspeople
   Immigration: KE4458.B87
   Legal works for: KE450.B87

C

Cadastral plans
   Quebec: KEQ336.C3
Cadets
   Air Force: KE7096
   Armed Forces: KE6906
   Army: KE6966
   Navy: KE7036
Caisses populaires
   Quebec: KEQ482.C7
Cameron's Digest: KEO105.2
Campaign expenditures
   House of Commons: KE4646
   KE provincial table: KEA-KEY 468.5.R4

INDEX

Campaign expenditures
- Legislative Assembly
  - KE provincial table: KEA-KEY 468.5.C3
  - Ontario: KEO841
  - Quebec: KEQ775.C35

Canada Gazette, Part 3: KE91

Canada Pension Plan: KE3432

Canadian Bar Association: KE365+

Canadian Bill of Rights: KE4381

Canadian Broadcasting Corporation: KE2649.C3

Canadian Charter of Rights and Freedoms: KE4381.5

Canadian Institute of Patent Solicitors: KE2975.A65

Canadian Pension Commission: KE6886

Canadian Radio-Television Commission: KE2614

Canadian Security Intelligence Service: KE7210.C35

Canadian Transport Commission: KE2082

Canadian Transport Commission Railway Transport Committee: KE2152

Canals
- Navigation and pilotage: KE2381
- Public property: KE5159

Capacity and disability: KE507+
- KE provincial table: KEA-KEY 190+
- Ontario: KEO206+
- Quebec: KEQ233+

Capacity to give and receive by will
- Quebec: KEQ354.C3

Capital: KE1408+
- KE provincial table: KEA-KEY 317+
- Ontario: KEO405+
- Quebec: KEQ496+

Capital cost allowances: KE5810

Capital gains tax: KE5785+

Capital investment
- Income tax: KE5785+

Capital punishment: KE8824.C3

Carriage by air: KE1102

Carriage by land: KE1100

Carriage by land
- Quebec: KEQ588

Carriage by sea: KE1105+
- KE provincial table: KEA-KEY 279+
- Ontario: KEO339+, KEO571
- Quebec: KEQ618+, KEQ620

Carriage of goods and passengers: KE2130+
- Contracts: KE1099+
  - KE provincial table: KEA-KEY 278+
  - Ontario: KEO336+
- Regulation of road traffic
  - Ontario: KEO538+
  - Quebec: KEQ597+

Carriage of passengers and goods
- Regulation of road traffic
  - KE provincial table: KEA-KEY 382.5+

Carriers
- Contracts: KE1099+
  - KE provincial table: KEA-KEY 278+
  - Ontario: KEO336+
  - Quebec: KEQ585+

Cas fortuit
- Obligations
  - Quebec: KEQ379.F6

Case load
- Courts
  - Ontario: KEO1057.2

Casebooks: KE442
- Quebec: KEQ200

Casualty insurance: KE1192+
- KE provincial table: KEA-KEY 285+
- Ontario: KEO350+
- Quebec: KEQ490+

Catholic Church: KE4514.C3

Cattle raising: KE1723+

Cause
- Contracts
  - Quebec: KEQ393.C65

Cautionement: KEQ304

Censorship
- Motion pictures: KE3982
  - KE provincial table: KEA-KEY 448.6+
  - Ontario: KEO800.5
  - Quebec: KEQ971.5

INDEX

Census registration: KE521
Central Mortgage and Housing Corporation: KE5302
Certification
Merchant mariners: KE1126
Certiorari: KE8568
Chambers cases
Law reports
Ontario: KEO108
Charitable contributions
Income tax: KE5814
Charitable trusts: KE793
Chattel mortgages: KE1045
Ontario: KEO323
Chattels
Civil procedure: KE8560.C4
Chattels, Torts affecting: KE1261
Ontario: KEO364.5
Checks: KE983+
Quebec: KEQ480.5
Chemical industries
Collective bargaining
Quebec: KEQ656.C4
Regulation: KE1840+
Chemical products
Products liability: KE1283.C48
Chemists
Quebec: KEQ988.C4
Child abuse
Criminal law: KE8926
Ontario: KEO1171.C45
Child health services: KE3652.C47
Child labor: KE3348
Child sexual abuse
Criminal law: KE8926
Torts: KE1312.5.C56
Child support
Parent and child: KE602
Child welfare
Ontario: KEO706+
Public welfare
KE provincial table: KEA-KEY 418.5.C55
Children
Capacity and disability: KE512
Liability: KE512

Children
Native peoples
KE provincial table: KEA-KEY 529.5.C45
Public welfare: KE3515+
KE provincial table: KEA-KEY 418.5.C55
Ontario: KEO706+
Quebec: KEQ723
Children, Access to: KE600+
Children, Law pertaining to
Legal education: KE298.C4
Chinese
Aliens: KE4479
KE provincial table: KEA-KEY 460.5.C4
Chiropodists: KE2714.P6
Ontario: KEO617.P6
Chiropractors: KE2717.C5
Church and education: KE3809
KE provincial table: KEA-KEY 438.5
Ontario: KEO771
Quebec: KEQ923
Church and state: KE4502+
KE provincial table: KEA-KEY 462+
Ontario: KEO831+
Quebec: KEQ762+
Church property: KE4505+
C.I.F. clause: KE964
Circumstantial evidence: KE8455
Cities and towns
Administrative organization
Quebec: KEQ824
Citizen participation in the administrative process: KE5026
Citizen suits: KE8404
KE provincial table: KEA-KEY 557.8
Citizenship: KE4345+
Citizenship requirements
Merchant mariners: KE1124
City councils
Ontario: KEO875.5.C5
City redevelopment: KE5295+
KE provincial table: KEA-KEY 505+
Ontario: KEO929+
Quebec: KEQ872+

INDEX

Civil and political rights and liberties
KE provincial table: KEA-KEY 458+
Civil code
Quebec: KEQ214.5+
Civil Code Revision Office
Quebec: KEQ224+
Civil defense: KE7213
Civil divorces and religious divorces, Relationship between
Domestic relations: KE572
Civil law
Quebec: KEQ211+
Civil procedure: KE8341+
KE provincial table: KEA-KEY 541+
Ontario: KEO1111+
Quebec: KEQ1101+
Civil responsibility
Quebec: KEQ451+
Civil rights: KE4381+
Native peoples: KE7722.C5
Ontario: KEO1045.C5
Ontario: KEO811+
Quebec: KEQ749+
Civil status
Natural persons: KE499+
KE provincial table: KEA-KEY 188
Ontario: KEO204
Quebec: KEQ229+
Civil trials: KE234+
Civil unions: KE591
Claims
Native peoples: KE7718
KE provincial table: KEA-KEY 529.4
Class action: KE8402
Quebec: KEQ1122
Clergy reserves: KE4507
Ontario: KEO831.5.C5
Clerks of court: KE8298
Close companies: KE1450
KE provincial table: KEA-KEY 321.P74
Quebec: KEQ500.P74
Clothing
Import regulation: KE1957.T4
Clothing industry
Collective bargaining
Quebec: KEQ656.C6

Co-ownership
Land tenure: KE673+
Quebec: KEQ277.C6
Coal mining: KE1795
KE provincial table: KEA-KEY 349.3
Coastal zone management
Public land law: KE5198
Coastwise navigation: KE2372
Coastwise shipping: KE2440
Cod: KE1765.C6
Code of Civil Procedure
Quebec: KEQ1104.5+
Coercive imprisonment
Quebec: KEQ1152.5.I5
Cohabitants
Ontario: KEO225.5
Coinage: KE5602
Collection agencies: KE1987.C6
KE provincial table: KEA-KEY 373.C6
Ontario: KEO502.C6
Collection laws: KE1018
KE provincial table: KEA-KEY 266
Collective bargaining: KE3193+
KE provincial table: KEA-KEY 402+
Ontario: KEO645+
Quebec: KEQ655+
Collective labor agreements: KE3193+
KE provincial table: KEA-KEY 402+
Ontario: KEO645+
Quebec: KEQ655+
Collective labor disputes: KE3204+
Colleges and universities: KE3904+
KE provincial table: KEA-KEY 446+
Ontario: KEO793+
Quebec: KEQ946+
Collèges d'enseignement générale et professionnel
Quebec: KEQ954
Collisions at sea: KE1107
Combines: KE1631+
Commercial arbitration: KE8618
KE provincial table: KEA-KEY 567.6
Ontario: KEO1160
Quebec: KEQ1162
Commercial espionage: KE2999
Commercial law: KE911+
KE provincial table: KEA-KEY 257

INDEX

Commercial law
  Quebec: KEQ477+
  Study and teaching: KE298.C6
Commercial leases: KE695.C6
  KE provincial table: KEA-KEY 225.C6
  Ontario: KEO261.C65
Commercial pledge
  Quebec: KEQ327
Commission merchants: KE1332.B7
Commissioners' court
  Quebec: KEQ1076.C6
Commissions of inquiry: KE4765+
  KE provincial table: KEA-KEY 476
  Ontario: KEO858
Committees of adjustment
  Land tenure
    Ontario: KEO921.2
Commodity exchanges: KE1093+
  Ontario: KEO334
Common jails
  KE provincial table: KEA-KEY 590.5
  Quebec: KEQ1195
Common law: KE454
  Quebec: KEQ205.3
Common law courts
  Ontario: KEO1061+
Communication: KE2460+
  KE provincial table: KEA-KEY 390+
  Ontario: KEO596+
  Quebec: KEQ628+
Community antenna television: KE2644
Community-based corrections: KE9436
Community legal services: KE376+
  KE provincial table: KEA-KEY 160+
  Ontario: KEO173+
  Quebec: KEQ180+
Community property: KE556
  Quebec: KEQ246+
Companies: KE1381+
  KE provincial table: KEA-KEY 306+
  Ontario: KEO391+
  Quebec: KEQ495+
Compensation for judicial error:
  KE9440
Compensation, War damage: KE12 3.5
Compensatory payments
  Income tax: KE5799.C6

Competition: KE1631+
Composition and draftsmanship, Legal:
  KE265
  Quebec: KEQ143
Compromise: KE8615
  KE provincial table: KEA-KEY 567.5
  Ontario: KEO1159
  Quebec: KEQ443
Compulsory education: KE3835+
  KE provincial table: KEA-KEY 440+
  Ontario: KEO778+
  Quebec: KEQ930+
Compulsory insurance
  Motor vehicles: KE2105
    KE provincial table: KEA-KEY 381.5
Compulsory licenses
  Patents: KE2955
Computation of tax: KE5835+
Computers: KE452.C6
  Legal works on
    Quebec: KEQ205.C65
Computers and privacy: KE1242.C6
  Quebec: KEQ456.3.C6
Conciliation
  Labor disputes: KE3206
    KE provincial table: KEA-KEY 404.3
    Ontario: KEO650
    Quebec: KEQ659
Conditional sale: KE1047
  Ontario: KEO324
Conditions
  Sales contracts: KE949.C6
    Ontario: KEO310.5.C6
Condominium
  Real property
    Quebec: KEQ277.C64
Condominium insurance: KE1187.C6
Conduct of legislators
  Ontario: KEO850.C6
Confederation Debates, 1865: KE4143
Confessions
  Criminal procedure
    Canada: KE9316
Conflict-of-interest laws, Violation of:
  KE9022
Conflict of interests
  Constitutional law: KE4244

INDEX

Conflict of interests
- Constitutional law
  - KE provincial table: KEA-KEY 455
- Legal ethics: KE344.C58
- Legislative Assembly
  - KE provincial table: KEA-KEY 471.C6
- Municipal officials: KE4923.C6
  - KE provincial table: KEA-KEY 479.5.C6
  - Ontario: KEO875.5.C6
- Parliament: KE4582
- Conflict of laws: KE470+
  - KE provincial table: KEA-KEY 182
  - Quebec: KEQ208+

Confusion
- Obligations
  - Quebec: KEQ385

Congestion and delay
- Courts: KE8220
  - Ontario: KEO1057.2

Conjugal violence: KE8925.5

Conscription
- Armed Forces: KE6860+

Conseil Souverain (Supérior): KEQ102

Consent
- Contracts
  - Quebec: KEQ393.C6

Conservation and management of agricultural and forestry lands: KE1686
- KE provincial table: KEA-KEY 339

Conservation of natural resources: KE5110+
- KE provincial table: KEA-KEY 491
- Ontario: KEO896+
- Quebec: KEQ846

Conservation of oil and gas: KE1811
- KE provincial table: KEA-KEY 352

Conservatorship
- KE provincial table: KEA-KEY 208

Consideration
- Contracts
  - KE provincial table: KEA-KEY 250.5
  - Quebec: KEQ393.C65

Consolidation and merger of corporations: KE1462

Consolidation and merger of corporations
- KE provincial table: KEA-KEY 321.5
- Ontario: KEO412.5
- Quebec: KEQ500.7
- Trade regulation: KE1631+

Conspiracy
- Criminal law: KE9112

Constables: KE8308
- KE provincial table: KEA-KEY 540.7.C6
- Ontario: KEO1096
- Police: KE5006+
- Works about criminal law for: KE8809.8.P6
  - KE provincial table: KEA-KEY 569.3.P6

Constables, Works about criminal law for
- Ontario: KEO1165.5.P6

Constitutional Act, 1791: KE4138

Constitutional law: KE4125+
- KE provincial table: KEA-KEY 452+
- Ontario: KEO804+
- Quebec: KEQ738+

Constitutions, Canadian and foreign: KE4226

Construction and interpretation,
- Statutory: KE482.S84

Construction industry
- Collective bargaining
  - Quebec: KEQ656.C65
- Contracts: KE933
  - Government contracts: KE905
  - KE provincial table: KEA-KEY 259.8.B8
  - Quebec: KEQ431.B8
- Income tax: KE5914.C6
- Labor disputes
  - Quebec: KEQ663.C6
- Labor laws
  - Quebec: KEQ696.C6
- Management-labor relations: KE3240.C6
  - Ontario: KEO655.C6
  - Quebec: KEQ666.C6
- Ontario: KEO482

INDEX

Construction industry
- Quebec: KEQ553
- Regulation: KE1915
  - KE provincial table: KEA-KEY 362
  - Safety regulations: KE3370.C6
  - Quebec: KEQ694.C6
- Consumer credit: KE1034
  - KE provincial table: KEA-KEY 268
  - Ontario: KEO318
  - Quebec: KEQ436
- Consumer products: KE1858.A+
- Consumer protection: KE1591+
  - KE provincial table: KEA-KEY 330
  - Ontario: KEO430
  - Quebec: KEQ510+
- Contagious and infectious diseases: KE3589+
  - Quebec: KEQ882.5+
- Containers: KE1620+
- Contempt of court: KE9028
- Contested elections
  - House of Commons: KE4652+
  - Legislative Assembly
    - KE provincial table: KEA-KEY 468.8
    - Ontario: KEO843
    - Quebec: KEQ776
- Contingent fees
  - Legal ethics: KE344.C6
- Contingent remainders
  - Future estates and interests: KE664
- Contract of carriage
  - Quebec: KEQ587+
- Contractors: KE1915
  - KE provincial table: KEA-KEY 362
  - Ontario: KEO482
  - Quebec: KEQ553
- Contracts: KE850+
  - Conflict of laws: KE474.C64
    - Quebec: KEQ209.C64
  - KE provincial table: KEA-KEY 250+
  - Ontario: KEO299+
  - Quebec: KEQ390+
- Contracts through correspondence, telephone, teletype, wire, computer, etc
  - Quebec: KEQ391

Contracts to make wills
- Quebec: KEQ354.C66

Contractual liberty
- Quebec: KEQ393.C6

Contributory negligence: KE1266
- KE provincial table: KEA-KEY 294+

Control of aliens: KE4452+
- Ontario: KEO824
- Quebec: KEQ914+

Control of prices: KE12 2.5+

Control of unemployment: KE12 1.4

Conversion
- Torts: KE1261
  - Ontario: KEO364.5

Conveyances: KE731+
- KE provincial table: KEA-KEY 231
  - Ontario: KEO272+

Cooperative credit associations: KE1008

Cooperatives

Corporations: KE1454
- Ontario: KEO412.C6
- Quebec: KEQ500.C6
- Income tax: KE5900

Copper mining: KE1802.C6
- KE provincial table: KEA-KEY 350.3.C6

Copropriété
- Quebec: KEQ277.C64

Copyright: KE2791+

Coroners: KE8312
- KE provincial table: KEA-KEY 540.7.C67
- Ontario: KEO1097
- Quebec: KEQ1098.C6

Corporate charters and bylaws: KE1400
- Quebec: KEQ495.3

Corporate finance: KE1408+
- KE provincial table: KEA-KEY 317+
- Ontario: KEO405+
- Quebec: KEQ496+

Corporate legal departments: KE1403

Corporate reorganization
- Debtors' relief: KE1518.C6
- Income tax: KE5920.C6

INDEX

Corporations
- Associations: KE1369+
  - KE provincial table: KEA-KEY 305+
  - Ontario: KEO389+
  - Quebec: KEQ494+
- Income tax: KE5884+, KE5884
  - KE provincial table: KEA-KEY 513+
  - Ontario: KEO981+

Correctional institutions
- Collective bargaining: KE3196.C67

Corrections
- Collective bargaining: KE3196.C67
- Criminal procedure: KE9410+
  - KE provincial table: KEA-KEY 588+
  - Ontario: KEO1192+
  - Quebec: KEQ1193+

Corroboration
- Criminal procedure: KE9344

Corrupt practices
- Election law
  - House of Commons: KE4648
  - Legislative Assembly
    - Ontario: KEO842

Corruption and bribery: KE9020
- Judges: KE8293.J8

Cosmetics: KE3696+
- KE provincial table: KEA-KEY 427+
- Ontario: KEO734+
- Quebec: KEQ900+

Costs
- Civil procedure: KE8517+
  - Ontario: KEO1148+

County courts
- Ontario: KEO1148.4.C6

Courts
- Civil procedure
  - KE provincial table: KEA-KEY 562.3
  - Quebec: KEQ1144+
- Criminal procedure: KE9358

Counterclaims
- Civil procedure: KE8392

Counterfeiting: KE9088

County courts
- Ontario: KEO1067+, KEO1085

County government
- KE provincial table: KEA-KEY 481

Courses of instruction
- Educational law
  - Elementary and secondary education: KE3873+
    - KE provincial table: KEA-KEY 445+
    - Ontario: KEO788+
    - Quebec: KEQ940+

Court administration
- Data processing: KE254.C6
  - Ontario: KEO1057.5

Court employees: KE8285+
- KE provincial table: KEA-KEY 539+
- Ontario: KEO1094+
- Quebec: KEQ1093+

Court of Appeal
- Ontario: KEO1079
  - Law reports: KEO133
- Quebec
  - Post-1965: KEQ1079
  - Pre-1965: KEQ1072

Court of Chancery
- Ontario: KEO1064
  - Law reports: KEO107

Court of Common Pleas
- Ontario: KEO1062
  - Law reports: KEO106

Court of Error and Appeal
- Ontario: KEO1063
  - Law reports: KEO104

Court of King's Bench
- KE provincial table: KEA-KEY 535.4
- Ontario: KEO1061
  - Law reports: KEO105
- Quebec: KEQ1072
  - Law reports: KEQ112

Court of Queen's Bench
- KE provincial table: KEA-KEY 535.4
- Ontario: KEO1061
  - Law reports: KEO105
- Quebec: KEQ1072
  - Law reports: KEQ112

Court reporters: KE8315

Courts: KE8199.2+
- KE provincial table: KEA-KEY 531.2+
- Native peoples: KE7722.C67

Courts
Native peoples
KE provincial table: KEA-KEY 529.5.C6
Ontario: KEO1053.2+
Quebec: KEQ1067.2+
Courts-martial: KE7165+
Court Martial Appeal Court: KE7187
Quebec: KEQ1055+
Trials: KE7175+
Courts of appeal
KE provincial table: KEA-KEY 535.2
Courts of chancery
KE provincial table: KEA-KEY 535.6
Courts of General Sessions of the Peace
Ontario: KEO1067+
Courts of requests
Ontario: KEO1072
Courts of revision
Local finance
KE provincial table: KEA-KEY 522.2
Covenants running with the land:
KE719+
Ontario: KEO269.4
Credit bureaus: KE1987.C7
KE provincial table: KEA-KEY 373.C7
Credit information
Tort liability: KE1248.C7
Credit, Letters of: KE1022
Credit managers
Legal works for: KE450.C7
Credit unions: KE1008
KE provincial table: KEA-KEY 265.C7
Ontario: KEO315.C7
Quebec: KEQ482.C7
Creditors' rights: KE1485+
KE provincial table: KEA-KEY 322+
Ontario: KEO417+
Quebec: KEQ404+
Crime and publicity: KE8817
Crimes without victims: KE9059+
Criminal intent: KE8834
Criminal jurisdiction: KE8828
Criminal law: KE8801+
KE provincial table: KEA-KEY 569+
Native peoples: KE7722.C75

Criminal law
Native peoples
KE provincial table: KEA-KEY 529.5.C75
Ontario: KEO1165+
Quebec: KEQ1168+
Criminal liability: KE8833+
KE provincial table: KEA-KEY 570.5
Criminal negligence: KE8834
Criminal procedure: KE9260+
KE provincial table: KEA-KEY 572+
Ontario: KEO1175+
Quebec: KEQ1174+
Criminal registration
KE provincial table: KEA-KEY 591
Criminal statistics: KE203
KE provincial table: KEA-KEY 143+
Ontario: KEO153+
Quebec: KEQ137+
Criminal trials: KE225+
Crop insurance
KE provincial table: KEA-KEY 284.8.C7
Cross claims
Civil procedure: KE8392
Cross examination: KE8427
Crown: KE4709+
Proceedings by or against: KE8595+
Crown and Executive branch: KE4705+
KE provincial table: KEA-KEY 473+
Ontario: KEO853+
Quebec: KEQ785+
Crown corporations: KE1465
Quebec: KEQ816
Crown lands: KE5184
KE provincial table: KEA-KEY 497
Ontario: KEO912
Quebec: KEQ856
Crown liability: KE1305
Ontario: KEO377
Crown privilege: KE4715
CTC Review Committee: KE2076.54
Culpability
Criminal law: KE8834
Cultural rights
Native peoples: KE7722.I58
Ontario: KEO821

INDEX

Currency: KE5602
Current Legislative Digest: KE72
Curricula
- Educational law
  - Elementary and secondary education: KE3873+
  - KE provincial table: KEA-KEY 445+
  - Ontario: KEO788+
  - Quebec: KEQ940+

Curtesy: KE684
- KE provincial table: KEA-KEY 223

Custody: KE600+
- KE provincial table: KEA-KEY 206.7+

Customs duties: KE6081+
- KE provincial table: KEA-KEY 519.C8

D

Dairy industry
- Regulation: KE1887
  - KE provincial table: KEA-KEY 359.3.D3
  - Ontario: KEO479
  - Quebec: KEQ549.D3

Damage to property
- Railway liability: KE2197

Damages
- Breach of contract: KE892
  - KE provincial table: KEA-KEY 255.2
  - Quebec: KEQ411.5.D36
- Income tax: KE5920.D3
  - KE provincial table: KEA-KEY 511.5.D36
- Legal concept: KE484.D3
  - KE provincial table: KEA-KEY 184.D3
  - Quebec: KEQ207.D3
- Non-fulfilment of obligations
  - Quebec: KEQ378
- Torts: KE1232
  - Ontario: KEO358
  - Quebec: KEQ451

Dangerous goods
- Railway safety: KE2172.D3
- Ship cargo: KE2367.D3

Day care centers: KE1987.D3

Day care centers
- Ontario: KEO502.D3

Death
- Definition of: KE3663.D43
  - KE provincial table: KEA-KEY 424.8.D43

Death by wrongful act: KE1237
- KE provincial table: KEA-KEY 291

Death by wrongful acts
- Quebec: KEQ455

Death certificates: KE521
- KE provincial table: KEA-KEY 192
- Ontario: KEO209
- Quebec: KEQ236

Death registration: KE521
- KE provincial table: KEA-KEY 192
- Ontario: KEO209
- Quebec: KEQ236

Debtor and creditor: KE1030+
- Conflict of laws: KE474.C64
  - Quebec: KEQ209.C64
- KE provincial table: KEA-KEY 267+
- Ontario: KEO317+

Debtors' relief: KE1515+
- KE provincial table: KEA-KEY 324+
- Ontario: KEO419+

Decedents' estates
- Administration
  - KE provincial table: KEA-KEY 248
  - Ontario: KEO293
- Claims against
  - Ontario: KEO295.C4

Decedents' family maintenance
- Wills: KE814.D42

Deceit
- Torts: KE1255

Declaratory judgments: KE8522.D42
- Quebec: KEQ1145.D42

Declaratory power of Parliament: KE4278

Decorum
- Court procedure: KE8218
  - Quebec: KEQ1070.5.C65

Deductions
- Income tax: KE5808+

Deeds
- Real property: KE731

INDEX

Deeds
- Real property
  - KE provincial table: KEA-KEY 231
  - Ontario: KEO272

Defamation
- Criminal law: KE8948

Defense contracts: KE902

Defense research and development: KE3960.D4

Defenses: KE1309
- Criminal liability: KE8839+

Defenses and objections
- Civil procedure: KE8386+

Deferment
- Military service: KE6863+

Delegated legislation: KE5024+
- Administrative process
  - KE provincial table: KEA-KEY 488.2

Delicts
- Quebec: KEQ451+

Denominational schools: KE3809
- KE provincial table: KEA-KEY 438.5
- Ontario: KEO771
- Quebec: KEQ923

Dentistry
- Collective bargaining: KE3196.D4
  - Quebec: KEQ656.D4

Dentists
- Ontario: KEO617.D4

Dentists and dental specialists: KE2714.D4

Department of Justice: KE4752
- KE provincial table: KEA-KEY 475
- Quebec: KEQ787

Department of Labor and Manpower
- Quebec: KEQ643

Department of Labour: KE3117

Department of National Defense: KE6848

Department of National Revenue: KE5690

Deportation: KE4475

Deposition: KE8408

Deposition and discovery
- Ontario: KEO1130

Depositions
- KE provincial table: KEA-KEY 184.O2

Deposits
- Banking: KE1016
  - Quebec: KEQ439

Depreciation allowances
- Income tax: KE5810

Desertion and nonsupport
- Parent and child: KE602
  - KE provincial table: KEA-KEY 206.8

Designs and models
- Copyright: KE2885
- Patent law: KE2952

Dilapidations
- Real property: KE703

Diminished responsibility
- Criminal liability: KE8839+

Disability insurance
- Contracts
  - Ontario: KEO346

Disability pensions
- Air Force: KE7074
- Armed Forces: KE6884+
- Army: KE6944
- Navy: KE7014

Disallowance and reservation of provincial legislation
- KE provincial table: KEA-KEY 456.5.D5

Disbarment
- KE provincial table: KEA-KEY 153
- Ontario: KEO164
- Quebec: KEQ154.3

Discharge
- Air Force: KE7062
- Armed Forces: KE6872
- Army: KE6932
- Navy: KE7002

Discharge of contract: KE880+
- KE provincial table: KEA-KEY 254
- Quebec: KEQ409+

Discipline
- Higher education: KE3920
- Legal profession
  - KE provincial table: KEA-KEY 153
  - Ontario: KEO164
  - Quebec: KEQ154.3

Discipline of legislators: KE4572
- Ontario: KEO850.C6

INDEX

Discovery
- Criminal procedure: KE9300

Discrimination
- Employment: KE3254+
  - KE provincial table: KEA-KEY 406.4+
  - Ontario: KEO659+
  - Quebec: KEQ671+
- Housing: KE5307
  - Ontario: KEO931

Dismissal of employees: KE3247+
- KE provincial table: KEA-KEY 406.2+
- Ontario: KEO658+
- Quebec: KEQ670+

Disposal of the dead
- Public health: KE3581

Dispose of land, Right to: KE711+
- Ontario: KEO268

Disqualification
- Armed Forces: KE6863+

Dissemination
- Literary copyright: KE2835

Dissolution
- Corporations: KE1459
  - KE provincial table: KEA-KEY 321.3
  - Ontario: KEO412.3
  - Quebec: KEQ500.3

Distilleries: KE3736

Distress
- Land tenure
  - KE provincial table: KEA-KEY 227.D58

Distress, Mortgagees' right to: KE754.D5

District courts
- KE provincial table: KEA-KEY 536
- Ontario: KEO1067+, KEO1085

Dividends
- Corporations: KE1408+
  - KE provincial table: KEA-KEY 317+
  - Ontario: KEO405+
  - Quebec: KEQ496+
- Income tax: KE5785+

Division courts
- Ontario
  - Post-1881: KEO1090
  - Pre-1881: KEO1072

Divorce: KE561+
- Conflict of laws
  - Quebec: KEQ209.M2
  - KE provincial table: KEA-KEY 201+
  - Ontario: KEO224+
  - Quebec: KEQ250+
- Taxation: KE5726

Documentary evidence: KE8457
- KE provincial table: KEA-KEY 560.D63

Domestic relations
- Family law: KE531+
  - KE provincial table: KEA-KEY 194+
  - Ontario: KEO213+
  - Quebec: KEQ237+
- Native peoples: KE7722.D6
- Torts: KE1252

Domestic shipping: KE2440

Domicile
- Civil status: KE499
  - Quebec: KEQ229
- Public welfare: KE3505.D6

Dominion succession duty: KE5976+

Donation of organs, tissues, etc
- Medical legislation: KE3663.D65
  - KE provincial table: KEA-KEY 424.8.D65

Double taxation: KE5695

Dower: KE684
- KE provincial table: KEA-KEY 223

Draft
- Armed Forces: KE6860+

Draft evaders
- Legal works for: KE450.I4A+

Drainage
- Public health: KE3625
  - Ontario: KEO719
  - Quebec: KEQ886
- Public property: KE5194+
  - KE provincial table: KEA-KEY 498+
  - Ontario: KEO913+

Drivers' licenses: KE2103
- Ontario: KEO532.D75

Droit de rétention
- Civil law
  - Quebec: KEQ226.R4

Drug addiction
- Medical legislation: KE3660.N3

Drug laws: KE3714+
- KE provincial table: KEA-KEY 427.5+
- Ontario: KEO738
- Quebec: KEQ900+

Drugs of abuse
- KE provincial table: KEA-KEY 427.8

Drunk driving: KE2114
- KE provincial table: KEA-KEY 382+
- Ontario: KEO535+
- Quebec: KEQ594

Drunkenness
- Crimes without victims: KE9078
- Criminal liability: KE8843

Due process of law: KE4408

Dumping
- Customs administration: KE6129

Duration and renewal: KE2815

Duress
- KE provincial table: KEA-KEY 252
- Void and voidable contracts: KE874

E

Easements: KE715+
- Ontario: KEO269.2

Economic assistance
- Agriculture and forestry: KE1691+
  - KE provincial table: KEA-KEY 340
  - Quebec: KEQ524

Economic crises
- Government measures: KE5460+

Economic development: KE1570+
- KE provincial table: KEA-KEY 328+
- Ontario: KEO425+
- Quebec: KEQ506+

Economic planning: KE1570+
- KE provincial table: KEA-KEY 328+
- Ontario: KEO425+
- Quebec: KEQ506+

Economic policy: KE1570+
- KE provincial table: KEA-KEY 328+
- Ontario: KEO425+
- Quebec: KEQ506+

Economics of law practice: KE349+
- KE provincial table: KEA-KEY 154

Economics of law practice
- Ontario: KEO166
- Quebec: KEQ156+

Education: KE3805+
- Air Force: KE7064+
- Armed Forces: KE6874+
- Army: KE6934+
- Collective bargaining: KE3196.E37
- KE provincial table: KEA-KEY 438+
- Labor laws
  - Ontario: KEO676.T42
  - Quebec: KEQ696.T4
- Native peoples: KE7722.E3
  - KE provincial table: KEA-KEY 529.5.E38
- Navy: KE7004+
- Ontario: KEO770+
- Quebec: KEQ922+
- War veterans: KE7240.E3

Education, Legal: KE273+

Educators
- Legal works for: KE450.E3

Eggs and egg products: KE1882

Ejectment: KE709

Election districts
- House of Commons: KE4640
- Legislative Assembly
  - KE provincial table: KEA-KEY 468.5.A6
  - Quebec: KEQ775.E5

Election law
- House of Commons: KE4622+
- Legislative Assembly
  - KE provincial table: KEA-KEY 468+
  - Ontario: KEO838+
  - Quebec: KEQ774+

Elections, Municipal
- KE provincial table: KEA-KEY 478.5.E43
- Quebec: KEQ830.E43

Electoral franchise: KE4627+

Electric industries
- Regulation: KE1855.E4

Electric railways: KE2220

Electrical installations
- Building laws: KE5275

INDEX

Electrical installations
- Building laws
  - KE provincial table: KEA-KEY 504.57
  - Ontario: KEO925.2
  - Quebec: KEQ869

Electricity
- Export regulation: KE1952.E43
- Regulation: KE2041
  - KE provincial table: KEA-KEY 376.3
  - Ontario: KEO518
  - Quebec: KEQ578

Electronic data processing
- Legal research: KE252+
  - Quebec: KEQ141

Electronic data processing personnel
- Collective bargaining: KE3196.E43

Electronic industries
- Collective bargaining: KE3196.E44

Electronic listening and recording devices
- Criminal procedure: KE9328
  - KE provincial table: KEA-KEY 578.5
  - Quebec: KEQ1186.5

Elementary and secondary education: KE3865+
- KE provincial table: KEA-KEY 444+
- Ontario: KEO784+
- Quebec: KEQ936+

Elevators
- Building laws
  - Ontario: KEO925.3

Embezzlement: KE8968

Emergency economic legislation: KE5460+

Emergency powers: KE4713

Emphyteusis
- Quebec: KEQ298

Emphyteutic lease
- Quebec: KEQ298

Employees' inventions
- Patents: KE2945

Employers' liability: KE1301
- Ontario: KEO376
- Quebec: KEQ470

Employment: KE3247+
- KE provincial table: KEA-KEY 406.2+

Employment
- Ontario: KEO658+
- Quebec: KEQ670+
- War veterans: KE7240.E4

Employment agencies: KE1987.E5
- Quebec: KEQ568.E5

Employment discipline: KE4944+

Employment, Income from
- Income tax: KE5775

Endowments
- Income tax: KE5870
- Nonprofit corporations: KE1375.E5

Enemy property: KE621

Energy resources and development: KE2035+
- KE provincial table: KEA-KEY 376+
- Ontario: KEO514+
- Quebec: KEQ577+

Engineering contracts: KE933
- Quebec: KEQ431.B8

Engineers
- Collective bargaining: KE3196.E5
  - KE provincial table: KEA-KEY 403.E5
  - Ontario: KEO647.E5
  - Quebec: KEQ656.E53
- Regulation: KE2730
  - Quebec: KEQ987

English regime, 1759-1867
- Quebec legal history: KEQ189
- Quebec legislation: KEQ53+

Enlisted personnel
- Air Force: KE7094
- Armed Forces: KE6904
- Army: KE6964
- Navy: KE7034

Enlistment
- Air Force: KE7062
- Armed Forces: KE6872
- Army: KE6932
- Navy: KE7002

Entrapment
- Criminal procedure: KE9321

Enumeration of voters
- Canadian House of Commons: KE4633

INDEX

Enumeration of voters
- Legislative Assembly
  - KE provincial table: KEA-KEY 468.5.R4

Environmental damages
- Quebec: KEQ467.5
- Torts: KE1285
  - KE provincial table: KEA-KEY 295.5
  - Ontario: KEO371.5

Environmental planning: KE5110+
- KE provincial table: KEA-KEY 491
- Ontario: KEO896+
- Quebec: KEQ846

Environmental pollution: KE3575+
- KE provincial table: KEA-KEY 420+
- Ontario: KEO713+
- Quebec: KEQ885+

Equal pay for equal work: KE3254+

Equality before the law: KE4410

Equipment
- Air Force: KE7106
- Armed Forces: KE6916
- Army: KE6976
- Navy: KE7046

Equity: KE457
- Civil procedure: KE8360
  - Ontario: KEO1111+
- KE provincial table: KEA-KEY 180
- Ontario: KEO192
- Quebec: KEQ205.6

Erosion control: KE1686

Error
- Void and voidable contracts
  - Quebec: KEQ398.E7
- Wills: KE814.M57

Espionage: KE9002

Estate planning
- KE provincial table: KEA-KEY 515.3
- Ontario: KEO998
- Quebec: KEQ1026

Estate tax planning
- KE provincial table: KEA-KEY 515.3
- Ontario: KEO998
- Quebec: KEQ1026

Estate taxes: KE5970+

Estates and interests
- Real property: KE630+

Estates and interests
- Real property
  - KE provincial table: KEA-KEY 217+
  - Ontario: KEO240+

Estoppel by judgment: KE8514

Ethics in government: KE4244

Eugenics: KE3661
- KE provincial table: KEA-KEY 424.5

Euthanasia
- KE provincial table: KEA-KEY 424.8.E88
- Medical legislation: KE3663.E94

Evidence
- Civil procedure: KE8440+
  - KE provincial table: KEA-KEY 559+
  - Ontario: KEO1136+
  - Quebec: KEQ1126+
- Courts-martial: KE7168
- Criminal procedure: KE9312+
  - KE provincial table: KEA-KEY 578+
  - Quebec: KEQ1186+

Excess profits tax: KE5890

Exchange
- Contracts
  - Quebec: KEQ422

Excise duties: KE6005

Excise taxes
- Provincial finance: KE6230+
  - Quebec: KEQ1028+
- Public finance: KE5996+
  - KE provincial table: KEA-KEY 516+
  - Ontario: KEO1004+

Exclusion of evidence: KE8485+

Executive power: KE4705
- KE provincial table: KEA-KEY 473+
- Ontario: KEO853
- Quebec: KEQ785

Executives
- Taxation: KE5669.8.E94

Executory interests: KE664

Exempt income
- Income tax: KE5764

Exemption
- Criminal liability: KE8839+

Exemptions
- Armed Forces: KE6863+
- Local finance: KE6289

INDEX

Exoneration of liability clauses
- Torts
  - Quebec: KEQ451.5.E9

Expenditure control
- Local finance: KE6267
- Provincial finance: KE6178
- Public finance: KE5622
  - Quebec: KEQ997

Expenses
- Income tax: KE5820+

Experiments with humans in medicine: KE3663.M43

Expert evidence
- Civil procedure: KE8472+
  - KE provincial table: KEA-KEY 560.E8
  - Ontario: KEO1140+
  - Quebec: KEQ1132+
- Criminal procedure: KE9337

Expert witnesses
- Civil procedure: KE8472+
  - KE provincial table: KEA-KEY 560.E8
  - Ontario: KEO1140+
  - Quebec: KEQ1132+
- Criminal procedure: KE9337

Explosives: KE3766.E9
- Quebec: KEQ910.E9

Export and import controls: KE1940

Export trade: KE1940, KE1950+
- KE provincial table: KEA-KEY 369+

Expropriation
- Public property: KE5175
  - KE provincial table: KEA-KEY 495
  - Ontario: KEO910+
  - Quebec: KEQ853

Expulsion: KE4475

Expungement of trademarks: KE2998

Extortion: KE8980+

Extra-provincial corporations
- Government regulation and control: KE1398

Extracontractual liability: KE1232+
- KE provincial table: KEA-KEY 290+
- Ontario: KEO358+
- Quebec: KEQ451+

Extractive industries: KE1671+

Extractive industries
- KE provincial table: KEA-KEY 338+
- Ontario: KEO441+
- Quebec: KEQ522+

Extradition
- Criminal procedure: KE9275

F

Fabriques: KEQ834

Factors: KE1332.B7

Factory inspection: KE3367
- KE provincial table: KEA-KEY 409.5
- Quebec: KEQ693

Faculties
- Higher education: KE3917

Faculties Higher education
- Quebec: KEQ951

Fair and unfair labor practices: KE3160

False pretenses
- Criminal law: KE8973

Family allowances
- Public welfare: KE3517

Family companies: KE1450
- KE provincial table: KEA-KEY 321.P74
- Quebec: KEQ500.P74

Family courts: KE542
- KE provincial table: KEA-KEY 195
- Quebec: KEQ238

Family law: KE531+
- KE provincial table: KEA-KEY 194+
- Ontario: KEO213+
- Quebec: KEQ237+

Family provisions
- Succession upon death
  - KE provincial table: KEA-KEY 248.5.F34
  - Ontario: KEO295.F34

Farm buildings
- Building laws: KE5270.F37

Farm corporations
- KE provincial table: KEA-KEY 340.5

Farm land
- Taxation: KE6291.F3
  - KE provincial table: KEA-KEY 523.6.F3

INDEX

Farm land
- Taxation
  - Ontario: KEO1025.7.F3
- Farm loans: KE1700
- Farm mortgage credit: KE1700
- Farm tenancy
  - KE provincial table: KEA-KEY 225.F35
- Farmers
  - Debtors: KE1520.F3
  - Income tax: KE5864.F3
  - Legal works for
    - KE provincial table: KEA-KEY 177.F37
  - Works about income tax for: KE5759.8.F37
- Farms
  - Land use
    - Ontario: KEO921.7.F3
- Fear
  - Void and voidable contracts
    - Quebec: KEQ398.V5
- Federal aid to education: KE3822
- Federal Court of Canada: KE8265+
  - Law reports: KE142
- Federal courts: KE8240+
- Federal grants, loans, etc
  - Local finance: KE6328.F4
  - Provincial finance: KE6256.F4
- Federal-provincial relations: KE4270+
  - Quebec: KEQ744+
- Federal public service: KE4940+
- Federal public service employees
  - Collective bargaining: KE3196.F4
  - Labor discipline: KE3336.F4
  - Management-labor relations: KE3240.F4
- Fee simple: KE632+
  - KE provincial table: KEA-KEY 217+
  - Ontario: KEO240+
- Feed stuffs: KE1842.F4
- Fees
  - Courts
    - Civil procedure: KE8517+
      - KE provincial table: KEA-KEY 562.3
      - Ontario: KEO1148+

Fees
- Courts
  - Civil procedure
    - Quebec: KEQ1144+
  - Legal profession: KE350+
    - KE provincial table: KEA-KEY 154
    - Ontario: KEO166
    - Quebec: KEQ156.5.F4
  - Notaries
    - Quebec: KEQ176.F4
  - Patents: KE2935.F4
- Fences
  - Real property: KE705
    - Ontario: KEO265
- Fertilizers: KE1842.F4
  - Quebec: KEQ545.F4
- Fiduciary substitutions
  - Successions and gifts
    - Quebec: KEQ357
- Field irrigation: KE1686
- Finance
  - Airlines: KE2275
- Finance charges: KE1034
  - KE provincial table: KEA-KEY 268
  - Ontario: KEO318
  - Quebec: KEQ436
- Finance, Court: KE8226.5
- Financial responsibility laws
  - Motor vehicles: KE2105
- Financial statements
  - Associations: KE1347
  - Corporations: KE1430
    - Ontario: KEO409
    - Quebec: KEQ498
  - KE provincial table: KEA-KEY 319
- Fine arts: KE3968
- Fines
  - Criminal procedure: KE9429
- Fire accidents
  - Torts: KE1274.F57
- Fire insurance: KE1184.F5
  - KE provincial table: KEA-KEY 284.5.F5
  - Ontario: KEO348.5.F5
  - Quebec: KEQ489.5.F5
- Fire prevention and control: KE3778
  - KE provincial table: KEA-KEY 433

INDEX

Fire prevention and control
- Ontario: KEO764

Firearms: KE3758

Fish protection: KE5210+
- Ontario: KEO916+

Fisheries and wildlife cases
- Statistics
  - KE provincial table: KEA-KEY 144.F57

Fishermen
- Income tax: KE5864.F3

Fishery products: KE1896+

Fishing industry
- Regulation: KE1760+
  - KE provincial table: KEA-KEY 347
  - Ontario: KEO458
  - Quebec: KEQ534
- Safety regulations
  - KE provincial table: KEA-KEY 409.7.F5
- Wages: KE3292.F5
  - KE provincial table: KEA-KEY 407.7.F5
- Workers' compensation: KE3420.F5

Fishing rights
- Native peoples: KE7722.H8
  - KE provincial table: KEA-KEY 529.5.H8
  - Quebec: KEQ1062.H85

Fixtures
- Land tenure
  - KE provincial table: KEA-KEY 227.F59
- Real property: KE702

Flags: KE4795

F.O.B. clause: KE964

Food and drug convictions
- Judicial statistics: KE206.F6

Food law: KE3696+
- KE provincial table: KEA-KEY 427+
- Ontario: KEO734+
- Quebec: KEQ902

Food processing industries: KE1867+
- KE provincial table: KEA-KEY 359+
- Ontario: KEO475+
- Quebec: KEQ548+

Force majeure
- Obligations
  - Quebec: KEQ379.F6

Foreclosure: KE754.F6
- KE provincial table: KEA-KEY 235.5.F67
- Ontario: KEO278.5.F6

Foreign affairs
- Prerogative powers of the Crown: KE4719

Foreign claims settlement: KE12 3.5

Foreign corporations
- Government regulation and control: KE1398
- Taxation: KE5864.N6

Foreign exchange regulation: KE5612

Foreign investment
- Economic policy: KE1575
  - KE provincial table: KEA-KEY 328.5
  - Ontario: KEO425.5
  - Quebec: KEQ506.5
- Income tax: KE5787

Foreign investors
- Legal works for: KE450.B87

Foreign judgments: KE8222
- KE provincial table: KEA-KEY 533.3.F67

Foreign relations: KE4310
- Quebec: KEQ746.F6

Foreign service officers
- Collective bargaining: KE3196.F6

Forensic psychology: KE8429

Forest engineers
- Quebec: KEQ988.F6

Forest reserves: KE5203

Forestry: KE1671+
- Collective bargaining: KE3196.F67
  - KE provincial table: KEA-KEY 403.F6
- KE provincial table: KEA-KEY 338+
  - Ontario: KEO441+
  - Quebec: KEQ522+
- Taxation: KE6244.F6
  - KE provincial table: KEA-KEY 518.5.F6
  - Ontario: KEO1012.F6

INDEX

Forfeitures
- Criminal procedure: KE9431

Forgery: KE9088
- Quebec: KEQ1172.F6

Formalities
- Contracts
  - KE provincial table: KEA-KEY 250.5

Fortuitous event
- Obligations
  - Quebec: KEQ379.F6

Foundations: KE1375.E5
- Income tax: KE5870

Franchises, Retail: KE1973
- KE provincial table: KEA-KEY 371.4

Fraud
- Criminal law: KE8973
- Torts: KE1255
- Void and voidable contracts: KE875
  - KE provincial table: KEA-KEY 252
  - Quebec: KEQ398.F7

Fraudlent conveyances
- Bankruptcy
  - Ontario: KEO418.5.F73

Fraudulent conveyances: KE1506.F7

Freedom of assembly and association: KE4425
- KE provincial table: KEA-KEY 458.5.A7

Freedom of expression: KE4418+
- KE provincial table: KEA-KEY 458.5.E94
- Quebec: KEQ755+

Freedom of information: KE5325
- KE provincial table: KEA-KEY 505.62
- Ontario: KEO937
- Quebec: KEQ876

Freedom of religion and conscience: KE4430
- Quebec: KEQ759

Freedom of speech: KE4420

Freedom of the press and of information: KE4422
- Quebec: KEQ757

Freehold estates: KE632+
- KE provincial table: KEA-KEY 217+
- Ontario: KEO240+

Freight
- Railway rates: KE2179

French regime (New France), 1540-1759
- Legislation: KEQ48+
- Quebec legal history: KEQ188

Frequency allocations: KE2605

Fringe benefits
- Income tax: KE5775
- Labor standards: KE3298+
  - KE provincial table: KEA-KEY 408.5.N65
  - Ontario: KEO666+
  - Quebec: KEQ678+

Fruits and vegetables
- Marketing
  - Quebec: KEQ529.F7
- Regulation of food processing: KE1874

Funeral services: KE1987.U5
- KE provincial table: KEA-KEY 373.U5
- Ontario: KEO502.U5

Furs
- Export trade
  - KE provincial table: KEA-KEY 369.5.F8

Future estates and interests
- Land tenure: KE660+
  - KE provincial table: KEA-KEY 221+
  - Ontario: KEO245+

Futures trading: KE1093

G

Gage
- Property
  - Quebec: KEQ325

Gambling
- Contracts: KE1225
- Criminal law: KE9066
- KE provincial table: KEA-KEY 434.3.L67

Game laws: KE5210
- KE provincial table: KEA-KEY 499.6
- Ontario: KEO916
- Quebec: KEQ859

Game protection: KE5210+

INDEX

Game protection
  Ontario: KEO916+
Game wardens
  Collective bargaining
    Quebec: KEQ656.G35
Games of chance: KE3795
  KE provincial table: KEA-KEY 434.3.L67
Gaming contracts
  Quebec: KEQ444
Garnishment
  Civil procedure: KE8552+
    KE provincial table: KEA-KEY 564
    Ontario: KEO1153+
    Quebec: KEQ1151+
Gas
  Regulation: KE2046
    KE provincial table: KEA-KEY 376.4
    Ontario: KEO521
    Quebec: KEQ579
Gas containers and equipment
  Accident control
    KE provincial table: KEA-KEY 432.5.G3
Gas installations
  Building laws
    KE provincial table: KEA-KEY 504.55
Gases, Noxious, Control of: KE3630+
  Ontario: KEO720
  Quebec: KEQ888+
Gasoline
  Excise taxes
    Quebec: KEQ1030.G3
  Regulation: KE1980.G3
    KE provincial table: KEA-KEY 371.5.G3
Gays
  Civil and political rights: KE4390
Geologists: KE2742.G4
Gift tax
  Provincial finance: KE6222
    KE provincial table: KEA-KEY 515+
    Ontario: KEO997+
    Quebec: KEQ1025+
  Public finance: KE5970+

Gifts inter vivos
  Quebec: KEQ351+
Gold mining: KE1802.G6
  KE provincial table: KEA-KEY 350.3.G6
Golf courses
  Property taxes: KE6291.G6
    Ontario: KEO1025.7.G6
Good faith
  Insurance contracts: KE1163.B33
Good Samaritan laws: KE1314
  KE provincial table: KEA-KEY 298
Goodwill, Sale of
  Income tax: KE5781.G6
Government agencies
  Quebec: KEQ816
Government business organizations
  Quebec: KEQ816
Government contracts: KE899+
Government expenditures: KE5617
  KE provincial table: KEA-KEY 508.3
Government liability
  KE provincial table: KEA-KEY 296.5.G6
Government-owned corporations
  Quebec: KEQ816
Government property: KE5323+
  KE provincial table: KEA-KEY 505.6+
  Ontario: KEO936+
  Quebec: KEQ875
Government service
  Legal profession: KE332.G6
    Quebec: KEQ152.G6
Government spending power: KE5617
Government torts: KE1305
  Ontario: KEO377
Governor-General: KE4723
Grain
  Marketing: KE1714.G7
    Quebec: KEQ529.G7
  Price supports: KE1694.G7
  Ship cargo: KE2367.G7
  Standards, grading, and inspection: KE1719.G7
Grand jury: KE9282
  KE provincial table: KEA-KEY 573.4
  Quebec: KEQ1179

INDEX

Grazing lands: KE5201
  KE provincial table: KEA-KEY 499.3
Great Lakes
  Navigation and pilotage: KE2377
Grievances
  Labor law: KE3332+
    KE provincial table: KEA-KEY 408.5.G7
    Quebec: KEQ684
Ground-effect machines
  Safety regulations: KE2365.G7
Ground leases: KE695.G7
Grounds for divorce: KE581+
Guaranteed prices
  Agriculture: KE1693+
Guaranty
  Ontario: KEO321
Guaranty insurance: KE1211+
  KE provincial table: KEA-KEY 286
  Ontario: KEO353.S9
Guardian and ward: KE606
  KE provincial table: KEA-KEY 208
  Ontario: KEO230
Guidance workers
  Educational law
    KE provincial table: KEA-KEY 442.5.G8

H

Habeas corpus: KE8569
  Quebec: KEQ1147
Habitation
  Property
    Quebec: KEQ292
Habitual criminals: KE8822
Harbors and ports: KE2387
  KE provincial table: KEA-KEY 388.H3
Hate propaganda
  Criminal law: KE8952
Hazardous articles and processes
  KE provincial table: KEA-KEY 431+
  Public safety: KE3763+
    Ontario: KEO760
Hazardous occupations: KE3365+
  KE provincial table: KEA-KEY 409.4+
  Ontario: KEO673+

Hazardous occupations
  Quebec: KEQ692+
Health and safety regulations
  Federal public service: KE4979
Health facilities
  Safety regulations
    Ontario: KEO673.5.H66
Health insurance: KE1174
  Federal public service: KE4978
  Social insurance: KE3404+
    KE provincial table: KEA-KEY 412
    Ontario: KEO679
    Quebec: KEQ702
Health professions: KE2706+
  Ontario: KEO616+
  Quebec: KEQ982+
  Regulation
    KE provincial table: KEA-KEY 395.4.P5
Health services
  Quebec: KEQ718
Hearsay
  Evidence: KE8485
  Quebec: KEQ1139
Heating plants
  Collective bargaining: KE3196.H43
Heavy industries: KE1855.A+
Helicopters: KE2268
Herbicides: KE3766.P5
  Quebec: KEQ910.P47
High Court of Justice
  Ontario: KEO1081
    Law reports: KEO134
High schools
  Ontario: KEO787
Higher education: KE3904+
  KE provincial table: KEA-KEY 446+
  Ontario: KEO793+
  Quebec: KEQ946+
Highway law: KE5126
  Ontario: KEO899
  Quebec: KEQ848
Historians
  Collective bargaining: KE3196.H57
Historic buildings and monuments: KE3995

INDEX

Historical buildings and landmarks
  KE provincial table: KEA-KEY 448.9
Holding companies: KE1448
Holidays
  Labor law: KE3318
  Labor standards
    Quebec: KEQ682
Home economics
  Collective bargaining: KE3196.H6
Homemakers: KE1987.H6
  Ontario: KEO502.H6
Homestead rights: KE684
  KE provincial table: KEA-KEY 223
Homesteads: KE5232
Homicide: KE8908+
Horizontal property: KE641
Horse racing: KE3792
  KE provincial table: KEA-KEY
    434.3.H6, KEA-KEY 434.3.L67
  Ontario: KEO766.5.H65
  Quebec: KEQ919.H67
Horses
  Sales contracts: KE945.H6
Hospital records: KE3654.R42
  Ontario: KEO730.R42
Hospital workers
  Collective bargaining
    Quebec: KEQ656.H6
Hospitals
  Air Force: KE7109
  Armed Forces: KE6919
  Army: KE6979
  Collective bargaining: KE3196.H65
  Labor disputes
    Ontario: KEO653.H6
    Quebec: KEQ663.H6
  Management-labor relations
    Quebec: KEQ666.H6
  Medical legislation: KE3650+
    KE provincial table: KEA-KEY 423.2
    Ontario: KEO726
    Quebec: KEQ895
  Navy: KE7049
  Safety regulations
    Ontario: KEO673.5.H66
Hotels: KE1987.H65

Hotels
  Excise taxes
    Quebec: KEQ1030.M4
  KE provincial table: KEA-KEY
    373.H67
  Quebec: KEQ568.H6
Hours of labor: KE3312+
  KE provincial table: KEA-KEY 408
  Quebec: KEQ681
House of Commons: KE4620+
Housing
  Public property: KE5295+
    KE provincial table: KEA-KEY 505+
    Ontario: KEO929+
    Quebec: KEQ872+
Housing condominium: KE641
  KE provincial table: KEA-KEY 217
  Ontario: KEO240
Housing cooperatives: KE680
Housing for older people
  Public welfare: KE3526
Huissiers
  Quebec: KEQ1098.B3
Human reproductive technology:
  KE3660.5
Humans in medical experiments:
  KE3663.M43
Hunting rights
  Native peoples: KE7722.H8
    KE provincial table: KEA-KEY
      529.5.H8
    Quebec: KEQ1062.H85
Husband abuse: KE8925.5
Husband and wife
  Family law: KE544+
    KE provincial table: KEA-KEY 196+
    Ontario: KEO218+
    Quebec: KEQ240+
  Torts
    KE provincial table: KEA-KEY
      296.H8
Hygiene and safety, Labor: KE3346+
  KE provincial table: KEA-KEY 409+
  Ontario: KEO671+
  Quebec: KEQ689+

INDEX

I

Illegal disclosure of official secrets: KE9002
Illegitimate children: KE596
- KE provincial table: KEA-KEY 206.4
- Ontario: KEO227

Illicit liquor traffic: KE9090
Illicit political activities
- House of Commons: KE4648
- Legislative Assembly
  - Ontario: KEO842

Immigrants
- Legal works for: KE450.I4A+

Immigration: KE4454+
- Quebec: KEQ914

Immigration Appeal Board: KE4456
Immigration inspection: KE3599
Immoral contracts: KE872
Impact fees
- Local finance: KEO1029.I54

Impeachment
- Judges: KE8293.R4

Import trade: KE1955+
Imprisonment
- Criminal procedure: KE9415+
  - KE provincial table: KEA-KEY 588+
  - Ontario: KEO1192+
- Juvenile criminal law: KE9449.3+
  - Ontario: KEO1196.22+
  - Quebec: KEQ1193+

Imprisonment for debt
- Quebec: KEQ1152.5.I5

Improvements
- Land tenure
  - KE provincial table: KEA-KEY 227.F59
- Real property: KE702
- Taxation: KE6295.I4

Imputation of payment
- Obligations
  - Quebec: KEQ374

Inchoate offenses: KE8903
Income
- Public finance
  - Ontario: KEO975+

Income averaging: KE5840

Income tax
- Corporations
  - Quebec: KEQ1014+
- Provincial finance: KE6194
  - Quebec: KEQ1008+
- Public finance: KE5751+
  - KE provincial table: KEA-KEY 511+

Incompatibility of offices: KE4244
Incorporation: KE1400
- KE provincial table: KEA-KEY 316
- Ontario: KEO403
- Quebec: KEQ495.3

Incorporeal hereditaments: KE714+
Independent contractors: KE928+
- KE provincial table: KEA-KEY 259+
- Ontario: KEO308+
- Quebec: KEQ430+

Indians: KE7701+
- KE provincial table: KEA-KEY 529+
- Legal aid: KE378.N3
  - KE provincial table: KEA-KEY 163.I53

Legal education: KE318.N3
- Ontario: KEO1044+
- Quebec: KEQ1060+

Indictment: KE9280+
- KE provincial table: KEA-KEY 573+
- Quebec: KEQ1178+

Indigenous legal systems
- Native peoples: KE7735+

Individual and state: KE4345+
- KE provincial table: KEA-KEY 458+
- Ontario: KEO811+
- Quebec: KEQ749+

Individuals, Control of
- KE provincial table: KEA-KEY 460+
- Quebec: KEQ913.92+

Industrial allocations: KE12 3+
Industrial designs: KE2908+
Industrial Development Bank: KE1026.I5
Industrial espionage: KE2999
Industrial priorities: KE12 3+
Industrial property: KE2908+
- KE provincial table: KEA-KEY 396
- Quebec: KEQ637

Infant welfare: KE3510

INDEX

Information
- Criminal procedure: KE9280+
  - KE provincial table: KEA-KEY 573+
  - Quebec: KEQ1178+

Information retrieval
- Legal research: KE252+
  - Quebec: KEQ141

Informed consent
- Medical legislation: KE3663.I54
  - KE provincial table: KEA-KEY 424.8.I5
  - Ontario: KEO730.I53

Inheritance taxes: KE5970+

Initiative and referendum: KE4527
- Quebec: KEQ767

Injunctions: KE8536
- KE provincial table: KEA-KEY 563.5
  - Ontario: KEO1152

Inland water carriers: KE2440

Innkeeper and guest
- Quebec: KEQ439

Insane persons
- Capacity and disability
  - KE provincial table: KEA-KEY 190.3.I5
  - Ontario: KEO207.I5
  - Quebec: KEQ235.I5

Insanity
- Criminal liability: KE8841

Insider trading: KE1067.I5

Insolvency and bankruptcy: KE1491+
- KE provincial table: KEA-KEY 322+
- Ontario: KEO417+, KEO418+
- Quebec: KEQ503+

Inspection
- Agriculture and forestry: KE1717+
- Food law: KE3705
- Ships: KE2355

Installment sale: KE1047
- Quebec: KEQ416

Instructions to jury
- Civil procedure: KE8505
- Criminal procedure: KE9350

Insurance: KE1141+
- KE provincial table: KEA-KEY 282+
- Municipal officials
  - Ontario: KEO875.5.I54
  - Ontario: KEO343+
  - Quebec: KEQ487+

Insurance agents: KE1154
- KE provincial table: KEA-KEY 282
- Ontario: KEO343

Insurance brokers: KE1154
- KE provincial table: KEA-KEY 282
- Ontario: KEO343
- Quebec: KEQ487.5

Insurance business: KE1154
- KE provincial table: KEA-KEY 282
- Ontario: KEO343
- Quebec: KEQ487.5

Intellectual property: KE2771+
- KE provincial table: KEA-KEY 396
- Native peoples: KE7722.I58
- Quebec: KEQ637

Inter-spousal immunity
- Torts
  - KE provincial table: KEA-KEY 296.H8

Interest
- Income tax: KE5785
- Loan of money: KE1030+
  - KE provincial table: KEA-KEY 267+
  - Ontario: KEO317+
  - Quebec: KEQ435+
- Mortgages: KE754.I5

Intergovernmental tax relations: KE6166

Intermediate courts
- KE provincial table: KEA-KEY 536
- Ontario: KEO1067+, KEO1085

Internal security: KE4486

International and municipal law: KE4252

International trade: KE1940+

Interpleader: KE8399

Interpretation of contracts
- Quebec: KEQ400

Interprovincial relations: KE4270+

Interrogatories: KE8408

Intestate succession: KE827+
- KE provincial table: KEA-KEY 247
- Ontario: KEO291
- Quebec: KEQ347+

INDEX

Inuit: KE7701+
- KE provincial table: KEA-KEY 529+
- Legal aid: KE378.N3
- Legal education: KE318.N3
- Quebec: KEQ1060+

Invasion of privacy
- Criminal offenses: KE8940

Invention
- Patent law: KE2941+

Investigation commissioners
- Quebec: KEQ648

Investigation, Criminal: KE9265+

Investment companies: KE1089
- Ontario: KEO332

Investment trusts: KE1089
- Ontario: KEO332

Investments: KE1060+
- KE provincial table: KEA-KEY 273+
- Ontario: KEO327+
- Quebec: KEQ484+

Investments, Income from
- Income tax: KE5785+

Irrigation
- Public property: KE5194+
  - KE provincial table: KEA-KEY 498+
  - Ontario: KEO913+

J

Jesuit estates: KE4508

Jeu et pari
- Quebec: KEQ444

Jews
- Discrimination in employment
  - General: KE3256.R44
  - Ontario: KEO660.J4

Job security: KE3262+

Joint legislative committees: KE4556.2+

Joint-stock companies: KE1381+

Joint tenancy: KE675+

Joint ventures: KE1362
- Income tax: KE5878

Judges: KE8290+

Judgment
- Civil procedure: KE8512+
  - KE provincial table: KEA-KEY 562+
  - Ontario: KEO1147+

Judgment
- Civil procedure
  - Quebec: KEQ1143+
- Criminal procedure: KE9355+

Judgment, Execution of: KE8550+
- KE provincial table: KEA-KEY 564
- Ontario: KEO1153+
- Quebec: KEQ1149+

Judicature Act of 1881 (Ontario): KEO1111+

Judicial advisors
- Quebec: KEQ260+

Judicial Committee of the Privy Council
- Decisions: KE4216.2

Judicial discretion
- Criminal procedure: KE9355+

Judicial districts
- KE provincial table: KEA-KEY 532.3

Judicial education: KE296

Judicial error, Compensation for: KE9440

Judicial ethics: KE8293.J8

Judicial functions
- Administrative procedure: KE5029
  - KE provincial table: KEA-KEY 488.4

Judicial officers: KE8285+
- KE provincial table: KEA-KEY 539+
- Ontario: KEO1094+
- Quebec: KEQ1093+

Judicial review of administrative acts: KE5036
- KE provincial table: KEA-KEY 488.5
- Ontario: KEO891.5
- Quebec: KEQ809

Judicial review of legislation: KE4248

Judicial separation: KE585

Judicial statistics: KE198+
- KE provincial table: KEA-KEY 142+
- Ontario: KEO152+
- Quebec: KEQ136+

Judiciary: KE4775

Jurisdiction
- Civil procedure: KE8364
  - Ontario: KEO1121
  - Quebec: KEQ1115
- Constitutional law: KE4270+
  - KE provincial table: KEA-KEY 456+

INDEX

Jurisdiction
- Constitutional law
  - Ontario: KEO808+
  - Quebec: KEQ744+
- Jurisprudence and philosophy of
  - Canadian law: KE427
- Juristic persons
  - Associations: KE1369+
    - KE provincial table: KEA-KEY 305+
    - Ontario: KEO389+
    - Quebec: KEQ494+
  - Income tax: KE5884+
- Jury and jurors
  - Civil procedure: KE8495+
    - KE provincial table: KEA-KEY 561
    - Ontario: KEO1144
    - Quebec: KEQ1141
  - Criminal procedure: KE9348+
    - Quebec: KEQ1187
- Justice, Administration of: KE8199.2+
  - Ontario: KEO1053.2+
  - Quebec: KEQ1067.2+
- Justices of the peace: KE8325
  - Criminal procedure: KE9365+
  - KE provincial table: KEA-KEY 538.2+, KEA-KEY 540+
  - Ontario: KEO1099+
  - Quebec: KEQ1095+
- Juvenile courts
  - Criminal procedure: KE9446
  - KE provincial table: KEA-KEY 593
  - Ontario: KEO1195.5
- Juvenile crime
  - Statistics: KE204
  - KE provincial table: KEA-KEY 143.5
  - Ontario: KEO153.5
  - Quebec: KEQ137.5
- Juvenile criminal law: KE9445+
  - KE provincial table: KEA-KEY 592+
- Juvenile criminal procedure: KE9445+
  - KE provincial table: KEA-KEY 592+
  - Ontario: KEO1195+
- Juvenile detention homes: KE9450
  - Ontario: KEO1196.7
- Juvenile justice, Administration of: KE9445+
  - Quebec: KEO1195+

Juveniles
- Legal aid: KE378.J8

K

Kidnapping: KE8935
- Parental: KE600+

L

Labeling
- Drugs: KE3714
- Trade regulations: KE1616+
  - Quebec: KEQ514
- Labor conditions
  - KE provincial table: KEA-KEY 406
  - Ontario: KEO657
  - Quebec: KEQ668
- Labor discipline: KE3328+
  - Quebec: KEQ683+
- Labor disputes
  - KE provincial table: KEA-KEY 404+
  - Ontario: KEO649+
  - Quebec: KEQ658+
- Labor injunctions: KE3217
  - KE provincial table: KEA-KEY 404.5
  - Ontario: KEO652
  - Quebec: KEQ661
- Labor law: KE3101+
  - Administration
    - Quebec: KEQ643
  - Conflict of laws
    - Quebec: KEQ209.L3
  - KE provincial table: KEA-KEY 399+
  - Ontario: KEO629+
  - Quebec: KEQ642+
- Labor law, Maritime: KE1121+
  - Quebec: KEQ622.M3
- Labor relations boards: KE3153+
  - Quebec: KEQ647+
- Labor standards: KE3244+
  - KE provincial table: KEA-KEY 406+
  - Ontario: KEO657+
  - Quebec: KEQ668+
- Labor supply: KE3340
  - Quebec: KEQ686

Labor unions
- Labor law: KE3170+, KE3170
  - KE provincial table: KEA-KEY 401+
  - Ontario: KEO643+
  - Quebec: KEQ650+
- Tort liability: KE1288.L3
- Torts
  - Quebec: KEQ468.L32

Lake Louise
- Public land law: KE5217.L3

Lakes
- Public property: KE5145+
  - KE provincial table: KEA-KEY 493+
  - Ontario: KEO903
  - Quebec: KEQ850+

Land Compensation Board
- Ontario: KEO910.5

Land grants: KE5237+
- Quebec: KEQ862

Land law
- Native peoples: KE7715
- Property: KE625+
  - KE provincial table: KEA-KEY 214+
  - Ontario: KEO236+
  - Quebec: KEQ269+

Land speculation tax
- Ontario: KEO990

Land subdivision: KE5263
- KE provincial table: KEA-KEY 503
- Ontario: KEO921+
- Quebec: KEQ867+

Land tenure: KE628+
- KE provincial table: KEA-KEY 215+
- Native peoples: KE7739.L3
  - KE provincial table: KEA-KEY 529.5.L3
- Quebec: KEQ1062.L35
- Ontario: KEO237+
- Quebec: KEQ270+

Land titles
- Data processing: KE254.L36
- Land titles system: KE739
  - Ontario: KEO274

Land transfer: KE729
- KE provincial table: KEA-KEY 230+
- Ontario: KEO271+

Land transfer tax
- Ontario: KEO989

Land trusts: KE795

Land use: KE5263
- KE provincial table: KEA-KEY 503
- Ontario: KEO921+
- Quebec: KEQ867+

Land valuation
- KE provincial table: KEA-KEY 523.4
- Real property taxes
  - Ontario: KEO1025.5

Landlord and tenant: KE690+
- KE provincial table: KEA-KEY 224+
- Ontario: KEO251+
- Quebec: KEQ426+

Language training
- Elementary and secondary education: KE3878
- Ontario: KEO788.4

Larceny: KE8960

Law
- Elementary and secondary education: KE3883.L3
- KE provincial table: KEA-KEY 445.7.L37
- Ontario: KEO788.7.L3

Law as a career
- Quebec: KEQ151+

Law reform: KE429+
- Criminal law
  - Ontario: KEO1167.5
- KE provincial table: KEA-KEY 168
- Ontario: KEO180
- Quebec: KEQ196

Law Reform Commission of Canada: KE430

Law reporting: KE269
- Ontario: KEO158
- Quebec: KEQ144

Law reports: KE132+
- KE provincial table: KEA-KEY 104+
- Ontario: KEO103.2+
- Quebec: KEQ100+

Law schools: KE322.A+

Law societies: KE360+

Law students: KE313+

Lawyer and society: KE331

INDEX

Lawyer and society
- Quebec: KEQ151.5

Lawyers
- Collective bargaining: KE3196.L38
  - Quebec: KEQ656.L3
- Quebec: KEQ151+

Lease and hire
- Contracts
  - Quebec: KEQ424+

Lease purchase: KE1047

Leaseholds: KE690+
- KE provincial table: KEA-KEY 224+
- Ontario: KEO251+

Leave regulations
- Civil service: KE4976

Leaves of absence
- Labor law: KE3318
- Labor standards
  - Quebec: KEQ682

Lefroy and Cassel's Practice Cases: KEO108

Legal advertising
- KE provincial table: KEA-KEY 184.N66

Legal aid: KE376+
- KE provincial table: KEA-KEY 160+
- Ontario: KEO173+
- Quebec: KEQ180+

Legal assistance to the poor: KE376+
- KE provincial table: KEA-KEY 160+
- Ontario: KEO173+
- Quebec: KEQ180+

Legal assistants
- Law office management: KE355.L4
  - Ontario: KEO168.L43

Legal certainty
- Constitutional law: KE4239

Legal ethics: KE339+
- KE provincial table: KEA-KEY 153
- Ontario: KEO164
- Quebec: KEQ154+

Legal etiquette
- Quebec: KEQ154+

Legal investments: KE1085.L4
- KE provincial table: KEA-KEY 275.L43

Legal profession: KE330+

Legal profession
- KE provincial table: KEA-KEY 152.2+
- Ontario: KEO161.2+
- Quebec: KEQ151+

Legal status
- Higher education: KE3920

Legal writing: KE298.L4

Legality
- Constitutional law: KE4239

Legislation: KE77.9+
- KE provincial table: KEA-KEY 39+
- Ontario: KEO48.2+
- Quebec: KEQ48+

Legislative Assembly
- KE provincial table: KEA-KEY 467+
- Ontario: KEO837+
- Quebec: KEQ772+

Legislative Council
- KE provincial table: KEA-KEY 466
- Quebec: KEQ21+, KEQ768+

Legislative functions
- Administrative procedure: KE5024+

Legislative power: KE4529

Legislative process: KE4550+
- KE provincial table: KEA-KEY 469+
- Ontario: KEO845+
- Quebec: KEQ778+

Legislative reporting
- KE provincial table: KEA-KEY 471.L4

Legislature: KE4529+
- Ontario: KEO836+
- Quebec: KEQ768+

Legitimacy of children: KE595
- Ontario: KEO227
- Quebec: KEQ255

Lesion
- Void and voidable contracts
  - Quebec: KEQ398.L4

Liability: KE484.L5
- Airlines: KE2280
- Attorney and client
  - Quebec: KEQ155.5.L4
- Carriage of goods and passengers: KE1099
  - Ontario: KEO336
- Legal ethics: KE347.M3
- Maritime law: KE1107+

INDEX

Liability
- Railways: KE2197+
- Trusts and trustees: KE798.L5

Liability insurance
- KE provincial table: KEA-KEY 285

Liability without fault
- Torts: KE1277+
  - KE provincial table: KEA-KEY 295+
  - Ontario: KEO370+
  - Quebec: KEQ466+

Libel and slander
- Criminal law: KE8948
- Torts: KE1246
  - KE provincial table: KEA-KEY 293
  - Ontario: KEO363
  - Quebec: KEQ457

Liberté testamentaire
- Quebec: KEQ354.C3

Libraries: KE4000
- KE provincial table: KEA-KEY 449
- Ontario: KEO802
- Quebec: KEQ975

Library science
- Collective bargaining: KE3196.L5

Licenses
- Local finance: KE6310
- Marriage
  - Ontario: KEO220
- Patents: KE2955
- Property taxes
  - KE provincial table: KEA-KEY 525
  - Quebec: KEQ1022

Licensing
- Corporations: KE1396+
- Professions
  - KE provincial table: KEA-KEY 395
  - Radio and television: KE2605
  - Service trades: KE1985

Liens: KE1050+
- KE provincial table: KEA-KEY 271.5.L54

Lieutenant-Governor
- KE provincial table: KEA-KEY 474

Lieutenant-Governors: KE4726

Life insurance
- Contracts: KE1165+
  - KE provincial table: KEA-KEY 283+

Life insurance
- Contracts
  - Ontario: KEO345
  - Quebec: KEQ488
- Federal public service: KE4978

Life insurance proceeds
- Estate tax: KE5985
- Income tax: KE5799.L5

Life interests
- Land tenure: KE648+

Life-rents
- Quebec: KEQ441

Lifesaving apparatus
- Ship safety regulations: KE2357

Light industries: KE1858.A+

Lighthouses: KE2392

Lightkeepers
- Collective bargaining: KE3196.L53

Limitation of actions
- Civil procedure
  - KE provincial table: KEA-KEY 556.L56
- Legal concept: KE484.L54
  - KE provincial table: KEA-KEY 184.L55
  - Ontario: KEO197.L56

Linguistic and cultural rights: KE4413
- KE provincial table: KEA-KEY 458.5.L56
- Ontario: KEO821
- Quebec: KEQ752

Liquidation
- Corporations: KE1459
  - KE provincial table: KEA-KEY 321.3
  - Ontario: KEO412.3
  - Quebec: KEQ500.3

Liquor
- Advertising: KE1612.A4

Liquor laws: KE3734+
- KE provincial table: KEA-KEY 428+
- Ontario: KEO741+
- Quebec: KEQ906+

Liquor taxes: KE6009.A43

Lis pendens: KE8388
- Ontario: KEO1125

Literary copyright: KE2825+

Livestock industry and trade: KE1723+

INDEX

Living accommodations for older people
  Public welfare: KE3526
Living wills: KE3663.E94
  KE provincial table: KEA-KEY 424.8.E88
Load line
  Ship safety regulations: KE2359
Loan of money: KE1030+
  KE provincial table: KEA-KEY 267+
  Ontario: KEO317+
  Quebec: KEQ435+
Loans
  Public finance: KE5627
    Quebec: KEQ998
Lobbying: KE4559
Local courts
  KE provincial table: KEA-KEY 538+
  Ontario: KEO1072+
  Quebec: KEQ1086+
Local finance: KE6265+
  KE provincial table: KEA-KEY 520+
  Ontario: KEO1017+
  Quebec: KEQ1034+
Local government: KE4900+
  Debts: KE6270
    Quebec: KEQ1036
  KE provincial table: KEA-KEY 477+
  Ontario: KEO860+
  Quebec: KEQ818+
Local transit: KE2220
  Ontario: KEO563
  Quebec: KEQ610
Locus standi: KE8396
Logging
  Taxation: KE6244.F6
    KE provincial table: KEA-KEY 518.5.F6
Loss of citizenship: KE4349+
Losses
  Income tax: KE5825
Lotteries: KE3795
  Criminal law: KE9066
  KE provincial table: KEA-KEY 434.3.L67
  Quebec: KEQ919.L6
Louage
  Quebec: KEQ424+

Lower courts
  Ontario: KEO1090+
  Quebec: KEQ1086+
Lumbering
  Safety regulations: KE3370.L8
    Ontario: KEO673.5.L8

M

Machine industry
  Collective bargaining
    Quebec: KEQ656.M3
Machine-readable bibliographic data
  Copyright: KE2829.M32
Magistrates: KE8325
  KE provincial table: KEA-KEY 540+
  Ontario: KEO1099+
  Quebec: KEQ1095+
Magistrates' courts: KE9365+
Magistrates' handbooks: KE9365+
  KE provincial table: KEA-KEY 583
  Ontario: KEO1188
Mail
  Classification of: KE2488+
Maintenance
  Divorce
    Quebec: KEQ252
Maintenance and advancement
  Trusts
    KE provincial table: KEA-KEY 242.M3
    Ontario: KEO284.5.M3
Malicious prosecution
  Torts: KE1253
Malpractice
  Legal ethics: KE347.M3
    KE provincial table: KEA-KEY 157.M34
  Physicians: KE2710.M34
  Torts: KE1271
    Ontario: KEO366
    Quebec: KEQ460
  Trial practice: KE8432.M34
Management
  Corporations: KE1402
    KE provincial table: KEA-KEY 316.5
    Ontario: KEO404

INDEX

Management
- Corporations
  - Quebec: KEQ495.7
- Courts: KEO1057+
- Law offices: KE352+
  - Ontario: KEO167
  - Quebec: KEQ157+
- Management-labor relations: KE3141+
  - KE provincial table: KEA-KEY 400+
  - Ontario: KEO631+
  - Quebec: KEQ645+
- Mandamus: KE8570

Mandate
- Contracts
  - Quebec: KEQ433

Manitoba, Law of: KEM1+

Manpower controls: KE3340
- Quebec: KEQ686

Manslaughter: KE8912

Manufacturing industries
- Labor disputes
  - Ontario: KEO653.M3
- Regulation: KE1840+
  - KE provincial table: KEA-KEY 356+
  - Ontario: KEO472+
  - Quebec: KEQ544+

Marijuana: KE3722.M3

Marine insurance: KE1135
- Quebec: KEQ622.I56

Maritime (Commercial) law
- KE provincial table: KEA-KEY 279+

Maritime commercial law: KE1105+
- Ontario: KEO339+
- Quebec: KEQ620

Maritime Court
- Ontario: KEO340

Maritime liens: KE1114.B6
- KE provincial table: KEA-KEY 280.5.B6

Maritime torts: KE1107

Marketing
- Agriculture and forestry: KE1712+
  - KE provincial table: KEA-KEY 341
  - Ontario: KEO448
  - Quebec: KEQ528+
- KE provincial table: KEA-KEY 341

Marketing of legal services: KE350.5

Marriage: KE544+
- Conflict of laws
  - Quebec: KEQ209.M2
- KE provincial table: KEA-KEY 196+
- Ontario: KEO218+
- Quebec: KEQ240+

Marriage certificates: KE546
- Ontario: KEO209
- Quebec: KEQ236

Marriage registration: KE521
- KE provincial table: KEA-KEY 192
- Ontario: KEO209
- Quebec: KEQ236

Marriage settlements: KE559

Marshes: KE5196.S9
- KE provincial table: KEA-KEY 498.5.S9
- Ontario: KEO914.S9

Mass media: KE2460+

Master and servant
- Contracts: KE924+
  - Quebec: KEQ429

Maternal and infant welfare: KE3510

Mathematicians
- Collective bargaining: KE3196.M27

Matrimonial property relationships
- Conflict of laws
  - Quebec: KEQ209.M2
- KE provincial table: KEA-KEY 198
- Ontario: KEO222
- Quebec: KEQ245+

McGill University: KEQ959.M3

Meals
- Excise taxes
  - Quebec: KEQ1030.M4

Meat
- Inspection: KE1878
- Marketing
  - Quebec: KEQ529.M4

Meat industry: KE1878+

Mechanical reproduction
- Copyright
  - Literary copyright: KE2835

Mechanics' liens: KE930
- KE provincial table: KEA-KEY 259.5
- Ontario: KEO308.3
- Quebec: KEQ315.M4

INDEX

Medical care
- Air Force: KE7082
- Armed Forces: KE6892
- Army: KE6952
- Navy: KE7022
- Social insurance: KE3404+
  - KE provincial table: KEA-KEY 412
  - Ontario: KEO679
  - Quebec: KEQ702
- War veterans: KE7240.M4

Medical care insurance: KE1174

Medical evidence
- Civil procedure
  - KE provincial table: KEA-KEY 560.E8
  - Ontario: KEO1141
  - Quebec: KEQ1133
- Criminal procedure: KE8475

Medical examiners: KEO1097
- Court employees: KE8312
  - KE provincial table: KEA-KEY 540.7.C67
  - Ontario: KEO1097
  - Quebec: KEQ1098.C6

Medical experiments with humans: KE3663.M43

Medical genetics: KE3663.G45

Medical institutions: KE3650+
- KE provincial table: KEA-KEY 423.2
- Ontario: KEO726+
- Quebec: KEQ895+

Medical legislation: KE3646+
- KE provincial table: KEA-KEY 423+
- Ontario: KEO724+
- Quebec: KEQ893+

Medical personnel
- Collective bargaining: KE3196.M35
  - KE provincial table: KEA-KEY 403.M4

Medical records: KE3654.R42
- Ontario: KEO730.R42

Medical witnesses
- Civil procedure
  - Ontario: KEO1141
  - Quebec: KEQ1133
- Criminal procedure: KE8475

Medicare: KE3405

Meetings
- Legal works on: KE452.M44

Mennonite lawyers: KE332.M45

Mens rea: KE8834

Mental cruelty
- Divorce: KE582.M4

Mental health courts: KE3659

Mental health facilities: KE3658
- Quebec: KEQ898

Mental incompetency proceedings: KE515

Mentally ill
- Capacity and disability: KE514+
- Medical legislation: KE3658
  - KE provincial table: KEA-KEY 424
  - Ontario: KEO729
  - Quebec: KEQ898

Mercantile law: KE911+
- KE provincial table: KEA-KEY 257
- Ontario: KEO306

Mercantile transactions
- Ontario: KEO306
- Quebec: KEQ477+

Merchant marine: KE2402+

Merchant mariners: KE1121+
- Quebec: KEQ622.M3

Metal products industry
- Collective bargaining
  - Quebec: KEQ656.M4

Metals
- Real property: KE636

Meteorology
- Collective bargaining: KE3196.M4

Midwives
- Quebec: KEQ983.M53

Migratory birds, Protection of: KE5210

Military colleges and schools
- Air Force: KE7065
- Armed Forces: KE6875+
- Army: KE6935
- Navy: KE7005

Military criminal law: KE7146+
- Quebec: KEQ1055+

Military discipline: KE7135

Military justice: KE7160+

Military law: KE6800+
- KE provincial table: KEA-KEY 527+

INDEX

Military law
- Quebec: KEQ1052+

Militia: KE6966
- Quebec: KEQ1053

Milk production and distribution
- Regulation: KE1887
  - Quebec: KEQ549.D3

Minerals
- Real property: KE636

Minimum wage: KE3275+
- KE provincial table: KEA-KEY 407+
  - Ontario: KEO663
  - Quebec: KEQ675

Mining: KE1790+
- Collective bargaining
  - Quebec: KEQ656.M5
- Income tax: KE5914.M5
  - Ontario: KEO983.M5
- KE provincial table: KEA-KEY 349+
  - Ontario: KEO461+
  - Quebec: KEQ537+
- Safety regulations
  - KE provincial table: KEA-KEY 409.7.M5
  - Quebec: KEQ694.M56
- Taxation: KE6035.M5
  - KE provincial table: KEA-KEY 518.5.M5
  - Ontario: KEO1012.M5

Minority lawyers: KE332.M56

Minority stockholders
- Ontario: KEO410.6

Minors
- Capacity and disability: KE512
  - KE provincial table: KEA-KEY 190.3.M5
  - Ontario: KEO207.M5
  - Quebec: KEQ235.M5
- Liability: KE512

Misbranding
- Trade regulation: KE1616+

Mise en demeure
- Quebec: KEQ379.D4

Misrepresentation
- Void and voidable contracts: KE875

Missing persons: KE503
- Quebec: KEQ231

Mistake
- Void and voidable contracts: KE875
  - KE provincial table: KEA-KEY 252
- Wills: KE814.M57

Mobile homes: KE5312.M6
- KE provincial table: KEA-KEY 505.4.M63
- Ontario: KEO933.M6

Money: KE5602

Money laundering
- Banking: KE1024.R42

Monopolies: KE1631+

Moot courts
- Legal education: KE302+

Moratorium
- Debtors' relief
  - KE provincial table: KEA-KEY 324.5.M6

Mortgages: KE752+
- KE provincial table: KEA-KEY 235+
  - Ontario: KEO278+

Mothers' allowances
- Public welfare: KE3517
  - Ontario: KEO706.5

Motion pictures: KE3980+
- KE provincial table: KEA-KEY 448.6+
  - Ontario: KEO800.3+
  - Quebec: KEQ971+

Motor boats
- Safety regulations: KE2365.M6

Motor carriers
- KE provincial table: KEA-KEY 382.5+
  - Ontario: KEO538+
  - Quebec: KEQ597+

Motor vehicle insurance: KE1202+
- Ontario: KEO351.3.A+
- Quebec: KEQ490+

Motor vehicle laws
- KE provincial table: KEA-KEY 381
  - Ontario: KEO531
  - Quebec: KEQ590

Multinational enterprises
- Government regulation and control: KE1398

Municipal bonds and debentures: KE6270
- Quebec: KEQ1036

INDEX

Municipal charters and ordinances: KE4913
- Quebec: KEQ828

Municipal Code
- Quebec: KEQ822

Municipal contracts: KE900

Municipal corporations: KE4904
- KE provincial table: KEA-KEY 478+, KEA-KEY 478
- Ontario: KEO861+
- Quebec: KEQ820

Municipal courts
- Quebec
  - Post-1965: KEQ1090
  - Pre-1965: KEQ1076.M8

Municipal elections: KE4917
- Ontario: KEO874

Municipal government: KE4904+
- KE provincial table: KEA-KEY 478+
- Ontario: KEO861+
- Quebec: KEQ820+

Municipal officials: KE4919+
- KE provincial table: KEA-KEY 479+
- Ontario: KEO875+
- Quebec: KEQ832+

Municipal public service: KE4995
- KE provincial table: KEA-KEY 484
- Ontario: KEO884+
- Quebec: KEQ840+

Municipal public service employees
- Collective bargaining: KE3196.P8
- Management-labor relations: KE3240.P8

Municipal services: KE4904+
- KE provincial table: KEA-KEY 478+
- Ontario: KEO861+
- Quebec: KEQ820+

Municipalities
- Tax powers: KE6275
  - KE provincial table: KEA-KEY 521
  - Ontario: KEO1022
- Torts: KE1288.M8
  - KE provincial table: KEA-KEY 296.M8

Munitions: KE3758

Murder: KE8910
- Trials: KE226.M8

Museums and galleries: KE3990
- Ontario: KEO800.9
- Quebec: KEQ973

Musical copyright: KE2850

Musicians
- Legal works for: KE450.M87

Mutual funds: KE1089
- Ontario: KEO332

N

Name
- Civil status: KE501
  - KE provincial table: KEA-KEY 188
  - Ontario: KEO204
  - Quebec: KEQ230

Narcotic addiction
- Medical legislation: KE3660.N3

Narcotics
- Criminal law: KE9050
- Drug laws: KE3720+
  - KE provincial table: KEA-KEY 427.8

Nasciturus: KE517

National anthem: KE4795

National Assembly
- Quebec: KEQ772+

National defense: KE6800+

National emblem: KE4795

National emergency, Government measures in time of: KE5460+

National Energy Board: KE2036

National parks and monuments: KE5207+

National preserves: KE5201+

National revenue: KE5631.5+

Nationality: KE4345+

Natissement
- Quebec: KEQ323+

Native peoples: KE7701+
- Administration: KE7742
- Legal aid: KE378.N3
- Legal education: KE318.N3
- Quebec: KEQ1060+

Natural children
- Quebec: KEQ256

Natural gas: KE1827
- Ontario: KEO469

INDEX

Natural persons: KE499+
- KE provincial table: KEA-KEY 187+
- Ontario: KEO203+
- Quebec: KEQ229+

Natural resources
- Taxation
  - KE provincial table: KEA-KEY 518+
  - National revenue: KE6030+
  - Ontario: KEO1010+
  - Provincial finance: KE6242+

Naturalization: KE4351

Navigation and pilotage: KE2372+

Navigation and shipping: KE2345+
- KE provincial table: KEA-KEY 387+
- Ontario: KEO571
- Quebec: KEQ618+

Navy: KE6997+

Negligence: KE1264+
- Ontario: KEO365+
- Quebec: KEQ459+
- Torts
  - KE provincial table: KEA-KEY 294+
- Trial practice: KE8432.N4

Negotiable instruments: KE980+
- Quebec: KEQ479+

Negotiated settlement: KE8615
- KE provincial table: KEA-KEY 567.5
- Ontario: KEO1159
- Quebec: KEQ443

Networks
- Radio and television: KE2605

Night work
- Labor standards: KE3312+
  - KE provincial table: KEA-KEY 408
  - Quebec: KEQ681

No-fault insurance: KE1205
- Quebec: KEO351.3.N6

Noise control: KE3635
- Ontario: KEO721
- Quebec: KEQ890

Nolo contendere: KE9297
- KE provincial table: KEA-KEY 575.5

Noncontentious (ex parte) jurisdiction
- Civil procedure: KE8605+

Noncontentious (ex-parte) jurisdiction
- Civil procedure
  - Quebec: KEQ1159+

Nonferrous metals: KE1800+
- KE provincial table: KEA-KEY 350+

Nonprofit corporations: KE1373+
- Income tax: KE5870
- KE provincial table: KEA-KEY 305.4
- Ontario: KEO389.5
- Quebec: KEQ494.4

Nonresidents
- Taxation: KE5864.N6

Nonwage payments: KE3298+
- KE provincial table: KEA-KEY 408.5.N65
- Ontario: KEO666+
- Quebec: KEQ678+

Notaries: KE8328
- Collective bargaining
  - Quebec: KEQ656.L3
- KE provincial table: KEA-KEY 540.7.N67
- Quebec: KEQ169+

Notice
- KE provincial table: KEA-KEY 184.N66

Novation
- Obligations
  - Quebec: KEQ384

Noxious gases, Control of
- Ontario: KEO720
- Quebec: KEQ888+

Nuisance
- Torts: KE1259

Nullity
- Legal concept: KE484.N8
- Marriage: KE550
  - Quebec: KEQ243

Nursery schools: KE1987.D3
- Ontario: KEO502.D3

Nurses: KE2714.N8
- Collective bargaining
  - KE provincial table: KEA-KEY 403.N85
  - Quebec: KEQ656.H6

O

Oath and affirmation
- Civil procedure: KE8464

INDEX

Oath and affirmation
- Civil procedure
  - KE provincial table: KEA-KEY 560.W5
  - Ontario: KEO1138.3
- Legal concept
  - KE provincial table: KEA-KEY 184.O2

Oats
- Marketing: KE1714.G7
- Price supports: KE1694.G7
- Standards, grading, and inspection: KE1719.G7

Obligations
- Conflict of laws: KE474.C64
  - Quebec: KEQ209.C64
- Quebec: KEQ365+

Oblique action
- Obligations
  - Quebec: KEQ404

Obscenity: KE9070

Occupational law: KE1589+
- KE provincial table: KEA-KEY 330+
- Ontario: KEO430+

Occupational therapists
- Collective bargaining: KE3196.P58

Occupations: KE2700+
- Quebec: KEQ980+

Occupiers' liability: KE1269
- KE provincial table: KEA-KEY 294.3.L5
- Ontario: KEO367.L5

Ocean bills of lading: KE1110

Offenses against the person
- KE provincial table: KEA-KEY 570.7.P47

Officers
- Air Force: KE7092
- Armed Forces: KE6902
- Army: KE6962
- Business corporations: KE1402
- KE provincial table: KEA-KEY 316.5
- Navy: KE7032

Offshore drilling: KE1815

Oil and gas
- Export regulation: KE1952.P4
- Leases
  - KE provincial table: KEA-KEY 353.L4
- Pipelines: KE2231
- Regulation: KE1808+
  - KE provincial table: KEA-KEY 351+
  - Ontario: KEO465+
  - Quebec: KEQ540

Oil and gas leases: KE1822

Oil sands
- KE provincial table: KEA-KEY 353.O36

Old age homes
- Public welfare: KE3526

Old age pensions
- Public welfare: KE3524

Older people
- Discrimination in employment: KE3256.A4
  - Ontario: KEO660.A4
- Legal works for: KE450.O43
  - KE provincial table: KEA-KEY 177.A34
- Public welfare: KE3522+
  - Ontario: KEO707
  - Quebec: KEQ725

Ombudsman: KE5034
- KE provincial table: KEA-KEY 488.6
- Ontario: KEO892.O4
- Quebec: KEQ808.3

Ontario appeal cases: KEO117.6

Ontario Energy Board: KEO515

Ontario Gazette, 1868-1950: KEO84

Ontario Labour Relations Board: KEO641

Ontario, Law of: KEO1+

Ontario Law Reports: KEO117.2
- New Series: KEO117.4

Ontario Municipal Board: KEO872

Ontario Reports: KEO117

Ontario Securities Commission: KEO407.5

Ontario Weekly Notes: KEO115
- New Series: KEO115.2

Ontario Weekly Reporter: KEO111

Ordinances: KE4254

INDEX

Ordinances
  KE provincial table: KEA-KEY 39+
Organization
  Armed Forces: KE6848
    Air Force: KE7057
    Army: KE6928
    Navy: KE6997
  House of Commons: KE4658+
  Legislative Assembly
    Ontario: KEO845+
    Quebec: KEQ778+
  Organized crime: KE8984
    KE provincial table: KEA-KEY 570.7.R3
    Ontario: KEO1171.R3
  Overseas sales: KE964
Ownership
  Property: KE618
    KE provincial table: KEA-KEY 212
    Ontario: KEO234
    Personal property: KE769.2+
    Quebec: KEQ267+
Ownership, Concurrent
  Land tenure: KE673+

P

Paralegal personnel
  Law office management: KE355.L4
    Ontario: KEO168.L43
Parcel post: KE2490.P3
Pardon
  Criminal procedure: KE9380
Parent and child: KE593+
  KE provincial table: KEA-KEY 206+
    Ontario: KEO226+
    Quebec: KEQ254+
Parental kidnapping: KE600+
Parental rights and duties: KE600+
  KE provincial table: KEA-KEY 206.7+
Parishes: KE4512.P3
  Quebec: KEQ834
Parliament
  Canada: KE4533+
Parliamentary divorce: KE576+
Parliamentary immunity and privileges: KE4578

Parliamentary reporting: KE4540
Parole
  Criminal procedure: KE9434
    Quebec: KEQ1197
Parties
  Civil procedure: KE8394+
    KE provincial table: KEA-KEY 557+
    Ontario: KEO1128+
    Quebec: KEQ1121+
  Contracts
    Quebec: KEQ402+
Partition
  Land tenure
    KE provincial table: KEA-KEY 227.P37
  Real property: KE678
Partnership
  Associations: KE1356+
    KE provincial table: KEA-KEY 304
    Ontario: KEO387
    Quebec: KEQ493
  Income tax: KE5878
Partnership of acquests
  Quebec: KEQ247
Party walls
  Real property: KE716.P3
    Quebec: KEQ296.P3
Passenger fares
  Railways: KE2189
Passports: KE4445
Patent and Copyright Office: KE2929+
Patent attorneys: KE2975
Patent medicines: KE3725.P3
Patents: KE2908+
  KE provincial table: KEA-KEY 396
  Quebec: KEQ637
Paternity: KE595
  Ontario: KEO227
  Quebec: KEQ255
Patients' rights: KE3648
Pawn
  Property
    Quebec: KEQ325
Pay
  Air Force: KE7070+
  Armed Forces: KE6880+
  Army: KE6940+

INDEX

Pay
- Navy: KE7010+

Payment
- Obligations
  - Quebec: KEQ374

Payroll deductions
- Income tax: KE5855+

Penitentiaries: KE9420

Pension and retirement plans: KE3432+
- Air Force: KE7072, KE7074
  - Military officers: KE7092
- Armed Forces: KE6882, KE6884+
  - Military officers: KE6902
- Army: KE6942, KE6944
  - Military officers: KE6962

Judges
- Pensions: KE8293.S3
- Retirement: KE8293.A6

Labor standards: KE3300
- Ontario: KEO666.2
- Quebec: KEQ679

Navy: KE7012, KE7014
- Military officers: KE7032

Ontario: KEO693

Parliament: KE4579

Public service: KE4972
- KE provincial table: KEA-KEY 483.5.T4
- Ontario: KEO885.T4
- Quebec: KEQ838.T4

Social insurance
- KE provincial table: KEA-KEY 415
- Quebec: KEQ709+

Teachers: KE3854.S3
- KE provincial table: KEA-KEY 441.5.S3
- Ontario: KEO782.S3
- Quebec: KEQ934.S25

War veterans: KE7230

Pension trust funds
- Income tax: KE5870

Pensions
- Income tax: KE5799.P4

People, The
- Constitutional law: KE4527+
  - Quebec: KEQ767+

People with disabilities
- Employment: KEA-KEY 406.5.P46
- Public welfare: KE3532+
  - Ontario: KEO708
  - Quebec: KEQ727

People with disabilities, Access for
- KE provincial table: KEA-KEY 504.7

People with mental disabilities
- Capacity and disability: KE514+

People with physical disabilities
- Capacity and disability: KE514+

Performance
- Contracts: KE882
- Sales contracts: KE963+

Performing arts: KE3972+
- KE provincial table: KEA-KEY 448.4+
- Ontario: KEO800+
- Quebec: KEQ970+

Perjury: KE9033

Perpetuities
- Land tenure: KE668
  - Ontario: KEO245

Personal actions: KE765

Personal exemptions
- Income tax: KE5808+

Personal income tax: KE5751+
- KE provincial table: KEA-KEY 511
- Ontario: KEO975
- Quebec: KEQ1008

Personal injuries
- Civil procedure: KE8432.P4
- Railway liability: KE2203
- Torts: KE1237
  - KE provincial table: KEA-KEY 291
  - Ontario: KEO359
  - Quebec: KEQ454

Personal property: KE765+
- KE provincial table: KEA-KEY 238+
- Ontario: KEO280+

Personal property, Recovery of: KE781

Personal property taxes: KE6300

Personnel
- Air Force: KE7060+
- Armed Forces: KE6870+
- Army: KE6930+
- Navy: KE7000+

Persons: KE498+

Persons
KE provincial table: KEA-KEY 186+
Ontario: KEO202+
Quebec: KEQ228+
Pesticides: KE3766.P5
Quebec: KEQ910.P47
Petroleum industry
Export regulation: KE1952.P4
Income tax: KE5914.M5
Regulation: KE1808+
KE provincial table: KEA-KEY 351+
Ontario: KEO465+
Quebec: KEQ540
Taxation: KE6035.M5
KE provincial table: KEA-KEY 518.5.M5
Ontario: KEO1012.M5
Pharmacists: KE2714.P4
Ontario: KEO617.P4
Quebec: KEQ983.P5
Pharmacy
Collective bargaining: KE3196.P5
Photography
Copyright: KE2868+
Physical therapists
Collective bargaining: KE3196.P58
Physician and patient
Privileged communications
Quebec: KEQ1131.5.P4
Physicians
Collective bargaining
Quebec: KEQ656.P5
Legal works for: KE450.P5
Regulation: KE2708+
KE provincial table: KEA-KEY 395.4.P5
Ontario: KEO616
Quebec: KEQ982
Picketing
Labor disputes: KE3213+
Ontario: KEO651+
Quebec: KEQ660+
Pilotage: KE2372+
Pipelines: KE2230+
Plants
Air Force: KE7106
Armed Forces: KE6916

Plants
Army: KE6976
Navy: KE7046
Plea bargaining: KE9297
Criminal procedure
KE provincial table: KEA-KEY 575.5
Pleading and motions
Civil procedure: KE8375+
KE provincial table: KEA-KEY 555+
Ontario: KEO1124+
Quebec: KEQ1119
Pleas
Criminal procedure: KE9293+
KE provincial table: KEA-KEY 574+
Pleas of guilty
Criminal procedure: KE9297
KE provincial table: KEA-KEY 575+
Pleasure craft
Safety regulations: KE2365.P5
Pledge
Property
Quebec: KEQ323+
Plumbing
Building laws: KE5281
Ontario: KEO925.25
Quebec: KEQ870
Podiatrists: KE2714.P6
Ontario: KEO617.P6
Police: KE5006+
Collective bargaining
Quebec: KEQ656.P64
KE provincial table: KEA-KEY 486
Ontario: KEO887
Works about criminal law for:
KE8809.8.P6
KE provincial table: KEA-KEY 569.3.P6
Ontario: KEO1165.5.P6
Police power
Constitutional law: KE4335
Quebec: KEQ842
Political activity
Provincial government employees
KE provincial table: KEA-KEY 483.5.P6
Ontario: KEO882.P64

INDEX

Political disabilities
  Criminal procedure: KE9431
Political offenses
  Criminal trials: KE226.P6
Political parties: KE4438
Political rights: KE4381+
  Ontario: KEO811+
  Quebec: KEQ749+
Pollution liability insurance: KE1207.P64
Polychlorinated biphenyls: KE3766.P64
Poor
  Legal protection: KE452.P6
    Ontario: KEO190.P6
    Quebec: KEQ205.P6
  Legal protection of
    KE provincial table: KEA-KEY 178.P6
Poor laws
  KE provincial table: KEA-KEY 418+
Possession
  Property: KE618
    Personal property: KE769.2+
    Quebec: KEQ286
Possessory estates
  Land tenure: KE648+
Postal offenses
  Canada: KE9095
Postal service
  Collective bargaining: KE3196.P65
  Regulation: KE2464+
Postal workers
  Labor disputes: KE3236.P6+
Poultry
  Marketing
    Quebec: KEQ529.M4
Poultry industry: KE1729
Poultry products: KE1882
Poverty
  Legal works: KE452.P6
    Ontario: KEO190.P6
    Quebec: KEQ205.P6
  Legal works on
    KE provincial table: KEA-KEY 178.P6
Power of appointment: KE662
Power of attorney: KE1330

Power of attorney
  KE provincial table: KEA-KEY 299.3
  Ontario: KEO382.5
  Quebec: KEQ433
Power supply
  KE provincial table: KEA-KEY 376+
  Public utilities: KE2035+
    Ontario: KEO514+
    Quebec: KEQ577+
Practice court
  Law reports
    Ontario: KEO108
Practice of law: KE335+
  KE provincial table: KEA-KEY 152.2+
  Ontario: KEO161.2+
  Quebec: KEQ153+
Precious metals
  Trade regulations: KE1622.P7
Preferential employment
  Quebec: KEQ670.2+
Preliminary crimes: KE8903
Premarital examinations: KE546
  Ontario: KEO220
Presbyterians: KE4514.P7
Prescription
  Property: KE725.P7
    Ontario: KEO269.5.P7
    Quebec: KEQ290+
  Real property
    KE provincial table: KEA-KEY 227.P7
Press
  Privileged communications
    Quebec: KEQ1131.5.P74
Press censorship: KE4422
Press law: KE2550
  Ontario: KEO601
  Quebec: KEQ629
Presumption of death: KE503
  Quebec: KEQ231
Presumptions
  Civil procedure: KE8447.P7
Prêt
  Loan of money
    Quebec: KEQ435+
Pretrial procedure: KE8408+
  Ontario: KEO1130+

Prevention of cruelty to animals: KE3676
Preventive detention: KE8822
Prévôté de Quebec: KEQ1076.P7
Price control: KE12 2.5+
Price discrimination: KE1651
Price fixing: KE1651
Price supports
Agriculture: KE1693+
Primary production: KE1671+
KE provincial table: KEA-KEY 338+
Ontario: KEO441+
Quebec: KEQ522+
Prime Minister and Cabinet: KE4730
Printing industry
Collective bargaining: KE3196.P7
Quebec: KEQ656.P7
Labor disputes
Ontario: KEO653.P7
Priorities, Industrial: KE12 3+
Priorities of claims and liens
Bankruptcy: KE1506.P74
KE provincial table: KEA-KEY 323.5.P74
Prisoners: KE9416
Prisoners' rights
Ontario: KEO1193
Prisons: KE9420
Administration: KE9415
Discipline: KE9415
Private bill procedure: KE4564
KE provincial table: KEA-KEY 471.P85
Quebec: KEQ782
Private charities: KE3500+
Private companies: KE1450
KE provincial table: KEA-KEY 321.P74
Quebec: KEQ500.P74
Private education and schools: KE3895
Quebec: KEQ944
Private international law
Quebec: KEQ208+
Private police: KE5010.P74
Private property, Public restraints on: KE5105+
KE provincial table: KEA-KEY 490+

Private property, Public restraints on
Ontario: KEO895+
Quebec: KEQ844+
Privileged (confidential) communications
Witnesses: KE8468+
Ontario: KEO1139
Quebec: KEQ1131+
Privileges and hypothecs
Property
Quebec: KEQ309+
Prizefighting: KE3792
Probate and proof
Wills
Quebec: KEQ354.P7
Probate law and practice: KE820+
KE provincial table: KEA-KEY 246
Ontario: KEO289
Probation
Criminal procedure: KE9434
Quebec: KEQ1197
Procuring
Criminal law: KE9075
Procuring miscarriage: KE8920
Produce exchanges: KE1093+
Ontario: KEO334
Product safety: KE3763+
KE provincial table: KEA-KEY 431+
Ontario: KEO760
Products liability: KE1282+
KE provincial table: KEA-KEY 295.3
Ontario: KEO371
Quebec: KEQ467
Products liability claims
Trial practice: KE8432.P76
Professional associations: KE2703
Professional corporations: KE2700
Income tax: KE5914.P7
Quebec: KEQ980
Professions: KE2700+
KE provincial table: KEA-KEY 395+
Ontario: KEO615+
Quebec: KEQ980+
Profiteering: KE12 2.5+
Prohibition: KE3734+
KE provincial table: KEA-KEY 428+
Ontario: KEO741+
Quebec: KEQ906+

INDEX

Promissory notes: KE986
  Quebec: KEQ480.8
Promoters
  Corporations: KE1400
    Quebec: KEQ495.3
Promotions
  Air Force officers: KE7092
  Army officers: KE6962
  Military officers: KE6902
  Navy officers: KE7032
  Public service employees: KE4969
Property: KE618+
  KE provincial table: KEA-KEY 212+
  Ontario: KEO234+
  Quebec: KEQ264+
Property insurance: KE1181+
  KE provincial table: KEA-KEY 284+
  Ontario: KEO348+
  Quebec: KEQ489+
Property of minors
  KE provincial table: KEA-KEY 206.7+
Property taxes
  Local finance: KE6280+
    KE provincial table: KEA-KEY 522+
    Ontario: KEO1024+
    Quebec: KEQ1040+
  Provincial revenue: KE6204+
    KE provincial table: KEA-KEY 514+
    Ontario: KEO985+
    Quebec: KEQ1018+
Proprietary drugs: KE3725.P3
Prospectus
  Corporations: KE1400
    Quebec: KEQ495.3
Prostitution
  Criminal law: KE9075
Protected works
  Copyright: KE2826+
Protecteur du citoyen
  Quebec: KEQ808.3
Protection of labor: KE3346+
  KE provincial table: KEA-KEY 409+
  Ontario: KEO671+
  Quebec: KEQ689+
Prothonotaries
  Quebec: KEQ1098.P7

Provincial Court
  Quebec: KEQ1086+
Provincial courts (Family division)
  Ontario: KEO214+
Provincial finance: KE6172+
Provincial grants, loans, etc:
  KE6328.P7
Provincial parks and forests
  KE provincial table: KEA-KEY 499+
  Ontario: KEO915+
  Quebec: KEQ858+
Provincial public service
  KE provincial table: KEA-KEY 483+
  Ontario: KEO881+
  Quebec: KEQ837+
Provincial public service employees
  Collective bargaining: KE3196.P8
  Management-labor relations:
    KE3240.P8
Provincial revenue
  KE provincial table: KEA-KEY 509+
  Ontario: KEO955+
  Quebec: KEQ1000+
Provisional remedies: KE8536
  KE provincial table: KEA-KEY 563.5
  Ontario: KEO1152
Psychiatric hospitals: KE3658
  Quebec: KEQ898
Psychiatrists
  Ontario: KEO617.P79
Psychologists
  Collective bargaining: KE3196.P87
  Ontario: KEO617.P79
Psychotherapists
  Ontario: KEO617.P79
Public assistance: KE3500+
  KE provincial table: KEA-KEY 418+
  Ontario: KEO703+
  Quebec: KEQ715+
Public auditing and accounting: KE5622
Public contracts
  Quebec: KEQ804
Public debts
  Provincial finance: KE6182
  Public finance: KE5627
    Quebec: KEQ998
Public defenders: KE9289

Public education: KE3805+
- KE provincial table: KEA-KEY 438+
- Ontario: KEO770+
- Quebec: KEQ922+

Public employees: KE4940+
- Collective bargaining: KE3196.P9
  - KE provincial table: KEA-KEY 403.P8
  - Ontario: KEO647.P4
  - Quebec: KEQ656.P8
- KE provincial table: KEA-KEY 483+
- Labor discipline: KE3336.P9
- Labor disputes: KE3236.P8+
  - Quebec: KEQ663.P8
- Labor laws
  - Quebec: KEQ696.P8
- Management-labor relations: KE3240.P9
  - Quebec: KEQ837+
  - Ontario: KEO881+
- Tort liability: KE1288.P8

Public finance: KE5600+
- KE provincial table: KEA-KEY 508+
- Ontario: KEO950+
- Quebec: KEQ995+

Public health: KE3575+
- KE provincial table: KEA-KEY 420+
- Ontario: KEO713+
- Quebec: KEQ882+

Public health hazards
- Quebec: KEQ882.5+

Public health measures
- Quebec: KEQ882.5+

Public interest lawyers: KE332.P82

Public intoxication: KE9078

Public land law: KE5184+
- KE provincial table: KEA-KEY 497+
- Ontario: KEO912+
- Quebec: KEQ856+

Public law: KE4120
- Quebec: KEQ735

Public lending rights
- Copyright: KE2839

Public officers
- Tort liability: KE1288.P8
  - KE provincial table: KEA-KEY 296.P8

Public policy: KE4335
- Quebec: KEQ207.P8

Public property: KE5105+
- KE provincial table: KEA-KEY 490+
- Ontario: KEO895+
- Quebec: KEQ844+

Public prosecutor: KE9280+
- KE provincial table: KEA-KEY 573+
- Quebec: KEQ1178+

Public records, Access to: KE5325
- KE provincial table: KEA-KEY 505.62
- Ontario: KEO937
- Quebec: KEQ876

Public safety: KE3756+
- KE provincial table: KEA-KEY 430+
- Ontario: KEO759+
- Quebec: KEQ908.92+

Public schools
- Ontario: KEO786

Public service: KE4940+
- KE provincial table: KEA-KEY 483+
- Ontario: KEO881+
- Quebec: KEQ837+

Public Service Commission: KE4941

Public utilities: KE2020+
- Regulation
  - KE provincial table: KEA-KEY 375+
  - Ontario: KEO512+
  - Quebec: KEQ575+
- Taxation
  - KE provincial table: KEA-KEY 513.5.P83

Public welfare
- Native peoples: KE7722.P8
- Social law: KE3500+
  - KE provincial table: KEA-KEY 418+
  - Ontario: KEO703+
  - Quebec: KEQ715+

Public works: KE5420
- KE provincial table: KEA-KEY 505.8
- Quebec: KEQ878

Publishing contract: KE2900

Punishment and penalties
- Criminal law: KE8820+
- Military law: KE7197

Purchasing and procurement: KE899+

Putting in default
- Obligations
  - Quebec: KEQ379.D4

Q

Qualification of voters
- Canadian House of Commons: KE4633
- Legislative Assembly
  - KE provincial table: KEA-KEY 468.5.R4

Qualifications
- Federal public service: KE4940+

Quantum meruit
- Breach of contract: KE892
  - KE provincial table: KEA-KEY 255.2

Quarantine
- Immigrants: KE3599

Quarrying: KE1790+
- KE provincial table: KEA-KEY 349+
- Ontario: KEO461+
- Quebec: KEQ537+

Quasi contracts: KE1229
- Quebec: KEQ448

Quasi delicts
- Quebec: KEQ451+

Quasi-marital relationships: KE591

Quebec Act, 1774: KE4136

Quebec Conference, 1864: KE4142

Quebec Gazette, 1764-1874: KEQ77

Quebec Gazette, 1822-1848: KEQ78

Quebec, Law of: KEQ1+

Quebec Official Gazette, 1869-: KEQ79

Quebec Pension Board: KEQ710

Quebec pension plan: KEQ709+

Queen's Bench Division
- KE provincial table: KEA-KEY 535.4

Quo warranto: KE8572

R

Racial and ethnic minorities
- Civil and political rights: KE4395

Racial discrimination
- Employment: KE3254
  - Ontario: KEO659

Racial discrimination
- Employment
  - Quebec: KEQ671

Racketeering: KE8984
- KE provincial table: KEA-KEY 570.7.R3
- Ontario: KEO1171.R3

Radio communication: KE2601+
- Quebec: KEQ635

Radio stations: KE2605

Radiotelegraph: KE2575

Railway safety: KE2170+

Railway sanitation: KE2170+

Railways
- Labor disputes: KE3232+
- Regulation: KE2141+
  - KE provincial table: KEA-KEY 383+
  - Ontario: KEO546+
  - Quebec: KEQ602+

Rape: KE8930.R3

Rates and ratemaking
- Mail: KE2488+
- Railways: KE2177+

Rationing: KE12 2+

Readings: KE442
- Quebec: KEQ200

Real estate agents: KE1987.R4
- KE provincial table: KEA-KEY 373.R4
- Ontario: KEO502.R43

Real estate business
- Income tax: KE5914.R4

Real estate development
- Ontario: KEO921.3

Real estate transactions
- KE provincial table: KEA-KEY 230
- Transfer of rights: KE729
  - Ontario: KEO271+

Real property: KE625+
- KE provincial table: KEA-KEY 214+
- Ontario: KEO236+
- Quebec: KEQ269+

Real property assessment
- Ontario: KEO1025.5

Real property taxes: KE6283+
- Local finance
  - KE provincial table: KEA-KEY 523+
  - Ontario: KEO1025+

INDEX

Real property taxes
- Local finance
  - Quebec: KEQ1042+
- Public finance: KE6204
  - Ontario: KEO987+
  - Quebec: KEQ1019+

Real servitudes
- Quebec: KEQ295+

Receivers
- Civil procedure: KE8540
  - Ontario: KEO1152.5
- Receivers in bankruptcy: KE1506.R43
- KE provincial table: KEA-KEY 323.5.R43

Recidivists: KE8822

Reclamation
- Public land: KE5194+
  - KE provincial table: KEA-KEY 498+
- Public property
  - Ontario: KEO913+

Record keeping
- Banking: KE1024.R42

Record keeping and retention
- Ontario: KEO385.5.B87

Recording and registration: KE521
- KE provincial table: KEA-KEY 192
- Ontario: KEO209
- Quebec: KEQ236

Records management
- Medical legislation: KE3654.R42
  - Ontario: KEO730.R42

Recovery of personal property: KE781

Recreation: KE3788+
- Quebec: KEQ918+

Recruiting
- Air Force: KE7062
- Armed Forces: KE6872
- Army: KE6932
- Navy: KE7002

Referees
- Civil procedure
  - KE provincial table: KEA-KEY 561.5

Reference cases
- Constitutional law: KE4216.3+

Reformatories: KE9422

Refugees: KE4472

Refuse disposal
- Public health: KE3606.R4
  - Ontario: KEO715.R4

Regional and city planning: KE5258+
- KE provincial table: KEA-KEY 502+
- Ontario: KEO920+
- Quebec: KEQ865+

Regional communities
- Local government
  - Quebec: KEQ826

Regional governments
- Ontario: KEO861+

Registers
- Property
  - Quebec: KEQ334+

Registrars
- Court employees
  - KE provincial table: KEA-KEY 540.7.R43

Registration
- Copyright: KE2810
- Land titles: KE739
  - KE provincial table: KEA-KEY 231
  - Ontario: KEO274
- Motor vehicles: KE2100
- Real rights
  - Quebec: KEQ332+
- Ships: KE2352

Registration of birth
- KE provincial table: KEA-KEY 192

Registration of death
- KE provincial table: KEA-KEY 192

Registration of marriages
- KE provincial table: KEA-KEY 192

Registration of voters
- Canadian House of Commons: KE4633
- Legislative Assembly
  - KE provincial table: KEA-KEY 468.5.R4

Registry offices
- Property
  - Quebec: KEQ334+

Regulation of corporations: KE1396+

Regulation of industry, trade, and commerce: KE1589+
- KE provincial table: KEA-KEY 330+

INDEX

Regulation of industry, trade, and commerce
- Ontario: KEO430+
- Quebec: KEQ510+

Regulation of trade and commerce: KE1935+
- KE provincial table: KEA-KEY 368+
- Ontario: KEO488+
- Quebec: KEQ558+

Regulatory agencies: KE5019+
- KE provincial table: KEA-KEY 488+

Relationship between civil and religious divorces
- Domestic relations: KE572

Release
- Obligations
  - Quebec: KEQ386

Religious and patriotic observances
- Educational law: KE3839.R4
- Ontario: KEO779.R4

Religious corporations: KE4502
- KE provincial table: KEA-KEY 462
- Ontario: KEO831

Religious discrimination
- Employment: KE3256.R44

Religious divorces and civil divorces, Relationship between
- Domestic relations: KE572

Religious instruction
- Educational law: KE3839.R4
  - KE provincial table: KEA-KEY 440.5.R4
  - Ontario: KEO779.R4

Remainders
- Future estates and interests: KE664

Remedies: KE6118
- Breach of contract: KE890+
  - KE provincial table: KEA-KEY 255+
  - Ontario: KEO304
  - Quebec: KEQ411+
- Civil procedure: KE8532+
  - KE provincial table: KEA-KEY 563+
  - Ontario: KEO1151+
  - Quebec: KEQ1146+

Remise
- Obligations
  - Quebec: KEQ386

Removal of judges: KE8293.R4

Removal of justices of the peace and magistrates
- KE provincial table: KEA-KEY 540.5.R4
- Ontario: KEO1099.5.R4
- Quebec: KEQ1096.R4

Remuneration
- Public service: KE4962+
  - KE provincial table: KEA-KEY 483.5.T4
  - Ontario: KEO882.T4

Rent: KE692
- KE provincial table: KEA-KEY 224.5
- Ontario: KEO260.5
- Quebec: KEQ427.R45

Rent control: KE692
- KE provincial table: KEA-KEY 224.5
- Ontario: KEO260.5
- Quebec: KEQ427.R45

Repairmen's liens: KE931
- Ontario: KEO308.4

Repairs
- Real property: KE703

Reparation: KE1312+
- KE provincial table: KEA-KEY 297
- Ontario: KEO379
- Quebec: KEQ473

Replevin: KE781
- KE provincial table: KEA-KEY 238.5.R44

Representation
- Contracts
  - Quebec: KEQ433

Representative government: KE4241

Reprinting
- Literary copyright: KE2835

Res judicata: KE8514
- Quebec: KEQ1135

Resale price maintenance: KE1653

Rescission contracts: KE896

Research: KE3950+
- KE provincial table: KEA-KEY 448+
- Ontario: KEO798+
- Quebec: KEQ968+

Reserved property
- Marriage law
  - Quebec: KEQ246.5.R4

Reserves
- Air Force: KE7096
- Armed Forces: KE6906
- Army: KE6966
- Navy: KE7036

Reserves and settlements
- Native peoples: KE7715

Resignation
- Employment: KE3262+

Respondentia: KE1114.B6
- KE provincial table: KEA-KEY 280.5.B6

Responsible government: KE4241

Restaurants: KE1987.H65
- KE provincial table: KEA-KEY 373.H67
- Quebec: KEQ568.H6

Restitution: KE1229
- Breach of contract: KE896

Restraint of trade: KE1631+

Restrictive trade practices: KE1649+

Retail sales tax: KE6232
- KE provincial table: KEA-KEY 516.4
- Ontario: KEO1005
- Quebec: KEQ1029

Retail trade: KE1967+
- KE provincial table: KEA-KEY 371+
- Ontario: KEO495+
- Quebec: KEQ563+

Retention
- Civil law
  - Quebec: KEQ226.R4

Retired persons
- Legal works for: KE450.O43
  - KE provincial table: KEA-KEY 177.A34

Retroactive law: KE476
- Quebec: KEQ205.9

Revenue sharing: KE6166

Reversions: KE663

Review courts
- Local property taxes
  - Ontario: KEO1024.5

Revocation
- Merchant mariners: KE1126

Revocatory action
- Creditors' rights
  - Quebec: KEQ405

Right to counsel
- Criminal procedure: KE9289
  - KE provincial table: KEA-KEY 574.2
  - Ontario: KEO1179

Right to die: KE3663.E94
- KE provincial table: KEA-KEY 424.8.E88

Rights as to the use and profits of another's land: KE714+
- KE provincial table: KEA-KEY 227.R54
- Ontario: KEO269+

Rights of suspects
- Criminal procedure: KE9265+
  - KE provincial table: KEA-KEY 572.3
  - Ontario: KEO1176
  - Quebec: KEQ1175

Rights of user
- Real property: KE703

Rights of way
- Roads: KE5134

Riots: KE9041

Riparian rights: KE707
- KE provincial table: KEA-KEY 227.R57
- Ontario: KEO266
- Quebec: KEQ283.R5

Rivers
- Navigation and pilotage regulations: KE2383
- Public property: KE5145+
  - KE provincial table: KEA-KEY 493+
  - Ontario: KEO903
  - Quebec: KEQ850+

Road traffic: KE2095+
- KE provincial table: KEA-KEY 381+
- Ontario: KEO531+
- Quebec: KEQ590+

Roads
- Public property: KE5126+
  - Ontario: KEO899
  - Quebec: KEQ848

INDEX

Roadside protection: KE5134
Royal Canadian Mounted Police: KE5008
Royal Military College: KE6877
Rule against perpetuities
  Land tenure: KE668
  KE provincial table: KEA-KEY 221
  Ontario: KEO245
Rule in Shelley's case: KE660
Rule of law
  Constitutional law: KE4238
Rulemaking power
  Administrative law
    KE provincial table: KEA-KEY 488.2
    Quebec: KEQ800
Rules
  House of Commons: KE4658.A351+
  Legislative Assembly
    KE provincial table: KEA-KEY 470
    Ontario: KEO846.A329+
  Sources of law: KE4254
Rural development and rehabilitation: KE1691
  KE provincial table: KEA-KEY 340
  Quebec: KEQ524
Rural municipalities and districts
  Ontario: KEO861+
  Quebec: KEQ822

S

Safety equipment
  Motor vehicles: KE2097
Safety regulations
  Labor law
    KE provincial table: KEA-KEY 409.4+
    Ontario: KEO673+
    Quebec: KEQ692+
Safety responsibility laws
  Motor vehicles: KE2105
    KE provincial table: KEA-KEY 381.5
Saint Lawrence Seaway: KE5157
  Navigation and pilotage regulations: KE2379
Salaries
  Income tax: KE5775

Salaries
  Judges: KE8293.S3
  Parliament: KE4579
  Public service: KE4967
    KE provincial table: KEA-KEY 483.5.T4
    Ontario: KEO885.T4
    Quebec: KEQ838.T4
  Teachers: KE3854.S3
    KE provincial table: KEA-KEY 441.5.S3
    Ontario: KEO782.S3
    Quebec: KEQ934.S25
Sale of goods: KE943+
  KE provincial table: KEA-KEY 261+
  Ontario: KEO310+
  Quebec: KEQ415+
Sales tax: KE6002
Sales tax, Retail: KE6232
  Ontario: KEO1005
  Quebec: KEQ1029
Same-sex marriage: KE591
Sanitation: KE3575+
  KE provincial table: KEA-KEY 420+
  Ontario: KEO713+
Scholarships
  Higher education
    Quebec: KEQ949
School boards: KE3814
  Education
    KE provincial table: KEA-KEY 439.3
    Ontario: KEO774
    Quebec: KEQ926
  Torts: KE1288.S3
School buildings
  Building laws
    KE provincial table: KEA-KEY 504.4.S35
School buses: KE2122
  KE provincial table: KEA-KEY 382.7.S3
School districts: KE3814
  KE provincial table: KEA-KEY 439.3
  Ontario: KEO774
  Quebec: KEQ926
School government and finance: KE3812+

School government and finance
KE provincial table: KEA-KEY 439+
Ontario: KEO773+
Quebec: KEQ925+
School lands: KE3820
School personnel, Nonteaching
KE provincial table: KEA-KEY 442+
School safety patrols
KE provincial table: KEA-KEY 439.6.T7
Science and the arts: KE3950+
KE provincial table: KEA-KEY 448+
Ontario: KEO798+
Quebec: KEQ968+
Scientists
Collective bargaining: KE3196.S34
Seafood industry: KE1896+
Seal of government: KE4795
Seals, Protection of: KE5215.S4
Searches and seizures
Criminal procedure: KE9270
KE provincial table: KEA-KEY 572.5
Ontario: KEO1177
Seat of government: KE4795
Secondary education: KEO787
Secretaries, Legal
Handbooks
KE provincial table: KEA-KEY 155
Ontario: KEO167
Secured transactions: KE1042+
KE provincial table: KEA-KEY 271+
Ontario: KEO322+
Securities
Investment: KE1065+
KE provincial table: KEA-KEY 274+
Ontario: KEO329+
Quebec: KEQ485+
Issue and sale: KE1411+
KE provincial table: KEA-KEY 318
Ontario: KEO407+
Quebec: KEQ497
Provincial finance: KE6182
Sedition: KE9005
Criminal trials: KE226.P6
Seduction: KE8930.S43
Seigneurial tenure
Quebec: KEQ271+

Seizure
Civil procedure
Quebec: KEQ1150+
Self-incrimination
Criminal procedure: KE9321
Senate: KE4593+
Seniority
Employment
Quebec: KEQ670.3
Sentence
Criminal procedure: KE9355+
Sentence, Execution of
Criminal procedure: KE9410+
KE provincial table: KEA-KEY 588+
Ontario: KEO1192+
Quebec: KEQ1193+
Juvenile criminal procedure:
KE9449.2+
Ontario: KEO1196.2+
Military criminal law: KE7197
Separate maintenance
Marriage law
KE provincial table: KEA-KEY 203
Ontario: KEO225
Separate property
Marriage law: KE557
Quebec: KEQ248
Separation
Marriage law: KE561+
KE provincial table: KEA-KEY 201+
Ontario: KEO224+
Quebec: KEQ250+
Separation from bed and board
Quebec: KEQ251
Sequestration
Contracts
Quebec: KEQ439
Service, Contract of: KE924+
Quebec: KEQ429
Service trades: KE1985+
KE provincial table: KEA-KEY 372+
Ontario: KEO501+
Quebec: KEQ567+
Services
Air Force: KE7060+
Armed Forces: KE6870+
Army: KE6930+

INDEX

Services
- Navy: KE7000+

Servitudes
- Real property
  - Quebec: KEQ295+

Settlement of foreign claims: KE12 3.5

Settlements
- Income tax
  - KE provincial table: KEA-KEY 511.5.D36

Sex discrimination: KE4399

Sex-oriented businesses
- Quebec: KEQ867.5.S48

Sexual offenses: KE8928+

Shareholders' meetings: KE1434
- Quebec: KEQ499.5

Shares and shareholders' rights: KE1432+
- KE provincial table: KEA-KEY 320
- Ontario: KEO410+
- Quebec: KEQ499+

Sheep raising: KE1726

Shelley's case, Rule in: KE660

Sheriffs: KE8332
- KE provincial table: KEA-KEY 540.7.S53
- Ontario: KEO1101
- Quebec: KEQ1098.S5

Shipbuilding industry
- Regulation: KE1855.S5

Shipbuilding workers
- Collective bargaining: KE3196.S54

Shipping laws: KE2402+

Ships
- Mortgages: KE1114.B6
  - KE provincial table: KEA-KEY 280.5.B6
- Property taxes
  - KE provincial table: KEA-KEY 524.3.S5
- Regulation: KE2350+

Shore protection
- Public land law: KE5198

Sick leave: KE3320

Signboards, Restrictions on roadside: KE5134

Slum clearance: KE5295+

Slum clearance
- KE provincial table: KEA-KEY 505+
- Ontario: KEO929+
- Quebec: KEQ872+

Small business
- Regulation: KE1658
  - KE provincial table: KEA-KEY 334
  - Ontario: KEO438
  - Quebec: KEQ519

Small business corporations: KE5906+

Small Claims Court
- Quebec: KEQ1087

Small claims courts: KE8276
- KE provincial table: KEA-KEY 538
- Ontario: KEO1090

Small loans: KE1034
- KE provincial table: KEA-KEY 268
- Ontario: KEO318
- Quebec: KEQ436

Smoke control
- Public health: KE3630+
  - Ontario: KEO720
  - Quebec: KEQ888+

Smuggling: KE6123
- KE provincial table: KEA-KEY 519.C8

Snowmobiles: KE2107.S6
- KE provincial table: KEA-KEY 381.7.S66
- Ontario: KEO533.S6
- Quebec: KEQ592.S6

Social insurance: KE3400+
- KE provincial table: KEA-KEY 411+
- Ontario: KEO678+
- Quebec: KEQ700+

Social law and legislation
- KE provincial table: KEA-KEY 398+

Social legislation: KE3098+
- Indians
  - Ontario: KEO1045.S63
- Ontario: KEO628+
- Quebec: KEQ640+

Social scientists
- Collective bargaining: KE3196.S62

Social security
- Quebec: KEQ700+

Social services
- Quebec: KEQ718

INDEX

Social work: KE3502
Social workers: KE3502
Collective bargaining: KE3196.S63
KE provincial table: KEA-KEY 403.S6
Soil conservation: KE1686
KE provincial table: KEA-KEY 339
Solar access zoning
Ontario: KEO921.5
Soldiers
Suffrage: KE4629
Sovereignty of Parliament: KE4241
Speakers' decisions
House of Commons: KE4658.A356
Legislative Assembly
KE provincial table: KEA-KEY 470.A329+
Speculation
Contracts: KE1225
Investments
Ontario: KEO333.S6
Speedy trial
Criminal law: KE8815
Sports: KE3792
Sports accidents
Torts: KE1274.S65
KE provincial table: KEA-KEY 294.3.S66
Spouses
Bankruptcy: KE1506.T56
Stamp duties: KE6060
Standards and grading
Agriculture: KE1717+
Standing
Civil procedure: KE8396
Standing orders
House of Commons: KE4658.A351+
Legislative Assembly
KE provincial table: KEA-KEY 470.A329+
Ontario: KEO846.A329+
Stare decisis: KE482.S83
Statistics, Vital, Registration of: KE521
Ontario: KEO209, KEA-KEY 192
Quebec: KEQ236

Statutes
Dominion of Canada (1867-):
KE86.9+
KE provincial table: KEA-KEY 39+
Ontario: KEO48.22+
Province of Canada (1841-1867):
KE77.9+
Quebec: KEQ63+
Statutory law and delegated legislation:
KE4254
Steam boilers
Public safety: KE3773
KE provincial table: KEA-KEY 432.5.S7
Steam-power plants
Collective bargaining: KE3196.H43
Steamboats
Safety regulations: KE2365.S7
Steel industry
Labor disputes: KE3236.S8+
Sterilization: KE3661
KE provincial table: KEA-KEY 424.5
Stict liability
Torts
Quebec: KEQ466+
Stock exchange transactions:
KE1065+, KEQ485+
KE provincial table: KEA-KEY 274+
Ontario: KEO329+
Quebec: KEQ485+
Stock transfers: KE1432+
KE provincial table: KEA-KEY 320
Ontario: KEO410+
Quebec: KEQ499+
Stockbrokers: KE1062
Street railways
Ontario: KEO563
Quebec: KEQ610
Streetcar lines: KE2220
Strict liability
Criminal law: KE8834
Torts: KE1277+
KE provincial table: KEA-KEY 295+
Ontario: KEO370+
Strikes and lockouts: KE3213+
KE provincial table: KEA-KEY 404.5
Ontario: KEO651+

INDEX

Strikes and lockouts
- Quebec: KEQ660+

Student aid
- Higher education
  - Quebec: KEQ949

Student counselors
- Educational law
  - KE provincial table: KEA-KEY 442.5.G8

Student government
- Higer education: KE3920

Students: KE3835+
- Higher education: KE3920
- Immigration: KE4458.S76
- KE provincial table: KEA-KEY 440+

Students with mental disabilities
- Elementary and secondary education: KE3890.M46

Subcontracting: KE3266.S9

Submerged land legislation
- KE provincial table: KEA-KEY 353.S92

Submerged lands: KE1815

Subornation of perjury: KE9033

Subpoena
- KE provincial table: KEA-KEY 560.W5

Subrogation
- Contracts: KE865
- Social insurance: KE3408.S9

Subrogatory action
- Obligations
  - Quebec: KEQ404

Subsidiary and parent companies: KE1448

Substitutions
- Successions and gifts
  - Quebec: KEQ356+

Subversive activities
- Constitutional law: KE4486
- Criminal law: KE9005

Subways: KE2220
- Ontario: KEO563
- Quebec: KEQ610

Succession duties
- Provincial finance: KE6222
  - KE provincial table: KEA-KEY 515+

Succession duties
- Provincial finance
  - Ontario: KEO997+
  - Quebec: KEQ1025+

Succession upon death: KE806+
- KE provincial table: KEA-KEY 244+
- Ontario: KEO286+

Successions and gifts
- Quebec: KEQ345+

Successions et libéralités
- Quebec: KEQ345+

Suffrage: KE4627+
- Ontario: KEO839

Summary conviction appeals
- Criminal procedure
  - Ontario: KEO1190.5

Summary convictions: KE9368
- Quebec: KEQ1191.5

Summary judgment: KE8522.S8

Sunday legislation: KE1971
- KE provincial table: KEA-KEY 371.3
- Ontario: KEO495.2
- Quebec: KEQ564

Superficies
- Quebec: KEQ283.S86

Superior Court
- Law reports
  - Quebec: KEQ113
- Quebec
  - Post-1965: KEQ1082
  - Pre-1965: KEQ1074

Superior courts
- KE provincial table: KEA-KEY 535
- Ontario: KEO1061+
- Quebec: KEQ1079+

Supervening impossibility: KE886
- KE provincial table: KEA-KEY 254

Supplies and stores
- Air Force: KE7106
- Armed Forces: KE6916
- Army: KE6976
- Navy: KE7046

Support
- Income tax: KE5799.A44
- Parent and child
  - KE provincial table: KEA-KEY 206.8

INDEX

Supreme Court
- KE provincial table: KEA-KEY 535.4
- Ontario: KEO1075+
  - Law reports: KEO132+
  - Rules: KEO1111+

Supreme Court of Canada: KE8244+
- Costs: KE8519
- Law reports: KE140

Sûretés personnelles et réelles
- Quebec: KEQ302+

Surety, Personal and real
- Quebec: KEQ302+

Suretyship
- KE provincial table: KEA-KEY 270
- Ontario: KEO321
- Quebec: KEQ304

Suretyship insurance: KE1211+
- KE provincial table: KEA-KEY 286
- Ontario: KEO353.S9

Surface rights
- Quebec: KEQ283.S87

Surgeons: KE2714.S9

Surrogate courts: KE820
- KE provincial table: KEA-KEY 246
- Ontario: KEO289

Surtaxes
- Income tax: KE5890

Surveying
- Land transfer: KE742
  - Ontario: KEO275

Survivors' benefits: KE3432+
- KE provincial table: KEA-KEY 415
- Ontario: KEO693
- Quebec: KEQ709+

Survivors' pensions and benefits
- Air Force: KE7074
- Armed Forces: KE6884+
- Army: KE6944
- Navy: KE7014

Suspension
- Labor discipline: KE3329
- Merchant mariners: KE1126

Swamps: KE5196.S9
- KE provincial table: KEA-KEY 498.5.S9
- Ontario: KEO914.S9

Syndicates, Professional
- Quebec: KEQ651

T

Tariff: KE6081+

Tariff Board: KE6096

Tax accounting: KE5705

Tax administration: KE5688+

Tax appeals: KE5715+

Tax collection: KE5700+

Tax Court of Canada: KE5717

Tax credits: KE5842

Tax evasion: KE5728

Tax exemption: KE5723
- Quebec: KEQ1006.E9

Tax procedure: KE5688+

Tax Review Board: KE5717

Taxation
- Local finance: KE6275+
  - KE provincial table: KEA-KEY 521+
  - Ontario: KEO1022+
  - Quebec: KEQ1038+
- Native peoples: KE7722.T39
- Provincial finance: KE6190+
  - Quebec: KEQ1002+
- Public finance: KE5661+
  - KE provincial table: KEA-KEY 510+
  - Ontario: KEO961+

Taxation of capital: KE6204+
- KE provincial table: KEA-KEY 514+
- Ontario: KEO985+
- Quebec: KEQ1018+

Taxation of transactions
- KE provincial table: KEA-KEY 516+
- Ontario: KEO1004+
- Quebec: KEQ1028+

Taxicabs
- Quebec: KEQ597.5.T38

Teachers
- Collective bargaining: KE3196.T4
  - KE provincial table: KEA-KEY 403.T4
  - Ontario: KEO647.T4
  - Quebec: KEQ656.T42
- Education: KE3850+
  - KE provincial table: KEA-KEY 441+

INDEX

Teachers
- Education
  - Ontario: KEO781+
  - Quebec: KEQ933+
- Labor laws
  - Ontario: KEO676.T42
  - Quebec: KEQ696.T4
- Legal status: KE3917
- Torts: KE1288.S3
- Technical education
  - Quebec: KEQ942.V6
- Telecommunication: KE2560+
  - KE provincial table: KEA-KEY 393+
  - Ontario: KEO606+
  - Quebec: KEQ632+
- Telecommunication facilities
  - Excise taxes
    - Quebec: KEQ1030.T4
- Telegraph: KE2575
- Telephone: KE2580
  - KE provincial table: KEA-KEY 393
  - Ontario: KEO606
- Telephone workers
  - Collective bargaining: KE3196.T44
- Telesat Canada: KE2649.T4
- Teletype: KE2575
- Television broadcasting: KE2640+
- Tenancy: KE690+
  - KE provincial table: KEA-KEY 224+
  - Ontario: KEO251+
- Tenancy in common: KE675+
- Tender
  - Obligations
    - Quebec: KEQ374
- Tenure
  - Judges: KE8293.A6
  - Public service: KE4962+
    - KE provincial table: KEA-KEY 483.5.T4
    - Ontario: KEO882.T4
    - Quebec: KEQ838.T4
  - Teachers
    - KE provincial table: KEA-KEY 441.5.T4
- Territory
  - Jurisdiction
    - Quebec: KEQ746.B6

Terrorism: KE9007
- Testate succession: KE808+
  - KE provincial table: KEA-KEY 245
  - Ontario: KEO287
  - Quebec: KEQ353+
- Testimony
  - Civil procedure
    - Ontario: KEO1138+
    - Quebec: KEQ1130+
- Textile industry
  - Collective bargaining
    - Quebec: KEQ656.T48
- Textiles
  - Import regulation: KE1957.T4
- Theaters
  - Building laws: KE5270.T4
    - KE provincial table: KEA-KEY 504.4.T4
- Thievery: KE8960
- Third parties
  - Bankruptcy: KE1506.T56
- Third parties, Contracts in favor of
  - Quebec: KEQ402
- Third party liability: KE3408.S9
- Threats
  - Criminal law: KE8980+
- Tidal oil: KE1815
  - KE provincial table: KEA-KEY 353.S92
- Timber laws: KE1740
  - KE provincial table: KEA-KEY 345
  - Ontario: KEO455
  - Quebec: KEQ532
- Title, Documents of
  - Sales contracts: KE955+
- Title insurance: KE1211+
  - KE provincial table: KEA-KEY 286
- Title investigation: KE731+
  - KE provincial table: KEA-KEY 231
  - Ontario: KEO273+
- Title transfer
  - Motor vehicles: KE2100
- Tobacco
  - Excise taxes
    - Quebec: KEQ1030.T6
  - Marketing
    - Quebec: KEQ529.T6

Tobacco smoking: KE3632
- Public health
  - Quebec: KEQ888.5

Toronto courts
- Domestic relations: KEO214.5

Toronto Stock Exchange: KEO330+

Torts: KE1232+
- KE provincial table: KEA-KEY 290+
- Ontario: KEO358+
- Quebec: KEQ451+

Toys
- Regulation: KE1858.T6

Trade associations: KE1660

Trade regulation: KEO430
- KE provincial table: KEA-KEY 330

Trade secrets: KE2999

Trademarks: KE2908+
- KE provincial table: KEA-KEY 396
- Quebec: KEQ637

Traffic courts
- KE provincial table: KEA-KEY 382.2
- Ontario: KEO535.3

Traffic regulations: KE2112+
- KE provincial table: KEA-KEY 382+
- Ontario: KEO535+
- Quebec: KEQ594

Traffic violations: KE2114
- KE provincial table: KEA-KEY 382+
- Ontario: KEO535+
- Quebec: KEQ594

Trailers: KE2107.T7

Training
- Air Force: KE7064+
- Armed Forces: KE6874+
- Army: KE6934+
- Navy: KE7004+
- War veterans: KE7240.E3

Training schools
- Juvenile criminal procedure: KE9450
  - Ontario: KEO1196.7

Transaction
- Contracts
  - Quebec: KEQ443

Transfer inter vivos
- Land transfer: KE729+
  - Ontario: KEO271+

Translators
- Collective bargaining: KE3196.T73

Transportation
- Collective bargaining
  - Quebec: KEQ656.T73

Transportation and communication: KE2071+
- KE provincial table: KEA-KEY 379+
- Ontario: KEO528+
- Quebec: KEQ585+

Transportation of students
- KE provincial table: KEA-KEY 439.6.T7
- Quebec: KEQ928.T7

Travel agents: KE1987.T73
- Ontario: KEO502.T73
- Quebec: KEQ568.T73

Travel regulations
- Federal public service: KE4980

Travelers' checks: KE984

Treason: KE9000
- Criminal trials: KE226.P6

Treaties
- Constitutional law: KE4252
- Native peoples: KE7702.7

Treatymaking power
- Prerogative powers of the Crown: KE4719

Trees
- Public property
  - Ontario: KEO896.7

Trespass to goods
- Torts: KE1261
  - Ontario: KEO364.5

Trespass to land
- Torts: KE1257
  - Ontario: KEO364

Trial
- Civil procedure: KE8420+
  - KE provincial table: KEA-KEY 558+
  - Ontario: KEO1133+
  - Quebec: KEQ1124+
- Criminal procedure: KE9304+, KEA-KEY 576+
  - Quebec: KEQ1184+
- Preparation: KE9286+

INDEX

Trial courts
- KE provincial table: KEA-KEY 535.4

Trial practice
- Civil procedure: KE8422+
  - KE provincial table: KEA-KEY 558+
  - Ontario: KEO1133+
  - Quebec: KEQ1124+
- Criminal procedure: KE9306
  - KE provincial table: KEA-KEY 577

Trial tactics
- Civil procedure: KE8422+
  - KE provincial table: KEA-KEY 558+
  - Ontario: KEO1133+
  - Quebec: KEQ1124+
- Criminal procedure: KE9306
  - KE provincial table: KEA-KEY 577

Trover: KE1261
- Ontario: KEO364.5

Trucks
- KE provincial table: KEA-KEY 382.7.T76
- Ontario: KEO541.T78

Trust companies: KE797
- KE provincial table: KEA-KEY 241
- Ontario: KEO284

Trust investments: KE1085.L4
- KE provincial table: KEA-KEY 275.L43

Trusts and trustees: KE787+
- Income tax: KE5864.T7
- KE provincial table: KEA-KEY 240+
- Ontario: KEO282+
- Quebec: KEQ342

Tunneling
- Safety regulations
  - Quebec: KEQ694.T8

Tutorship and curatorship
- Quebec: KEQ260+

U

Ultra vires
- Corporations: KE1371.U4

Unauthorized practice of law
- Quebec: KEQ154.3

Unauthorized publication of picture: KE1242.U5

Unborn children: KE517

Unconscionable transactions: KE872
- KE provincial table: KEA-KEY 252

Undertakers: KE1987.U5
- KE provincial table: KEA-KEY 373.U5
- Ontario: KEO502.U5

Undue influence
- Void and voidable contracts: KE874

Unemployment, Control of: KE12 1.4

Unemployment insurance: KE3451+

Unfair competition: KE2908+

Unfair trade practices: KE1649+

Uniform Law Conference of Canada: KE432.A65

Unincorporated associations: KE1351+
- KE provincial table: KEA-KEY 303+
- Ontario: KEO386+
- Quebec: KEQ492.5+

Union organization
- Quebec: KEQ653

Union shop: KE3172
- Quebec: KEQ652

Université de Sherbrooke: KEQ959.S5

Unjust enrichment: KE1229
- Quebec: KEQ448

Unlawful contracts: KE871.A+
- KE provincial table: KEA-KEY 252
- Quebec: KEQ396.A+

Unmarried couples: KE590
- Ontario: KEO225.5
- Quebec: KEQ253

Unsatisfied judgment funds: KE1204
- KE provincial table: KEA-KEY 285.4
- Ontario: KEO351.3.U5

Unusual receipts
- Income tax: KE5799.C6

Upper Canada Gazette: KEO83

Urban communities
- Local government
  - Quebec: KEQ826

Urban studies, Legal works on: KE452.U7

Usage and custom, Legal: KE482.U8
- Quebec: KEQ206.U8

Use
- Property
  - Quebec: KEQ292

INDEX

Use tax
- KE provincial table: KEA-KEY 516.5

Usufruct
- Quebec: KEQ292

Usury
- Loans: KE1030+
  - KE provincial table: KEA-KEY 267+
  - Ontario: KEO317+
  - Void and voidable contracts: KE871.U8

V

Vacations
- Labor law: KE3318
- Labor standards
  - Quebec: KEQ682

Vagrancy: KE9080

Value-added tax: KE6002

Vendor and purchaser: KE729
- KE provincial table: KEA-KEY 230
- Ontario: KEO271

Vendor's liability: KE729
- KE provincial table: KEA-KEY 230+

Venereal diseases: KE3593.V4
- Ontario: KEO714.5.V4

Vente
- Contracts
  - Quebec: KEQ415+

Vente à tempérament: KEQ416

Vente de la chose d'autrui
- Quebec: KEQ417

Venue
- Civil procedure: KE8364
  - Ontario: KEO1121
  - Quebec: KEQ1115

Veterans
- Land grants: KE5240

Veterinarians
- Quebec: KEQ988.V4

Veterinary hygiene
- KE provincial table: KEA-KEY 426

Veterinary laws
- KE provincial table: KEA-KEY 426

Veterinary medicine and hygiene: KE3668+

Veterinary public health: KE3668+

Vicarious liability: KE1295+
- Ontario: KEO374+
- Quebec: KEQ470+

Victims of crimes
- Criminal procedure: KE9443+

Victims of crimes, Compensation to
- KE provincial table: KEA-KEY 297

Violation of privacy
- Torts: KE1240+
  - KE provincial table: KEA-KEY 292+
  - Ontario: KEO361
  - Quebec: KEQ456+

Violence

Void and voidable contracts
- Quebec: KEQ398.V5

Visiting nurses: KE1987.H6
- Ontario: KEO502.H6

Vocational education
- Quebec: KEQ942.V6

Vocational rehabilitation
- Public welfare: KE3532+
  - Ontario: KEO708
  - Quebec: KEQ727

Void and voidable contracts: KE869+
- KE provincial table: KEA-KEY 252
- Quebec: KEQ395+

Void and voidable marriages: KE550
- Quebec: KEQ243

Voting age: KE4627+

W

Wage and hour laws: KE3275+

Wagering
- Contracts: KE1225

Wages
- Income tax: KE5775
- Labor standards
  - KE provincial table: KEA-KEY 407+
  - Ontario: KEO663
  - Quebec: KEQ675

Waiver
- Insurance contracts: KE1163.W3

Waiver, Legal works on: KE452.W35

War and emergency powers: KE4713

War contracts: KE902

War damage compensation: KE12 3.5

INDEX

War, Government measures in time of: KE5460+
War veterans: KE7230+
Warehouses: KE1995+
Warranties
- Sales contracts: KE949.C6
- KE provincial table: KEA-KEY 261.5.C6
- Ontario: KEO310.5.C6
Wartime and emergency legislation: KE6810+
- Wages: KE3277+
Wartime disputes
- Labor disputes: KE3226
Wartime finance: KE5632+
Waste
- Real property: KE703
Wastes
- Public safety
  - KE provincial table: KEA-KEY 431.5.W37
Water: KE2051
- KE provincial table: KEA-KEY 376.5
- Ontario: KEO524
- Quebec: KEQ580
Water pollution: KE3625
- KE provincial table: KEA-KEY 422.W3
- Ontario: KEO718+
- Quebec: KEQ886
Water power development: KE5145
Water resources: KE5145+
- KE provincial table: KEA-KEY 493+
- Ontario: KEO903
- Quebec: KEQ850+
Water rights: KE707
- Ontario: KEO266
Water transportation: KE2345+
- KE provincial table: KEA-KEY 387+
- Ontario: KEO571
- Quebec: KEQ618+
Watersheds: KE5145+
- KE provincial table: KEA-KEY 493+
- Ontario: KEO903
- Quebec: KEQ850+
Weapons
- Air Force: KE7106
- Armed Forces: KE6916
- Army: KE6976
- Export regulation: KE1952.W43
- Navy: KE7046
- Public safety: KE3758
Weekly day of rest legislation: KE3312+
Weights and measures: KE1620+
Wetlands: KE5196.S9
- KE provincial table: KEA-KEY 498.5.S9
- Ontario: KEO914.S9
Wheat
- Marketing: KE1714.G7
- Price supports: KE1694.G7
- Standards, grading, and inspection: KE1719.G7
White collar crime: KE8958+
Wholesale trade: KE1961
Wife abuse: KE8925.5
Wilderness preservation: KE5207+
- KE provincial table: KEA-KEY 499+
- Ontario: KEO915+
- Quebec: KEQ858+
Wildlife protection: KE5210+
- KE provincial table: KEA-KEY 499.6
- Ontario: KEO916+
- Quebec: KEQ859
Wills: KE808+
- Contracts to make
  - Quebec: KEQ354.C66
- KE provincial table: KEA-KEY 245
- Ontario: KEO287
- Quebec: KEQ353+
Wills, Execution of: KE831+
- KE provincial table: KEA-KEY 248
- Ontario: KEO293
Wiretapping
- Criminal offenses: KE8940
- Criminal procedure: KE9328
  - KE provincial table: KEA-KEY 578.5
  - Quebec: KEQ1186.5
Without par value stocks: KE1424.W5
Witness
- Civil procedure
  - Quebec: KEQ1130+

INDEX

Witnesses
- Civil procedure: KE8460+
  - KE provincial table: KEA-KEY 560.W5
  - Ontario: KEO1138+
- Criminal procedure: KE9335
  - KE provincial table: KEA-KEY 579
- Woman labor: KE3352
  - Quebec: KEQ690
- Women
  - Capacity and disability: KE509
    - KE provincial table: KEA-KEY 190.3.W6
    - Ontario: KEO207.W6
    - Quebec: KEQ234
  - Civil status of married women: KE552
    - Quebec: KEQ244
  - Discrimination in employment: KE3256.W6
    - Ontario: KEO660.W6
    - Quebec: KEQ672.W65
  - Legal aid: KE378.W65
  - Legal works for: KE450.W6
    - KE provincial table: KEA-KEY 177.W6
  - Native peoples: KE7722.W6
  - Public service: KE4955
- Women law students: KE318.W6
- Women lawyers: KE332.W6
  - Quebec: KEQ152.W65
- Wood-using industries
  - Collective bargaining
    - Quebec: KEQ656.W6
- Work and labor contractors: KE928+
- Work and labor contracts
  - KE provincial table: KEA-KEY 259+
  - Ontario: KEO308+
- Work rules: KE3328+
  - Quebec: KEQ683+
- Workers' compensation: KE3414+
  - KE provincial table: KEA-KEY 413
  - Ontario: KEO681+
  - Quebec: KEQ705+
- Workmen's Compensation Commission
  - Quebec: KEQ706
- World War I
  - Public finance: KE5636

World War II
- Public finance: KE5637

Y

Yachts
- Safety regulations: KE2365.P5

Youth services
- Public welfare: KE3515+
  - KE provincial table: KEA-KEY 418.5.C55
  - Ontario: KEO706+
  - Quebec: KEQ723

Z

Zoning: KE5258+, KE5263
- KE provincial table: KEA-KEY 502+
- Ontario: KEO920+, KEO921+
- Quebec: KEQ865+